Broken Irelands

Irish Studies
Kathleen Costello-Sullivan, *Series Editor*

Select Titles in Irish Studies

For a full list of titles in this series,
visit https://press.syr.edu/supressbook-series/irish-studies/.

Broken Irelands

Literary Form in Post-Crash Irish Fiction

MARY M. MCGLYNN

Syracuse University Press

∞ The paper used in this publication meets the minimum requirements
of the American National Standard for Information Sciences—Permanence
of Paper for Printed Library Materials, ANSI Z39.48-1992.

For a listing of books published and distributed by Syracuse University Press,
visit https://press.syr.edu/.

ISBN: 978-0-8156-3777-6 (hardcover)
      978-0-8156-3786-8 (paperback)
      978-0-8156-5570-1 (e-book)

Library of Congress Cataloging-in-Publication Data

Names: McGlynn, Mary M., 1970– author.
Title: Broken Irelands : literary form in post-crash Irish fiction / Mary M. McGlynn.
Description: First edition. | Syracuse, New York : Syracuse University Press, 2022. |
    Series: Irish studies | Includes bibliographical references and index.
Identifiers: LCCN 2022024776 (print) | LCCN 2022024777 (ebook) |
    ISBN 9780815637776 (hardcover ; alk. paper) | ISBN 9780815637868 (paperback ;
    alk. paper) | ISBN 9780815655701 (ebook)
Subjects: LCSH: English literature—Irish authors—History and criticism. |
    English literature—21st century—History and criticism. | Literature
    and society—Ireland. | Social problems in literature. | Financial crises
    in literature. | LCGFT: Literary criticism.
Classification: LCC PR8757 .M34 2022 (print) | LCC PR8757 (ebook) |
    DDC 823/.92099415—dc23/eng/20220815
LC record available at https://lccn.loc.gov/2022024776
LC ebook record available at https://lccn.loc.gov/2022024777

Is the philosopher not permitted to rise above a
faith in grammar?
> —Frederick Nietzsche, *Beyond Good
> and Evil* (1886)

spare the butter,
economise,

and for Christ's sake,
at all times,
watch your language.
> —Rita Ann Higgins, "Be Someone,"
> *The Witch in the Bushes* (1988)

Contents

Acknowledgments and Credits

Sometimes when I hit an impediment in the progress of this book, I would reach out to colleagues, panicked. The argument isn't defined enough. My points repeat themselves. I can't see how to revise this. I received encouragement, offers to read, valuable feedback from friends in related and more distant fields. I've been particularly thankful for the structural suggestions and morale boosts of Allison Deutermann, Stephanie Hershinow, and Laura Kolb, brilliant and inspiring women who have helped me remain calm and rethink; I am honored to call them friends as well as colleagues. Through the time of COVID lockdown, Allison's support has been immensely important. Sean O'Toole was a ready reader with astute editorial suggestions and a killer text game. Early conversations with Matt Eatough helped inspire the entire direction of inquiry, and he always knew what to recommend I should read. I am grateful for the encouragement of Peter Hitchcock, who provided smart, generous, and helpful guidance, always with penetrating insight and a flurry of jokes. I thank Tim Aubry for his feedback and friendship, not to mention his willingness to serve as department chair. Nancy Yousef and John Brennan have long been mentors, advocates, and friends. Shelly Eversley is my beloved fellow traveler, as is Liz Wollman, honorary department member. Jessica Lang, Cheryl Smith, and Lisa Blankenship were good interlocutors with excellent advice about my scholarship as well as amazing leaders who gave our administrative projects intellectual rigor. They are also each treasured friends who have provided much-needed emotional ballast. Working alongside Claudye James and Gina Parmar has been a pleasure, and I am indebted to them for their support and good cheer. Our department's environment of scholarly creativity is exciting right now, and I feel deep gratitude to and affection for my colleagues. I also want to thank those who trained me as an undergraduate and a graduate student, as many lessons resonate to this day; the impact of Kurt Heinzelman is visible in my attention to the economic, as well as every time I use the word "indeed"; Neil Nehring first helped me fuse culture and politics and form. Ursula Heise always blazed trails; David Damrosch and the late George Stade reminded me of the value of my own voice. The fingerprints of my mentors are everywhere on this work.

I thank people who know who they are, even if I don't, those anonymous readers who made reports for the journals in which some of these ideas first appeared, as well as the reviewers of the manuscript. My immense respect for the peer review process rests on the integrity and intelligence of these unsung folks.

It was sometimes terrifying, yet thrilling, to share this work with graduate students while it was in progress. I am especially grateful to Caleb Fridell, Carmel McMahon, and Destry Sibley for their insightful and generative critical engagements with the texts and concepts I was wrestling with. Nathan Nikolic and Jessica Lugo made contributions that helped me to remain alert to the way my biases could shape my methods.

I am grateful for institutional support I've received along the way. First, I was honored and inspired in the year I spent with the fellows at the Center for Place, Culture, and Politics, especially David Harvey and Ruth Gilmore. The activist scholarship there seeded my project. I was fortunate to teach undergraduates and graduate students at the University of Connecticut as the Lynn Wood Neag Visiting Professor in 2013, a break from administrative responsibilities that gave me space to begin developing the ideas that gave rise to this project. CUNY's ongoing support for faculty research has made a material difference, and I thank the CUNY Research Foundation, the PSC CUNY award, and the CUNY Book Completion Award. I am grateful to Baruch College for their support of scholarship via research reassigned time, which matters immensely. Support from

Baruch's Center for Teaching and Learning was vital as well. I also feel a deep debt to the facilities I used frequently in my work—the libraries at CUNY (with a special shout-out to the Interlibrary Loan folks at Baruch), the Seton Hall library, Columbia University's Inter-library Loan, and the New York Public Library.

Irish studies is a small enough community that I read the program of an international conference with a recognition of how many of its presenters have been helpful to me! I count myself lucky to have the support and friendship in this community of Mary Burke, Tara Harney-Mahajan, and Lucy McDiarmid, all of whom provided social outlets, as well as deadlines and feedback to me on portions of this project. Elizabeth Brewer Redwine has been a reliable, funny, and empathetic supporter, cheerleader, shoulder, and inspiration. Joe Cleary's work has blown me away since I first read it; writing for him was a productive challenge and getting to know him a blast. Barry McCrea is an incredibly insightful reader of the contemporary land-scape; his help on questions of Irish language was also key. Adam Kelly has been a perceptive reader and commenter whose work and feedback has shaped mine over and over. I've been grateful for and inspired by questions and conversations at conferences from Kate Costello-Sullivan, Mike Malouf, Diane Negra, Mike Rubenstein, and Kelly Sullivan. Cóilín Parsons I thank for his formidable and witty intelligence and his excellent sense of fun. Tom Ihde and Nick Wolf both helped me fill gaps about the history of Irish. The Columbia Irish Studies Seminar has been a marvelous place to hear new scholarship and discuss my work, and I thank my cochair and friend Seamus O'Malley, as well as our seminar members and the Columbia University Seminars Office for providing this forum.

Working on a project about contemporary Ireland makes me thankful for friends and family able to offer their perspectives on the crisis, recession, and current economic situation, as well as on the literary and cultural texts that have accompanied the period. I'm grateful to Marion Moynihan, Neil Bedford, all the O'Sullivans of Corbally, and particularly to Emmet Wafer, who has such interesting ideas and can discuss them on a distance run. I owe an incredible debt to my wonderful witty husband, Conor O'Sullivan, whose assistance has extended to material and physical care like cooking, cocktail mixing, doing laundry, and listening. Our amazing children, Tomás and Sally, are astute readers and clever interlocutors in their own right, skeptical as they may remain of "books about books." I also thank my parents, Ann and Dick McGlynn, for their ever and ongoing interest and the myriad invisible ways they shaped my progress. Sara and Joe Platz and Lizzy McGlynn and Mark Reilly have given me love, not to mention so many good times and such wonderful nephews and niece! Erin O'Connor read any book I shoved in front of her and let me worry on her porch; Karla was wonderful in thinking through the craft of fiction; I thank as well Kadee, Mary, Kim, Nikki, SJ, the Blue Angels, and all the wonderful friends and neighbors in our community. Andrea and Jennifer remain steadfast and indispensable.

I have long felt anxious sharing my work with peers, and it took me years to relax my hold enough to recognize the immense value of a writing group. Abby Bender, Claire Bracken, and I have met for over a decade now to exchange drafts, offer feedback, and talk about our plans (and our families and careers). This space has felt safe and challenging at once. Their encouragement and advice were instrumental in jump-starting my progress when I hit the associate professor stall that becalms some of us lucky enough to do our work in the tenure stream. Their critiques of my work taught me how to be incisive and supportive at the same time. The emotional and intellectual encouragement from Abby and Claire has been invaluable; this book would not exist without them and the careful attention they gave it, so I dedicate what follows to these two smart and caring women. Thank you, dearest friends!

Credits

My sincere gratitude to the following for permission to reproduce the following materials:

The cover image is reproduced with permission. "Icarus on the Motorway" hybrid photo collage 2015; www.seanhillen.com.

Excerpts from *Solar Bones* by Mike McCormack, copyright 2016 by Mike McCormack, are used by permission of Tramp Press.

The image from the Asylum Archive is reproduced courtesy of Vukašin Nedeljkovic.

I gratefully acknowledge permission to use material in chapter 2 that was originally published as "Greengos: Contemporary Irish Constructions of Latin America." In *Where Motley is Worn: Transnational Irish Literature*, edited by Moira Casey and Amanda Tucker, 43–64. Cork: Cork University Press, 2014.

I also gratefully acknowledge permission to use material in chapter 2 that was originally published as "Things Unexploded—The Calculus and Aesthetics of Risk in Two Post-Boom Irish Novels" in *boundary 2* 45, no. 1 (February 2018): 181–200. Duke University Press. All rights reserved. Republished by permission of the publisher. www.dukepress.edu.

I also gratefully acknowledge permission to use material in chapter 4 that was originally published as "'no difference between the different kinds of yesterday': The Neoliberal Present in *The Green Road*, *The Devil I Know*, and *The Lives of Women*." LIT: *Literature Interpretation Theory* 28, no. 1 (January 2017): 34–54. Reprinted by permission of Taylor & Francis Ltd, http://www.tandfonline.com.

I express appreciation to the Aaron Warner Fund at the University Seminars at Columbia University for their help in publication. The ideas presented have benefited from discussions in the University Seminar on Irish Studies.

Broken Irelands

Introduction

A Horse Called Forget The Past

Sean Mulryan comes from humble beginnings, hailing from a thatched cottage in Roscommon, where he grew up one of seven siblings. Born in 1954, Mulryan left school at seventeen to begin work as a bricklayer and became a developer within a decade. Soon he was one of the biggest builders of housing estates across central Ireland, his reach extending into commercial and residential properties in the United Kingdom and Europe as well. His status as construction mogul positioned him as a modern-day equivalent to the lord of a Big House: he kept an opulent 240-acre estate with a restored eighteenth-century mansion and a horse farm, as well as other Irish homes and a London residence. Mulryan's rise paralleled that of Ireland itself, each moving past a modest rural midcentury into the flush boom years of the Celtic Tiger. In the media, profile after profile extolled Mulryan's work ethic and business acumen. While his net worth in 2005 was officially only in the hundreds of millions of euro, his company, Ballymore Properties, was worth billions, with investments at the time that positioned him to earn €5 billion more. This lucrative vantage led journalist Kevin Murphy to argue in the *Irish Independent* (2005) that Mulryan stood likely to become the richest man in Ireland. Still, as Murphy presciently remarked, "that won't fall into his lap this year or next year, mind you, and it will only happen on condition that everything goes according to plan, and in property things don't always go to plan." The tone of the opinion piece is hard to parse, by turns lauding Mulryan's entrepreneurial determination and reminding readers of corruption allegations that had dogged him for decades, ending with the observation that his success derived from the willingness of Irish bankers to fund his projects more than those of other developers. Encapsulated in this strange, speculative column is the Celtic Tiger's relationship to the press, which was unwilling to critique Ireland's plutocratic class directly but recurrently signaled ambivalence about the symbiosis among banks, developers, and government officials.

Like his restored estate, Mulryan's embrace of horse racing recalls the Big House elite.[1] Mulryan's remark to reporters that "I don't know how many horses I own now. Somewhere between 50 and 100" performs the careless nonchalance of the lord of the manor.[2] This avocation, alongside his supranational investments and his cozy relationship with powerful financiers and politicians, foregrounds the continuities between an earlier aristocracy and a contemporary ruling class. Mulryan's lifestyle is redolent of the way wealth has expressed itself in Ireland for centuries. At the same time, throughout the Tiger era, frequent reminders that Mulryan was born into poverty, "self-made," and the protagonist of a "rags-to-riches" story sat alongside recurrent references to his generosity to charities, features that figure him more as an American-style millionaire than a neoteric pretender to the sort of inherited privilege evoked by an eighteenth-century manor.[3] Mulryan's image can be read as a site of resolution of the contradictions between two different iterations of affluence—old money and new, a contradiction that, paradoxically, underscores such shared traits as massive income disparities and economic policies that favor entrenched wealth.[4] The fact that one

1. In 1996, Joe Lee "described the Tiger as a driving force that changed Ireland from Europe's 'carthorse' to Europe's 'thoroughbred'" (quoted in Buchanan 2013, 138).

2. Goswami and Alderson (2006); see also Sheridan (2007).

3. Modern European welfare states are less dependent on charity than the United States, with the Anglo-Irish countries somewhere in between.

4. The persistence of inequality spurs Thomas Piketty's argument in *Capital in the Twenty-First Century* (2014) that the era of Keynesian midcentury consensus

of Mulryan's most successful thoroughbred horses happened to be named Forget The Past perfectly captures the irony: an age-old pastime of the rich assumes the guise of a new, forward-looking ethos, a metonymic encapsulation of the Irish Celtic Tiger Era desperate to shed its associations with the midcentury Republic and its reputation as stagnant, self-enclosed, and priest-ridden.

Both animals, tiger and thoroughbred, peaked in 2006–7. The Celtic Tiger—by most measures the first economic boom in Ireland's history—was marked by the same sorts of irrational exuberance and attendant critiques of materialism seen in the United States during its parallel economic expansion near the turn of the century. As prices climbed and speculation expanded, the government failed

> to do anything to curb the speculative housing bubble and the reckless lending by the banks which fuelled it, resulting in a profound systemic crisis at the heart of the economy . . . the contours of neoliberalism Irish-style, a model in which public authority favours market players, particularly major corporate players, and has actively used state power over the course of the Celtic Tiger boom to give ever greater freedom of action to these players, with disastrous consequences for sectors like construction and banking. (Kirby 2010, 164)

Ireland's crash was monumental, coming at the same time as the wider global financial crisis. The nation's real estate bubble burst and the overleveraged banks (including two, Bank of Ireland and Allied Irish Banks, that themselves date their origins to the Big House era) had to admit to billions of euro in losses. The collapse of the Irish "economic miracle" left behind "mass unemployment (peaking at 14.6%), large-scale emigration (net emigration of over 122,000 since April 2009), a broken banking sector (the country's six principal banking institutions were, at least partially, nationalized), an indebted

---

marks an anomaly in the inexorable accumulation of wealth and the persistence of inequality.

government (government debt standing at 117% of GDP) and public (1 in 8 households with a mortgage in arrears of 90 days or more), and a wrecked housing market (prices having dropped over 50% for houses and 60% for apartments) up to April 2013" (O'Callaghan et al. 2014, 121). These statistics only somewhat emphasize the degree to which the economic crisis spread throughout the public, who were deeply affected by the harsh terms imposed by the so-called troika of international financial institutions—the IMF (International Monetary Fund), the European Central Bank, and European commission—whose aid was available only upon acceptance of severe terms comprising tax increases and public spending cuts equaling $20 billion (over €15 billion) and high-interest loans and funds withdrawn from its pension plan (Faiola 2010).[5] The public austerity measures and cutbacks bailed out banks but left citizens impoverished and without support.

Not only were banks protected at the expense of the populace, but, within the citizenry, privation was not evenly distributed across the economic spectrum. As the economic crisis burgeoned and the property market was in free fall, the media reported upon the sorts of belt-tightening the rich were experiencing; this included a great deal of attention to private planes and helicopters. Mulryan was reported in 2008 to be selling a helicopter.[6] In another curious choice of journalistic emphasis, one news story devoted most of its attention to another, more expensive helicopter Mulryan was *not* selling and a €20 million airplane that the tycoon had named the Grey Goose, in a reference that merged Howard Hughes with high-end vodka.[7]

5. This €15 billion cut was applied to total expenditures of roughly €80 billion. See Norris (2013).

6. *The Likeness*, Tana French's 2008 installment in her Dublin Murder Squad series, notes that "the economic boom has given us too many people with helicopters" (11), an indication of the symbolic resonance of the Dedalian machines.

7. In addition to the two helicopters named in Quinlan's article (2008), Mulryan is reported to own a pair of Sikorskys: see Sheridan 2007. In Tiger-era

The clear message was that Mulryan was not experiencing the same financial gut punch as the populace at large. Rather, the wealthy were permitted to retain many properties and assets: although Mulryan would come to owe over €2.8 billion in debts to NAMA, the National Asset Management Agency that bought up bad debt from the 2008 crash, he and other developers were offered deals in which they received six-figure salaries to help sell their assets and move them off NAMA's books.[8]

There is substantial debate as to the degree to which such measures were successful in mitigating economic impact. In the ten plus years since the creation of NAMA, Ireland has experienced a massive recession, entered and, in 2013, exited a bailout, and seen its domestic employment rates and property market rebound. This recovery has been of debatable health, with some viewing it as anemic and others making analogies to magical creatures. Paul Krugman's ethnic-slur coinage of "leprechaun economics" (@paulkrugman 2016) refers to numbers that look extraordinary and bear little resemblance to economic conditions on the ground, while Paul Howard (2014), via Ross O'Carroll Kelly, ironically dubbed the recovery the "Celtic Phoenix," brilliantly capturing the supernatural component of an economic recovery in which unemployment goes down but wages don't go up, and economic gains remain concentrated at the upper end of the economic spectrum. Those who did not experience real growth during the Tiger years continue to struggle; while the big developers saw their debts taken into public hands, small mortgage holders were not offered any sort of amnesty. In the month that Ireland exited the bailout, one in ten of its citizens was food insecure on a daily basis. Moreover, the two-thirds of the Irish public whose annual incomes at the height of the boom were below €38,000 find

---

reporting, helicopters of Tiger moguls featured regularly, signaling a privileging of time over expense.

8. See "Myths and Realities about NAMA and Developers' Salaries" (2012); Reilly (2010); and "Why Does the State Pamper Sean Mulryan?" (2019).

themselves nevertheless on the hook for the domestic bailout and the servicing of the amount borrowed from the troika.[9] The economic recovery has thus been a vastly uneven one. Meanwhile, Mulryan's fate and that of the Irish economy seem to have continued in parallel, as he has again begun building in his native country and bought new horses to replace those he sold. One of Mulryan's new thoroughbreds is named Rolling Revenge (Webb 2017).

This book examines crisis-era novels of the country where Rolling Revenge and his owner have been optimistically hailed as augurs of a renewed prosperity. While this national narrative has been relentlessly sanguine, fiction has offered a more nuanced perspective in the aftermath of the crash, in novels by both well-established authors and emergent voices. Recurrently throughout the Tiger years, cultural commentators claimed that there was no sustained artistic engagement with the boom, a view many have convincingly disputed.[10] The belief in a dearth of critique during the Tiger has a corollary in the notion that the years since the crash represent a "renaissance," a figuration contested by Rosemary Meade (2012), who warily notes the appropriation of Irish artists for Brand Ireland. Even more critical is Adam Kelly, explaining the concerns of Angela Nagle: "For Nagle, the prevalent idea that Celtic Tiger wealth bred cultural conformity and that the crash reinvigorated aesthetic energy . . . is exactly the cover story that the Irish state and the capitalist class require to put

9. Coulter and Nagle (2015) list the amount owed by each household for the domestic bailout of 2008–10 as €37000 (7), a number coincidentally close to the €38000 maximum annual income in 2008 of over two-thirds of wage earners.

10. Cahill (2011) cites Julian Gough, Fintan O'Toole, and John Banville as having noted a dearth of literal engagements with the Tiger era. Cleary (2018) argues that the Tiger saw few challenges from Ireland's most prominent literary voices, those such as Edna O'Brien, Colum McCann, and Colm Tóibín. Countering these positions are Cahill herself, Claire Bracken (2013), Jason Buchanan (2013), Eoin Flannery (2014), and Adam Kelly (2020), who have written about various intraboom critiques by authors including Anne Enright, Anne Haverty, Paul Howard, Deirdre Madden, and Denis O'Driscoll.

a positive spin on a new wave of economic hardship. The very notion of a post-crash cultural renaissance is here seen to do ideological work on behalf of entrenched power in Irish society" (2020, 196). Kelly and Nagle offer a trenchant caution to a book exploring novels of the last dozen years; it is important not to overvalue the crash as a conceptual break, nor to see it as an unfortunate but ultimately beneficial event. An examination of works published since the crash reveals a spectrum of engagement, from continuities with earlier, unacknowledged critiques to some complicity with a neoliberal status quo, to innovations that represent new directions in Irish fiction. In no way does the attention to these innovations suggest that the ongoing privations for so many are an appropriate or acceptable exchange.

The idea of normalizing privation is one whose origins can be traced back to not just the Tiger years, but, as I shall outline in my next chapter, even to the mid-century Irish effort to open its borders and markets. Central to my argument about the post-boom period is that it represents a culmination or endpoint of a mindset deeply indebted to American notions of the individual as *homo economicus*, primarily an economic creature; this worldview fosters attention to the self as human capital, privileges personal optimization, and advocates commodified self-care. Such an investment in personal responsibility and individual will sits in tension with feelings of powerlessness and entrapment that arise from a globalized perspective. Contemporary public discourse, climate change and endless attendant natural disasters, the massive complexity of technological and policy frameworks, and a cultural investment in an "end of history" worldview can make us feel impotent, stuck. My contention is that the novels here explored, united in their use of formal techniques I gather under the terms ungrammaticality and irrealism, offer fictional resolutions to these contradictory affective states, speaking to temporal, spatial, and ideological dimensions.

In conjunction with a nation whose economic decisions have been so disastrous for its citizens, these notions of the irreal and ungrammatical, which I expand upon below, give rise to my sense of *broken* Irelands. This study casts a critical eye on a faulty iteration of statehood, a nation that has created different realities for different classes and, in misordering its priorities, has left swaths of its population without basic rights and protections. There is some consolation in the recognition that a broken construct is one that allows for examination, imagination, and new formation. In my next chapter, I will break down some of the theoretical components comprising *Broken Irelands*. First, however, to round out this introduction, I will explain my use of the concepts of irrealism and ungrammaticality, following this with a short précis of each chapter.

Irrealism and Ungrammaticality

Irish fiction in the latter half of the twentieth century was in large part quite distant from the modernist experimentation that preceded it; the last twenty years have witnessed something of a return to more formally adventurous texts in ways that are in conversation with the economic context I will explore in greater detail in the next chapter. In examining such convergences, the Warwick Research Collective (WReC) advocates the term "irrealism" (2015), which they derive from a piece by Michael Löwy, in which he describes the ideological dissidence of Romantic texts critical of industrial modernity, expressed in thematic resistance to dis-enchantment, rationality, quantification, mechanization, and the dissolution of social bonds (2008, 197–200). His discussion emphasizes "fantastic, supernatural, nightmarish, or simply *nonexistent* forms" (205) outside of literary realism, a sphere the WReC usefully extends to textual techniques as well. For the WReC, irrealism comprises a "range of formal features . . . typically addressed under the name of 'modernism,'" including

> anti-linear plot lines, meta-narratorial devices, un-rounded characters, unreliable narrators, contradictory points of view, and so on . . . we understand these techniques and devices more broadly as the determinate formal registers of the (semi-) peripherality in the

world-literary system, discernible wherever literary works are com-
posed that mediate the lived experience of capitalism's bewildering
creative destruction (or destructive creation). (2015, 51)

The WReC further argues that these formal features are in part
a consequence of "their authors' self-conscious conversation with,
and deployment of, relevant formal properties of adjacent forms
(often non-literary) within their local or regional cultural ecology"
(52). Key to this analysis is recognition of the fact that irrealism
is not the product of a particular environment or era so much as
a tool used to engage with it. One of the WReC's case studies is
of Scottish writer James Kelman. Kelman's interest in class, in the
complex identification that the Scots have to British identity, and
in the relationship of local and vernacular languages to the metro-
pole's Standard English qualify his fiction for "(semi-) peripheral"
status, a characterization that can be legitimately and productively
extended to many Irish writers as well.[11] The ongoing semiperipheral status of Irish works and continuing uneven capitalist development make the last twelve years fertile ground for irrealist novels in
Ireland, featuring a variety of formal irruptions in largely mimetic
texts, including the kaleidoscopic points of view in Donal Ryan's
The Spinning Heart (2012), Colum McCann's antilinear vignettes
in *Transatlantic* (2013), and the unreliable narrator of Claire Kilroy's *The Devil I Know* (2012).

The characterization of irrealism in Irish fiction since the
crisis can extend to include features at higher formal levels, like
genre choices. We see irrealist elements in novels activating genre

11. My earlier work on Kelman and his Scottish and Irish contemporaries
examined in particular their inheritance of modernist techniques and interests,
especially as seen in their formal experimentation. This work focused especially on
the absence of conventional hierarchies between narrator and character, evidenced
by such choices as the absence of quotation marks and the presence of nonstandard
constructions and transliterated pronunciations within the narrative framework,
analysis easily aligned with the WReC's characterization of irrealism.

conventions, from the thriller to the speculative to the magical. This suggestion is congruent with Löwy's original interest in oneiric texts as well as with the WReC's theories, as seen in WReC member Stephen Shapiro's work on the gothic. The gothic and related genres generate characters, plotlines, and other elements with supernatural dimensions. But even in texts that only skirt such classification, irrealist outgrowths can be detected. Novels like Anne Enright's *Green Road*, from 2015, which otherwise hews to strictures of verisimilitude, feature recurrent imagery of nonhuman actants and galvanized objects, anthropomorphically animated. This book's analysis of the actants in irrealist Irish novels connects to work about agency, causality, and assemblage from such scholars as Gilles Deleuze, Bruno Latour, and Jane Bennett, as well as to Bonnie Honig's discussion (2017) of the roles of things in the creative of a contemporary democratic public, and Mel Chen's analyses (2012) of grammatical animacy, in turn linking these analyses to discussions of literary form.

My primary goal in discussing irrealism is to connect it to crisis, austerity, and imbalanced recovery; for now I underscore the formal dimensions I note in aspects including genre, image, narrative choices, and even sentence structure. Indeed, a deliberate distance from the realist tradition expresses itself especially well at the level of the sentence, in what I am terming "ungrammaticality." To pick up on my last example, we can see a grammatical dimension to the displacement of agency away from traditional subjects. The use of passive voice, unclear grammatical subjects, and syntax emphasizing object positions can work to critique—or, in some cases, conform to—a structure of feeling in which citizens do not feel they are actively empowered or responsible. The implications extend from questions of individual efficacy and autonomy up to evaluations of who is accountable for the economic crisis.

The WReC proposes that the irrealist tendency can be traced at minute levels through attention to catachresis, as well as "disjunction and amalgamation as literary innovations" (72), including challenges in "both lexis and syntax," (142) a suggestive strain of argument that I shall flesh out further.[12] Before I do so, I want to clarify my use of the term "ungrammaticality." Linguists make a distinction between descriptive and prescriptive grammar, noting that the latter imposes rules on utterances by native speakers. Descriptive grammar, by contrast, derives its rules from those utterances. The fiction I investigate in this book plays with both types of grammar; some texts experiment with punctuation, which is part of a prescriptive grammar, while others are interested seeing what happens when we disrupt generative grammar—through the refusal of subject/verb agreement, for instance. Though all of these authors seek to remain, as Jan Mieszkowski characterizes it, "sensible" rather than "nonsensical" (2019, 26), generating sentences that are still coherent to speakers of English, many do not conform to rules imposed by an educational establishment and its gatekeepers. Rather, they use one part of speech as another, deploy unconventional word orders, render a transitive verb as intransitive. Of course, these sorts of experiments or departures from the norm are part of an Irish writer's literary inheritance from James Joyce, Samuel Beckett, Elizabeth Bowen, Flann O'Brien, and others. With a nod to domestic and international modernist forebears, I subsume under the idea of "ungrammaticality" the momentary estrangement or confusion that arises for a reader in the face of a writerly sentence, one calling attention to its own construction through departures from expectations and norms. To return to Mieszkowski, we can define ungrammaticality as "the extension of creativity in language use to transformations in the rules of syntax and grammar themselves . . . [a figure] on the border of figuration and disfiguration, [that] calls

12. "Catachresis" as a rhetorical term dates back to classical literature, referring to a metaphor that makes a radical departure from conventional usage, congruent to the idea of the mixed metaphor; its contemporary iteration hails back to Gayatri Spivak's application of deconstruction in postcolonial theory, where Western ideas are grafted onto former territories.

for a reconsideration of . . . what makes any syntax or grammar a syntax or grammar" (2009, 652–53).[13]

My investigation of Irish novels of the last dozen years tracks a marked presence of such performatively ungrammatical or unusual stylistic features, with profusions of specific formations like sentence fragments, run-on sentences, irreconcilable verb tenses, and, crucially, a proliferation of the use of present tense narration. Recent Irish novels features a variety of departures from standard prescriptive grammaticality, particularly with sentence fragments—a staccato whose numerical rise can be counted in novels by Colum McCann, for instance—and, on the other end, of run-on and otherwise extended sentences, as in Sebastian Barry's *On Canaan's Side* (2011), for one, as well as novels by Mike McCormack and Eimear McBride. In playing with sentence length and conjunction, Irish authors are in step with larger linguistic trends, phenomena noted even beyond the realm of literature: the Stanford Literary Lab found that in World Bank annual reports, the word "and" has roughly doubled in frequency since 1946, which is credited to "long lists of nouns that create the illusion of activity, sometimes despite a 'total absence of all logic'" (Schuessler 2017, C6). We can link this to recent examples of literary parataxis, noting the lack of methodical connection between ideas expressed in sentence fragments. The decline of hypotaxis, the use of subordinating conjunctions and clauses, can in some cases function as what Richard Lanham calls "syntactic democracy" (2003, 29), giving equal weight to ideas and deferring to a reader

---

13. Throughout his excellent scholarship, Mieszkowski himself does not refer to ungrammaticality, but rather uses the term "anacoluthon" (2009), a rhetorical figure that maps well onto much of what I discuss: a jarring departure from grammatical expectation. I have chosen "ungrammaticality" in part to afford myself a more expansive range of possible ungrammaticalities, but mainly because this characterization aligns better with the idea of irrealism, both of them defining their examples with clear reference to what they are *not*. "Anacoluthon" has the added disadvantage of its near resemblance to another rhetorical term, "anacoloutha," the substitution of one word for another in a nonreciprocal context.

for the assigning of relative values to them. But parataxis can also signal "a refusal to subordinate . . . to make complex, unequal connections, to relate, to explain" (30). Such disinclination, inability, or failure to articulate a relationship between ideas can signal an abdication of responsibility or reflect a feeling of paralysis and powerlessness. Parataxis offers us a parallel to ideas about the subjection to simultaneity as well as a connection to the diminished agency of the assemblage.

In documenting this rise of the deployment of ungrammatical expressions, I see a mode of writing that is to some extent evocative of other forms of communication emergent in this millennium—text messages, emoji, gifs, and memes. As linguist Gretchen McCullough has written, we can detect a "general principle of internet language these days that the more overwhelmed with emotions you are, the less sensical your sentence structure gets" (2014, n.p.). McCullough notes that first-generation Internet language often featured abbreviations and misspellings, modifications at the level of the typographical. She suggests that second-generation innovations are more likely to take place at the level of the grammatical: syntax changes and rhetorically jarring formulations like catechresis or anthimeria give rise to what she terms "stylized verbal incoherence" (n.p.).[14] The syntactic and grammatical variations she traces arise during the economic crisis and aftermath of austerity, both in the Internet-speak that she studies and in the novels discussed in the pages that follow. Acknowledging as well Jennifer DeVere Brody's keen insight that "punctuation marks historically have provided much of the affect of Western print culture since the Enlightenment" (2008, 2), I attend to the ways that contemporary conventions within print grammar in particular evoke feeling. My attention to ungrammaticality links such formal techniques

14. Anthimeria (or antimeria) is the use of one part of speech for another. I employ Greek classical rhetorical terminology like "catechresis" and "anthimeria" because it is useful for characterizing ungrammaticalities but also to pay tribute to another small EU nation whose citizens were asked to bear the brunt of the economic crisis and blamed for their role in propagating it.

to their structural effects. The move away from longtime realist norms—including standard grammar, narrative past tense, subordinating clauses, and even punctuation marks themselves—reaches for a new mode of expression congruent with a new era of financialized economic subjectivity, a structure of feeling akin to Lauren Berlant's "cruel optimism" (2011, 2) and its attendant "recession grimace" (196). Ungrammatical texts retain a faith in language's expressive capacities but only via modification of it as a means of communication. This need to experiment or modify can indicate a loss of faith in existing modes of human agency, a disenchantment that replaces rational thought with such innovations as new takes on animacy and textual representations of affective overload; relatedly, such novels also track a feeling of entrapment within the current moment and an evolving belief in the possibility of progress or change.

I see the sites at which texts venture into irrealism and ungrammaticality as irruptions of impossibility, recognitions of the gap between what is promised or expected and what is likely, often even in texts that are otherwise not overtly concerned with the economic crisis. For instance, the discussion of gothic elements in chapter 4 explores how authors press up against the limits of rational explanation, requiring irreal elements to round out their narratives or resolve contradictions, a catachrestic mimesis of an economy that rises and falls without clear rational motive. While I want to be cautious not to read all novels of the austerity periods as merely or primarily allegories of their historical moment, we can note the correlation of irrealist plots and techniques with a moment in which global economic wisdom has hewed to unproven and questionable remedies, a homeopathic placebo in which the victim (the public) is blamed for the disease while the virus that caused it remains un(der)regulated. The formal innovations of Irish novels of recession and austerity, the ways that they venture into unusual and unexpected linguistic constructions and genre formations, take place in conjunction with reconfigurations of the relationship of the novel to time, both at the granular levels of verb tense and syntax and in their choice of scope and period.

Layout of the Chapters

Broken Irelands is structured via examinations of various irruptions of neoliberal ideology in recent Irish fiction. The concept of irruption evokes the suddenness and pervasiveness of the changes the book tracks, suggesting as well an ecological dimension in which the environment of a book's composition, publication, and circulation applies pressure to its author, who likewise shapes the culture and conversation into which she intervenes. Pushing beyond a descriptive account of the place of Irish literature in a country in crisis, the book stops short of the expectation that literature direct policy or bear sole responsibility for focusing the attentions of what some metrics characterize as a shrinking reading public. Both arts and criticism of the arts can shape larger ideas of what constitutes "common sense" at the same time as evolving norms make space for or disallow some fictional responses to their contemporary moment. The book traces how irrealism and ungrammaticality articulate themselves in Irish fiction from 2007 through 2019, a period that spans the final excesses of the Irish boom, the massive bust of 2008, the period of austerity and "troika" control, and the time since Ireland was declared economically sovereign again, in December 2013.

I've chosen a small but tumultuous window, noting that literature, unlike journalism, does not respond immediately to external conditions. Even the hastiest of novels will take a year from germination to publication, and it's not unusual for this gestation to last more like three to five years. This means that the fiction I examine cannot be taken as literal or direct responses to its immediate conditions of publication: a novel appearing in 2008 is reflective not of the implosion of the real estate market but rather represents, reflects, or responds to the bubble of the preceding years.[15] Indeed, we can see the cruel ironies of the publication cycle in the appearance of such nonfiction titles as Roy Foster's *Luck and the Irish: A Brief History*

---

15. See Cleary (2018) for discussion of the job of literature in this context.

of Change from 1970, and Marc Coleman's *The Best Is Yet to Come*, triumphalist books that both hit the market in the fall of 2007 as the global economic crisis grew.

Conscious of the incubation period of a novel, I examine novels that reflect, overtly or obliquely, on the Irish social and economic conditions of their production. My finding is that we can see a distinct set of shared features, some of which they have in common with contemporaneous novels of other nations, as I discuss below. For now, however, I want to lay out the thematic concerns and formal traits of this period, in which I see sustained literary examinations of 1) American dominance; 2) infrastructure and environmental threats; 3) real estate; and 4) the lives of precarious and refugee subjects depicted as objects and objects themselves invested with animacy. The book's scope narrows from broad to minute, demonstrating that novels respond to neoliberalism and precarity at different levels of social organization: they take on the wholesale refashioning of the collective as well as the interaction of individuals with the commodities surrounding them. Each chapter juxtaposes its particular thematic concerns with specific textual techniques.

To begin I unpack the theoretical backdrops that have influenced my argument. Aware of my debts to postcolonialism, Irish studies, and world-systems theory, I situate my project within these contexts. I then examine the terminology of neoliberalism, with particular attention to its framing of class, its recognition of the role of American culture and economic influences, and its rhetorical reliance on mystification. From the intersection of these traits emerges an idea of neoliberal time, a stasis in which the present is supposedly becalmed. The chapter concludes with attention to theories of temporality and simultaneity and their implications for irrealist and ungrammatical texts.

My study then shifts to fiction, locating Irish novels of the dozen years under examination within a global context that I argue is shaped by the United States of America, neoliberalism's "planetary spearhead" (2009, x), as Loïc Wacquant has memorably put it. Chapter 2 claims that the climate in post-2008 Irish culture, one that uncritically accepts the primacy of the economic, is indebted to American ideas of social mobility and a related discourse of risk. The US worldview was, in the flush Celtic Tiger years, congruent with an individualist mentality in Ireland that fed nicely into rhetorics of meritocracy and boom. I demonstrate the sway of this outlook via attention to narrative focalization in two pre-crash novels, Joseph O'Connor's *Redemption Falls* (2007) and Colum McCann's National Book Award–winning *Let the Great World Spin* (2009). Turning next to Paul Lynch's *Red Sky in Morning* (2013), a novel written in the wake of the economic crisis, I argue that its experiments in syntax displace human subjects and thereby deny progress or agency for Irish characters, instead figuring America as the only site of a trajectory of progress. This move isolates the Irish economic crash from its larger global context and locates responsibility internally. I conclude with a section that reads McCann's *Transatlantic* (2013) alongside Sebastian Barry's *On Canaan's Side* (2011), arguing that the sentence fragments in the former and the run-ons in the latter both generate an affective ungrammaticality that privileges emotion over solutions. While Barry's vision is more comfortable with growing inequality, both accept and naturalize an American-inspired vision of personal risk as natural and beneficial.

If the American settings of all the novels in chapter 2 speak to the importance of US models (not to mention investment) in Ireland, chapter 3 attends to internal processes of networking and interconnection. Taking as its scope the national infrastructure, from the postapocalyptic steampunk power in the imagined *City of Bohane* (2011) by Kevin Barry, to the water-treatment plants in Mike McCormack's *Solar Bones* (2016), this chapter argues that water, power, roads, and bureaucracy, which function as sites of concrete, real, and shared social endeavor as well as communal environmental hazards, disclose anxieties and ambivalences about collective enterprise. Alongside this interest in connection, I focus specifically on grammatical conjunctions via attention to polysyndeton, parataxis, and hypotaxis, exploring the ways that coordinating and subordinating conjunctions create different logical—and, by extension, ideological—relationships among ideas. The irrealism of these novels, as well as their various formal disruptions, lay out visions of an Irish society that does not function as a public. While Barry's envisioned future points to social fragmentation, McCormack, with his single-sentence novel, offers some hope for a cohesive social identity.

Chapter 4 narrows from community projects to personal and commercial real estate, taking as its governing ungrammaticality the rhetorical trope of catachresis. Situating its focal texts within the colonial history of displacement and Anglo-Irish Big Houses, the chapter argues that contemporary fiction about Irish real estate reworks its long-standing tropes so that the uncanny home becomes converted into capital, creating disjunctions expressed via catachresis, which blurs the distinction between accountability and vulnerability. I first locate contemporary reworkings of the Big House novel in a modernist context via brief attention Elizabeth Bowen's *A World of Love* (1954), which I compare to Claire Kilroy's *The Devil I Know* (2012) and Anne Enright's *The Green Road* (2015). In the next section I focus on two series of Irish "development thrillers" in the tradition of American hard-boiled crime fiction, by Alan Glynn and Declan Hughes. In their larger neoliberal sense of timelessness, they transfer of the negative qualities of earlier Anglo-Irish characters and ideals onto the middle class, a precarious polity whose alleged overconsumption and riskiness is faulted for the economic crash. Finally, I consider Paul Murray's *The Mark and the Void* (2015), which, with Kilroy's *Devil*, are the only novels in my project that take finance as a central subject, engaging directly with questions of risk and environmental hazard.

I begin my final chapter with a reading of the coincident popularity of the ideas of a Celtic Phoenix and Marie Kondo's *The Life-Changing Magic of Tidying Up* (2014), both catachrestic and uncanny assemblages that functioned as projections of Irish feelings about time, consumerism, and culpability. I situate the use of these cultural artifacts in the context of steampunk aesthetics and Marx's dancing table as a means of introducing my final, most minute, level of focus, on domestic objects, domesticated animals, and systems of containment. I examine galvanized machines and uncanny objects as well as their ungrammatical effects in brief treatments of Christine Dwyer Hickey's *The Lives of Women*, Enright's *The Green Road*, and Lisa McInerney's *The Glorious Heresies* (all 2015), arguing in each case that grammatical choices restricting subjects on the page reflect the ways that each novel's characters find their options controlled by outside forces. Reading the surprising presence of chimerical sheep imagery in each novel, I suggest that the use of an animal known for its stupidity and collective nature acts as an indictment of the populace's passivity in a moment of austerity. The next segment of the chapter considers the affordances of second-person address in Sara Baume's *spill, simmer, falter wither* (2013) and a story from Melatu Okorie's collection *This Hostel Life* (2018), arguing that each text underscores marginalization and alternative relational networks that exceed conventional ideas of individual autonomy and agency. I conclude with a section about the period of Direct Provision to asylum seekers in Ireland, making an analysis of some photographs from Vukašin Nedeljkovic's Asylum Archive, a documentary photography project that engages with ungrammaticality through its attention to agency, enacting precisely the estrangement enforced by the Direct Provision system while it exposes the wages of a regime that treats people as objects.

As the first draft of this book neared completion, the 2020 Irish parliamentary elections showed results that suggested a nation ready for change. The combined share of the votes that went to the two main parties, Fianna Fáil and Fine Gael, came in at a historic low point. Sinn Féin won the most first-preference votes and second-most seats in the Dáil, its best result since 1923. While ultimately the party was not included in the coalition government that was formed, the strong showing in Ireland of a party whose nationalist platform was connected to progressive promises to spend more on health and housing signaled a revolt against the pro-business regime under Leo Varadkar and Fine Gael. As Michelle Murphy of Social Justice Ireland observes (2020), the "positive trajectories" in employment, consumption, and exports in Ireland contrast with "visible signs of distress and inequality . . . persistent poverty that remains hidden beneath the assumption that plenty for the lucky few will lead to prosperity for the many." Doubtless it was frustration with the zombie ideas of trickle-down economics that drove the vote, and not the Fine Gael campaign slogan "A Future to Look Forward To," the final preposition of which did, however, infuriate prescriptive lay linguists and motivated opinion writer Miriam Lord to note a "mangling" of time within the "grammatically off-key campaign slogan" (2020, n.p.). And yet the ungrammaticality was telling: a future looked forward to never arrives, suspending Fine Gael's Ireland in the neoliberal present. Certainly this makes a less appealing prescription than that of the United Nations Development Programme, whose 2019 report is called "Beyond Income, Beyond Averages and Beyond Today," a document that proposes to tackle inequity and climate change. Such a vision of motion, change, and progress can move beyond a broken Ireland.

1

The Economic and Cultural Contexts of Irrealism and Ungrammaticality

Broken Irelands: Other Irelands, Global Irelands

The notion of broken Irelands implies both a plural nation and a fracturing that is both destructive and generative, a sense of the many possibilities that exist. Within it are myriad stories and experiences, including many that were historically suppressed. An expectation of cultural unity and uniformity was advanced by early iterations of the new nation via its social, artistic, and political formations, as well as its partnership with the Catholic Church. While the cultural image projected was, of course, not uniform, its conours were recognizable inside the country and abroad, and the shape they assumed was one against which a great number of subsequent literary texts positioned themselves. The scholars who shaped the field of Irish studies from its origins brought attention to the contexts within which this art was produced.

Elizabeth Butler Cullingford's 2001 book, *Ireland's Others: Ethnicity and Gender in Irish Literature and Popular Culture*, intervened in the nationalism/revisionism debate of that time within Irish studies itself, as well as conversations about Ireland's place in postcolonialism, the value of cultural studies methodology, and the place of the increasingly prosperous Irish nation in an increasingly global cultural and economic milieu. This important book considered the contours of Ireland's colonial status, building upon work by David Lloyd, Seamus Deane, Edward Said, and others. It offhandedly interwove analysis of various cultural forms, enacting the obsolescence of the high/low culture divide. Moreover, it flipped a common, foundational critical practice in Irish studies: the analysis of representations of Irishness in British texts. Examining how non-Irish others are constructed in Irish texts, Cullingford notes the persistence of essentialist ideas about such marginalized populations as Jews and Native Americans, also breaking ground in her explorations in popular culture of the treatment of Travellers, abused children, and people who identify as LGBTQ. Due in part to Cullingford's work, many of these concerns have evolved, as has the important role of media and cultural studies, in which Diane Negra's work over the last two decades has also been instrumental. Developments in postcolonial, decolonial, and anticolonial studies have shifted the discussion of the contemporary Irish example to a frame attendant to the importance of Ireland's place within the EU, its interactions with the Global South, and its ongoing relationship with the United States. Given the economic and cultural ascendance of Ireland in recent decades, it feels important now to direct focus to other dimensions of Ireland, via attention to the dynamics of temporality, spatiality, and agency, as well as the relationship of form and ideology. To this end, I take as a starting point the idea of imagined communities in plural—the way that iterations of nation proliferate. This book acknowledges both domestic and exported Irelands, including the way that diaspora has created outposts of the Irish nation, each with its own versions. Because I examine works of fiction, these versions of course include all sorts of imaginaries and hypotheticals, varieties of Ireland that are by definition unreal and multiple. The unreal also links to the idea of irrealism, as developed in the Warwick Research Collective's (WReC) "combined and uneven development," a key concept that I discussed in the introduction. In recognition that there is no single thing such as Ireland, other Irelands are unreal Irelands, irreal Irelands.

But, in addition to the plural nation, we must think about the singular idea of the other. Grammatically, "other" is a determiner, which functions somewhat like an adjective, though it introduces a noun rather than modifying or providing more detail about it. Unlike an adjective, a determiner is a semantically indispensable part of a sentence, and I'd suggest, in keeping with Gayatri Spivak and Cullingford herself, that the other is likewise semantically indispensable. In attending to the other, I recognize the primacy of other colonized and formerly colonized subjects in the shaping of Ireland now. The interaction of Ireland with its dispersed descendants, with citizens of places affected by its tourists and economic policies, and with migrants, refugees, and asylum seekers in an unbalanced global economy, has transformed the nation since 2001, revealing, for instance, a nation less generous to those seeking shelter than we might expect, given its own history. Within *Broken Irelands* are the multiple others that a unified view of a nation would obscure.

The imagined nation has thus been formed by geopolitical pressures, always in conjunction with the economic. The fact that the boom and bust in Ireland were part of a larger global financial crisis; that Ireland serves as a tax haven for some of the world's most lucrative and powerful tech and pharmaceutical companies; that Ireland's net immigration hit an all-time high only to be followed by a return to record emigration as unemployment soared in 2009 and beyond; that Ireland now has a higher nonwhite population than at any time in its history; that London and New York remain major publishing outlets for Irish writers—all these circumstances underscore the fact that recent economic circumstances, including literary production and circulation, are inherently global. In the course of the book I argue that globalism is very much about Americanism in Ireland, but the articulation of American economic models through such institutions as the IMF and the World Bank means we must widen the lens beyond just Ireland and the United States.

Moreover, the twenty-first century literary conversation itself is very much a global one, with trends in current fiction extending beyond linguistic and national boundaries. The ongoing discussion of world literature—from David Damrosch, Franco Moretti, and Pascale Cassanova to Rebecca Walkowitz, Peter Hitchcock, and the

WReC—is a backdrop to interventions in the current Irish scene.[1] Moira Casey and Amanda Tucker's volume *Where Motley Is Worn: Transnational Irish Literatures*; Joe Cleary's important "'Horseman, Pass By!' The Neoliberal World System and the Crisis in Irish Literature"; and recent work by Sharae Deckard, Claire Bracken, Adam Kelly, Michael Rubenstein, and Matthew Eatough all reorient our focus to include not just discussions of non-Irish settings or characters in contemporary Irish texts, but the analysis of the ways in which a global framework shapes conditions of authorship, complicates notions of distinctly Irish voices, and activates questions of the roles and effects of literature in a time in which the economic overshadows the political, the ideological, the aesthetic, the natural.

The pervasive presence of the economic, of a pursuit of market efficiency, and of profit to the point that it drives politics and reshapes policy and even ideology, has earned this era the label of "neoliberalism." Although I find this term to be problematic—a feeling in which I am far from alone—it gestures efficiently to a set of conditions currently pervasive.[2] While acknowledging the limits to

1. This is the sort of footnote that could become its own book. With each intervention into the current world literature discussion, the issue and its complications become richer. See, in particular, Gloria Fisk, Sarah Brouillette, and *Comparative Literature Studies* 53, no. 3 (2016). My choice to work on an anglophone literature in a national context could be problematic for many of those whose work I find helpful and influential, but I hope that, in examining relevant local traditions and contours, I provide material for those seeking to make larger arguments at the same time as I test, in the specific, claims that they make in general.

2. I note briefly the disavowal of the term by such diverse scholars as Gargi Bhattacharyya, Terry Flew, and Seán Ó Riain; even those willing to use it—including Martijn Konigs, David Harvey, Wendy Brown, and Stuart Hall—disagree about its historical origins and attendant meanings. In his descriptions of the Mont Pèlerin society and those associated with it, such as Friedrich Hayek, Milton Friedman, and James M. Buchanan, Phillip Mirowski offers a coherent genealogy and some categorical limits to the term "neoliberalism"'s applicability; see "Hell Is the Truth Seen Too Late" and "Neoliberalism: The Movement That Dare Not Speak its Name."

its usefulness, I will justify momentarily my choice to engage with it; for now I want to emphasize that it is the free movement of capital across borders, with the attendant discussions about the supposed free movement of people and intellectual property, that gives rise to this neoliberal moment—that is, the world economic dimension of the twenty-first century is a necessary starting point. As Cleary succinctly frames it, "There can be no strong cultural materialist assessment of the condition of contemporary Irish writing that does not also attend to the wider literary system into which Irish literature is currently integrated or that does not address some of the more salient changes to that wider system, locally and globally, in recent decades" (2018, 145).

Such a wide scope can be useful in maintaining a balance between arguing for connectivity and uniqueness. Throughout the book, I remain conscious of the ways in which Irish texts participate in and flesh out larger global tendencies: for instance, the formal traits I examine, such as the rise in present tense and adjacent ungrammaticalities, are not unique to the Irish context, nor is the prevalence of such ideological responses to neoliberalism as magical thinking. I hope readers will see in my analysis of these features connections to other literatures, whether in a national or global context. At the same time, I want to trace out the ways in which the particular manifestations of these larger trends bear an imprint of their local conditions and traditions. For example, in Ireland, supposed beliefs about home ownership as the apotheosis of neoliberal individualism operate alongside and in tension with ingrained ideas about public and private spaces that arise from such historical conditions as the power of the Big House, the role of the Land League, and the persistence of ruins dotted across the landscape.[3] Not only do these economic

3. Importantly, as I discuss in chapter 4, enthusiasm for home ownership exists more as a concept than a reality; see O'Flynn et al. 2014b. "This notion of an Irish 'property-owning gene' rested on claims that the rate of home ownership is higher in Ireland than in other European countries—a view contradicted by any long-term comparison with European averages. In 2006, at the peak of the boom,

features have local and nonlocal dimensions, but the formal and generic choices authors make reflect a similar blend; in the case of real estate, for example, we see Irish writers engaging not only with tropes of Big House novels of the last two centuries but also with gothic tendencies that can be seen in fiction beyond Ireland's borders as well. This sort of activation of related but residual literary forms registers the specific local history of Irish homes, inflecting a larger generic attention to social relations among different classes.

Throughout *Broken Irelands*, I trace features of contemporary neoliberal life common across modernized settings that spring from a particularly American approach to class and consumption. The Irish resolution of what Louis Althusser has called the "imaginary relationship of individuals to their real conditions" (2001, 109)—what Terry Eagleton has seen as imaginative solutions to "real contradictions" (1995, 246)—is thus particular and discernible as part of a broader historical wave. Giovanni Arrighi offers a valuable paradigm in *The Long Twentieth Century* (1994), a book whose argument about a century of American economic dominance gains credibility through his attention to similar economic patterns in Genoese, Dutch, and British power in earlier eras. With this model in mind, I remain attuned throughout to larger geographic and temporal contexts so as to avoid the twin errors of missed patterns and mistaken assertions of novelty.

Neoliberalism, Individualism, and Economics

In structuring my argument, I have opted to refer to the current economic mode with the term "neoliberalism." Given its pervasive yet controversial presence in the critical conversations of this century, it feels important to recognize its mushiness and its traction and to

---

home ownership in Ireland stood at 76 per cent, putting Ireland at 16th in 'home-ownership' levels, out of the 27 nations listed by Eurostat (cited in McCabe, 2010)" (2014, 926). See also O'Callaghan et al. (2014); O'Callaghan et al. (2015); and Norris (2016).

clarify my meaning and intent in using it, however advisedly.[4] Those wary of neoliberalism as a conceptual category express concern about its capaciousness. Gargi Bhattacharyya sees it "as the term most burdened with explanatory expectation in recent times" and expresses discomfort with it as a "catch-all that loses all local detail and history," (2015, 17), further worrying that reliance upon it "fall[s] into accounts of predictability and inevitability" (18). In a like vein, Terry Flew pointedly identifies the ways in which "neoliberal" can come to stand for Everything That Is Wrong Right Now. He contends that the broad application of the term is "intellectually unsustainable" and calls for its use to be limited to analysis of the construction of "market and market-like relations' in the political-economic space" (2014, 51). Flew suggests that much of what is lumped under the term neoliberal today is rather about a "neo-Marxist hegemony theory" (51). Bryan Fanning's critiques have a methodological dimension; he argues that discussions of neoliberalism lack "concrete explanation . . . through steps that are not explained. . . . The leap from ideology in general to specific structural influences on society is rarely disentangled in detail" (2014, 161).

In response to these sorts of concerns, Phillip Mirowski (2018, 2019) argues that neoliberalism as a coherent philosophical orientation *is* historically traceable. He contends that the term is no more polysemous than others that its detractors use less critically, like "free market" or even "capitalism." Detailing eleven themes of what he labels, with knowing irony, the Neoliberal Thought Collective, Mirowski asserts that "people think the label 'neoliberalism' is an awful neologism because the neoliberals have been so good at covering their tracks, obscuring what they stand for, and denying the level of coherence which they have achieved in their long march to legitimacy" (2018, n.p.). In essence, he suggests that a refusal to use

---

4. For an excellent discussion that parallels and expands upon the issues I consider here, see Deckard and Shapiro's introduction to *World Literature, Neoliberalism, and the Culture of Discontent* (2019), which I came across too late to incorporate here.

the term plays into the hands of a school of thought that has sought to portray its ideology not as a coherent intellectual movement but rather as a natural view, mere common sense, a framing that owes a clear debt to Stuart Hall, not to mention Antonio Gramsci. Mirowski asserts the primacy of the market but also—in important contradistinction to many theorists who see a laissez-faire absence of intervention—the idea that, within neoliberalism's contours, there is an important role for government. Unlike Flew's more strictly economic framework, Mirowski's more epistemic criteria show how a theory of market society extends into "all areas of life," a line of argument that derives from Michel Foucault's early characterization of neoliberalism. As Joseph Henry Staten succinctly sets forth, neoliberalism extends beyond the economic into the "'production of subjectivity.' Neoliberalism does not impose itself on us coercively, via punitive measures or structures of discipline, but gently shapes our common-sense understandings of the world and ourselves through the medium of our everyday experiences, turning us into competitors, entrepreneurs, and round-the-clock workers. We are not exactly subjugated by neoliberalism, as one is subjugated by totalitarianism; instead, we are 'subjectified' by it" (2017, n.p.).

Such an extension of market logic is why, while mindful of Flew's concerns about mission creep, critics in the humanities must attend to connections between the economic and the cultural, the better to explore their interrelation and mutual construction. In this vein, Jeffrey Williams's trenchant definition of American neoliberal novels in "The Plutocratic Imagination" underscores the change in focus from the political to the economic: "The neoliberal novel shifts from moral allegory to a resigned realism. Instead of conspiracies underneath the surface of society, the machinations of the powerful are no longer hidden, nor expected to be. And power resides not with those in government but explicitly with the super-rich. . . . Their signature feeling is chagrin or numbness rather than outrage, and they are less oppositional than the previous generation's political fictions, which excoriated coterie power. The 'neoliberal novel,' in short, focuses on class and the force of political economy rather than conventional politics"

(2013, 94–96). Tracing what we could see as an evolution from a political unconscious to an economic conscious, Williams articulates the rise of a "plutocratic imagination" in which an (often avowedly left-wing) oligarchy makes decisions. He contends that the privileging of private over public, individual over group, and economic over political and cultural is so pervasive that even novels critical of their society operate within neoliberal constrictions.

The idea of a plutocratic novel would seem to suggest collaboration with the status quo, whereas the term "neoliberal novel" suggests more inadvertent complicity; Williams does not discuss novels that show overt antipathy to their historical moment. My own argument here begins with the position that even novels striving to offer critiques of Ireland's contemporary social and economic order find themselves embedded in it. For me, the key aspect of the neoliberal is the way in which—to offer a modification to Flew's characterization of hegemony—it advocates for a devolution, destruction, or distrust of social institutions, valorizing instead the personal, individual, and private. In keeping with Mirowski's position that this dissolution of the collective is conducted less against the state than with its assistance, I read the assault to be on democracy, using Gargi Bhattacharyya's suggestion that consent is no longer sought, which aligns with Bonnie Honig's useful formulation, in *Public Things*, of the opposition between a public, collective, or commons mindset and a "contemporary impulse to privatize everything" (2017, 3). The decline in collectivist thinking and institutions can be traced in part to the Reaganite and Thatcherite attack on unions, government, and even, if we take Margaret Thatcher (1987) at her word, society itself, given her famous assertion that "there is no such thing as society."

Thatcher's view reflected a move away from the sorts of Keynesian monetary policies that had helped to build the global economy in the middle of the twentieth century. The Keynesian model that governed the world economic order came under increasing pressure in the United Kingdom and United States during the terms of Thatcher and Ronald Reagan, respectively, with their efforts to lower taxes and trade barriers and their corresponding ideological interest in shifting responsibility from the collective to the individual. In the wake of these developments, the demise of the Eastern Bloc was read as evidence that government interventions on behalf of the collective (an overt collective, anyway, one of those working on for the polis) were infringements on individual liberty and agency.

Throughout the twentieth century, Ireland's social and political contract came to resemble those of other relatively prosperous Global North countries, even if its specific history diverges from this more general narrative. The economic boom and rampant growth of the stock market in the United Kingdom and United States in the 1980s, for instance, do not map easily onto Ireland, which remained mired in unemployment and recession. Still, Seán Ó Riain (2014, 2017) notes that the origins of Ireland's growth pre-date its eventual emergence by decades; the 1990s see the fruition of initiatives dating back to efforts to reject the isolationism during World War II. Locating "Irish developmentalism" in T. K. Whitaker's "First Programme of Economic Expansion" and the subsidies, lowered taxes, and end of protectionism evinced in the early 1960s, Ó Riain argues that "contemporary globalization appears to have found Ireland well before it found the rest of the globe. From the late 1950s forward, Ireland pursued an uninterrupted strategy of increasing integration in the global economy—actively pursuing foreign investment and becoming one of the most open economies in the world" (2017, 39). In Ireland, as elsewhere, the 1990s came to feature a light regulatory environment, the privatization of state corporations, and a further lowering of the corporate tax rate.

Alongside these sorts of pro-business policies, labor relations also played a role in Ireland's move from midcentury isolationism through prosperity and into economic crisis. Terrence McDonagh and Terry Dundon (2010) identify Ireland's unique labor/management model as one of "social partnership" structures that contributed, ultimately, to a move away from a collective mindset. McDonagh and Dundon note that, while Ireland in the twentieth century had "historically high levels of union membership" (15), its particular accommodations between labor and management differed in key ways from arrangements in Britain and the United States—namely, through adapting "voluntary partnership as an alternative and more inclusive social governance arrangement . . . [that] . . . facilitated a consensus around national identity rather than sectional self-interest" (15). McDonagh and Dundon argue that this collaborative approach did not so much circumvent problems as conceal them: "In many ways, the framework of social partnership created an appearance of industrial harmony which did not have deeper roots in parallel economic and social structures" (16). Ireland might appear less adversarial to the collective, but privatization, weak enforcement of EU directives, and a "minimalist welfare state in terms of social security and health care provision" (16) meant that Ireland experienced a decline in the notion of a civic society or public good broadly congruent with that in Britain and the United States.

Alongside these economic features, we can trace a decline in resonant iterations of the collective: the drop-off in church attendance, the rise in a two-tier system of medical care, the construction boom that created more private homes, the decline of rural communities alongside the upsurge of more impersonal versions of urbanization, and the growth in personal technology. My interest in the post-boom era stems in part from a concern that the structures that helped to assemble earlier unity—complex forces with positive and negative features—are now vanishing or being marshaled toward the goal of dismantling a civic collective. Neoliberalism may offer us one set of terms to use in considering the reconfiguration of social interactions in recent decades, but a parallel or embedded narrative about the changing relationship of the individual to the collective provides another important framework. I therefore also make connections to Ulrich Beck's ideas about reflexive modernity and individualization as society moved beyond industrial modernity (1986). Beck contends that in the latter half of the twentieth century, personal choice in identification replaces "class culture and consciousness, gender and family roles" (87), pointing out that increased choice and responsi-bility devolve to the individual.[5] The social shifts tracked by Beck were viewed in distinct though compatible lenses by Luc Boltanski and Ève Chiapello, who trace the emergence of networked organi-zations and the false "freedom" and "autonomy" of post-Fordist capitalism, as well as by Scott Lash and his idea of the "non-linear individual" (2005, ix). These late capitalist forms emerge alongside a decline in social safety nets and the rise of technology for the self, from the Walkman to the personal computer to the feed, a larger cultural movement toward atomization.

I've written elsewhere about the gains for working-class people in the United Kingdom and Ireland during the time of postwar con-sensus, as well as about the ways that a Thatcherite mindset worked to separate the "undeserving" from the rest of society (McGlynn 2016). This project of disassembling the welfare state has taken a different path in Ireland than in Britain, due in part to the different economic bases of each economy and the relative lack of power of unions in Ireland; because of the social partnership model, unions were never a huge foe to be vanquished as they were in Wales, the Midlands, and the Northeast. Moreover—and in extension of this fact—Ireland's economic worldview has come increasingly to bor-row from the American model, replacing its earlier collective identi-ties (of nation, culture, and religion) with increasingly individualized, consumption-oriented identities.[6] At the same time as Ireland joined

5. I discuss Beck's ideas further in the next chapter. See also Rasborg (2017); Lash (2001); and Beck and Beck-Gernsheim (2001).

6. Part of the attraction of the American model is that it provides a means to shed stodgy collectivism, meaning that when Ireland casts away what was charac-terized as an insular nationalism, it (perhaps inadvertently) also rejects class iden-tifications. See Coulter (2015, 25–26) for an excellent summary of what Ireland in the 1990s attempted to leave behind (including the dominance of the Catholic Church, sectarianism, and archaic ideas about divorce and homosexuality) and the myopia about the dangers of neoliberal capitalism that this effort caused.

Europe, eliminating trade boundaries and embracing a single market and currency, it retained similarities to the United States, from its sharp agrarian/urban divide (much less prominent in the United Kingdom) to its tax system organized to encourage, protect, and reward entrepreneurial activity. This American orientation will be discussed further in chapter 2.

At the moment, I merely point out that, at the height of the Celtic Tiger, the sitting government paid tribute to the "rugged individualism" of the United States as a way to distance itself from and critique its continental European neighbors, a mindset that appears to have helped to hasten and deepen Ireland's economic crisis and to have laid groundwork for a public particularly compliant and receptive to austerity measures. In the pages that follow, I contend that we can productively read the moment of the crash as the logical extension of not only "rapid globalization" but also, crucially, the *"Americanization* of the Irish economy and society during the Celtic Tiger years" (Kelly 2017, 51, emphasis mine). That is, the key dimension of the crash in Ireland is its indebtedness to economic models drawn not from the EU but from the United States. Such a mindset certainly informed Tánaiste Mary Harney's July 2000 praise of the "'American way . . . an economic model that is heavily based on enterprise and incentive, on individual effort and with limited government intervention'" (quoted in O'Toole 2010, 173). Decrying what she saw as a European tendency toward interventionism and instead emphasizing personal responsibility, Harney pledged Irish allegiance to American ideologies at just the moment that many observers would suggest a boom tipped into a bubble. I want to emphasize less the shift from supposedly healthy growth into irrational exuberance than the fundamental assumptions that unite both, calling attention to their debt to an ethos of speculation—of risk—and personal identity, factors that meld in what gets packaged as a "free market" ideology that decries government ownership, regulation, or even taxation. The distrust of collectivism embodied in Harney's remarks has shaped Irish responses to the crisis.

Austerity and Alchemy

With penetrating hindsight, the narrative of the rise and fall of the Celtic Tiger continues to solidify, though interpretations still differ. Many scholars, including Colin Coulter (2015) and Kieran Allen (2015), read the entire period of exponential growth as an untrammeled, uneven, poorly planned grab of capital. As Coulter notes in an excellent overview of the path to austerity, critiques of the Tiger can be found as early as Denis O'Hearn's 1998 warning *Inside the Celtic Tiger: The Irish Economy and the Asian Model*, which noted inequities in growth (as well as the role of US-led industrial sectors). Coulter suggests, however, that O'Hearn's heavy reliance on a neo-Marxist dependency theory meant that he "might not quite have succeeded in his attempt to vanquish the mainstream ideologies that venerated the boom" (2015, 31). Others, like Séan Ó Riain (2014), seek to distinguish an initial "healthy" phase from a subsequent overleveraging, particularly in domestic real estate, a debt-propelled property bubble. Both narratives connect the Irish economic trajectories—first up and then down, down, down—to the larger global economy.

The structuring of the terms of the 2009 bailout imposed a retroactive narrative on the boom and bust, one that underscores a worldview driven by nonstate economic actors and suggests an absence of alternatives.[7] Annie Galvin (2018) has concisely and compellingly

---

7. Clearly only the most protectionist economy operates in anything even resembling isolation, but in discussing the way that a relatively small economy like Ireland's is buffeted by larger forces, it is important that we do not fall into a rhetoric of inevitability. It is easy to absolve those in power of the consequences of their choices if we accept the idea of a massive, complex economic system that operates directed only by an "invisible hand." While Adam Smith's metaphor was long taken to be of a benevolent automaton, pervasive global precarity would suggest the hand to be indifferent and paring its fingernails, if it is indeed disconnected from any human agency. But, just as likely, the human agents who benefit from the idea of an uncontrolled system use the perception of an intricate and enfolded structure as a way of concealing their active control in the ongoing distribution

wedded economic and cultural insights about austerity, emphasizing austerity's discursive usefulness. She characterizes the position of the Irish economy within domestic, European, and global contexts, tracing the interaction among these levels through the lens of austerity and directing us to James Meadway's insight that, unlike "recession," which has a formulaic definition (two consecutive quarters of negative growth), austerity is a more flexible category, which accounts for its significance in our cultural imaginary (2018, 579). Gargi Bhattacharyya's *Crisis, Austerity, and Everyday Life: Living in a Time of Diminishing Expectations* (2015) examines this suppleness and rhetorical potential at length, noting the ways that the term encompasses the degradation of politics; the institutionalization of despair; and, ultimately, the overall diminishing of expectations. Bhattacharyya sees austerity as managing "the reframing of what people can expect [into] what people deserve" (145).

Bhattacharyya notes the usefulness of the Birmingham model of cultural studies and the work of Stuart Hall in particular. Hall's analysis of Thatcherism and Reaganism revealed the ways in which each leader sought and created consent for a dismantling of postwar-era consensus. Bhattacharyya argues that the ongoing austerity measures in practice (her focus is Great Britain) arose out of a similar discursive maneuver that seeks to use the economic crisis to advance an ideological project of redistributing economic assets. She locates the difference between the earlier moment of dispossession in the 1980s and the current one in the downplaying or even outright absence in the 2010s of a rhetoric of consent, recurrently demonstrating that now "we are encouraged to believe our consent is unnecessary" (11). Her analysis builds on that of John Clarke and Janet Newman (2012, 26), in their reading of austerity as "magical

---

of wealth among a small, and, increasingly, stratospherically wealthy elite. The contemporary rhetoric of inevitability serves as the logical extension of Thatcher's There Is No Alternative (TINA); a reasonable counterframe is Rob Nixon's, which acknowledges austerity as one facet of slow violence and structural violence as constitutive of a global economy grounded in inequality (2011, 10).

thinking" that "remake[s] our readings and articulations of events and likely futures." In such an instance, in which ideology is being rendered as "common sense," we can see fiction as a space in which the pillars of common sense are rattled. The direct line between novel and political action is rare, but, in looking at a cross-section of recent fiction, both B-format and mass market, we can discern patterns that both respond to and reconfigure the status quo.[8] Particularly in a landscape where so much weight is given to the symbolic and imaginary (we can think of indices of "consumer confidence" and the like), fiction is a source for counterimaginaries of the sort that sculpt a cultural structure of feeling.

Raymond Williams's "structure of feeling" is a touchstone for Adam Kelly as well, a backbone to his convincing case for the role of novels in an economic context where "the question of what is real and what is not cannot easily be settled," opening space for novels that reveal the limits of "a materialist commitment to the 'real economy'" but stop short of postmodernist embraces of "the unreality of contemporary life *tout court*" (2020, 198). In keeping with Kelly, Bhattacharyya, and Clarke and Newman, I underscore that, alongside the real-world food insecurity and housing struggles faced by Irish citizens due to the shape of the troika bailout, there is a discursive battlefield as well, the space where such struggles are made to seem acceptable or not. The nontangible qualities of the terrain in no way diminish the stakes of the encounter. Quite to the contrary, rhetorical interventions have massive effects on real-world people and policies.

The interaction of material and rhetorical forms the basis of the aforementioned concept of consumer confidence: the notion that economic actors who feel positively about the economy participate in more exchanges, from shoppers who buy more goods

8. I employ the term "B-format" rather than the more common "literary fiction" because the distinction among high-, middle-, and lowbrow is not only increasingly murky but also irrelevant, a holdover from an era in which hierarchy and privilege were under less critical scrutiny.

when they believe the economy is healthy to stock market investors whose choices to buy reflect and inspire further growth to
companies who hire more workers when economic indicators tell
them it is safe. Such a mindset follows from the neoliberal faith in
a market that knows more than any single participant in it could:
this Hayekian "unassimilable complexity" of the economy requires
consumer participation, not comprehension (Staten 2017, n.p.). Paul
Krugman evoked the "confidence fairy," in mocking the statement
of European Central Bank president Jean-Claude Trichet in 2011
that "'confidence-inspiring policies will foster and not hamper economic recovery'" (quoted in Clarke and Newman 2012, 300). The
imposition of austerity relies on a form of "voodoo economics" in
which the market's preference for untrammeled capital is taken as
a promise of growth that will—at least a little—trickle down to
government coffers and the wallets of the 99 percent. Clarke and
Newman dub this mindset the "alchemy of austerity," noting that it
"is not just a matter of persuading the populace to adopt a form of
'false consciousness'; alchemy, the investment in magical beliefs, is
itself part of the strategy for recovery" (300). These critiques would
seem to suggest that the rhetorical concept of consumer confidence
ought not be considered to have a major effect on the economy, but
the fact that people like Trichet believe in its importance means
that such numbers are tracked and invested with significance, to
the point that high consumer confidence is interpreted as a sign of
a healthy economy even if many citizens remain in economically
precarious positions.[9]

The flipside to this confidence game is the effort by those opposed
to a postwar consensus welfare state to suggest that public spending
and the public sector were somehow responsible for crisis and that

9. The tracking of unemployment rates and wages are similarly problematic, as a low unemployment rate and rising wages are read as indices of economic
health, although these numbers neither address chronic underemployment and the
exploitations of shift work nor demonstrate how people are managing with inadequate health and retirement plans.

their contraction is a moral and social good. This funhouse mirror of Piketty's argument (2014) sees the social agreements that underwrote Europe's economy after World War II—namely, the provision of cradle-to-grave health care, jobless benefits, and a right to basic housing—as an anomalous and inefficient economic mode that must be abandoned. Beginning in 2009, both the British and Irish safety nets began to be dismantled in ways that pushed benefits provision toward a more American-style, minimalist, last-ditch scenario. This is a crisis that is not being wasted by opponents of the welfare state: while the Irish economy lagged behind others in its return to official economic growth, turning economic indicators like employment rates, growth rates, and debt-to-GDP ratios in an upward direction only in 2013, as of 2020, it had registered continuous economic growth since then, by most measures the fastest in the EU.[10] Giovanni Arrighi (1994) has argued that systems of flexible accumulation evolve new solutions in new political contexts; much of what we see happening in the Irish public sphere represents an adjustment and accommodation designed to ensure the ongoing accumulation of capital by the very wealthy and a corresponding downward recalibration of expectations for an expanding precarious class.

Discussion of economic conditions continues to be shaped by recourse to rhetorics of complexity and even mysticism, as well as by the financialization of daily life and a normalization of precarity—such are the neoliberal contributions to our contemporary structures of feeling. Conversations about the economy that rely upon discourses of alchemy and unreality mystify complex mathematics and obscure the real-world dimensions of financialization.[11] Throughout *Broken*

---

10. The data on growth is complicated by the role Ireland has served in the enticingly named tax avoidance schemes (the Double Irish and Single Malt) for numerous major US companies including Apple, Google, and Starbucks. Such shell games ended in January 2020, with efforts by a new presidential administration in the United States in 2021 suggesting further reduction of Ireland's tax haven status to come.

11. See Finch (2015).

Irelands, I connect such discourse to the formal traits and generic tendencies of recent Irish fiction.[12] A crucial and related aspect of neoliberal society is its presentation of time as a static, individualized experience from which there is no escape. To this timeless time I now turn.

Timeless Time, Simultaneity, and the Neoliberal Present

In the twenty-first century, throughout the public sphere, instantaneity and sensation are privileged over logic or development, affording primacy to personal experience. It is easy to disparage a social milieu shaped by unboxing, haul, and reaction videos; YOLO (You Only Live Once); and social media influencers. Even such supposed counterforces as mindfulness, slow food, and media fasts are born of a worldview inflected by commodified self-care. Such an environment feels increasingly difficult to escape; we can see its effects on our language in the proliferation of texts—rebranded as "content"—that presume a reduction of attention spans. Numerous hallmarks of the new millennium such as Twitter; TLDR (Too Long, Didn't Read) summaries; and fragmentary text conversations laced with abbreviations and such nonverbal signifiers as gifs and emoji deliver content in discrete, easy-to-consume microdoses. Ironically, in the era in which we read in ever-smaller units, the total *amount* that we read has actually grown: Maryanne Wolf cites a research finding that the average person "consumes about 34 gigabytes across varied devices each day," which Jennifer Howard (2018) calculates as some one hundred thousand words. The only way for most of us to navigate so much material is through skimming, which lends a sense of haste and superficiality to our engagements.

12. I have made the connection elsewhere between magical thinking and texts that break with realist conventions, arguing that the focus of such films and novels on individual characters in Britain serves to obscure the processes by which the bulk of the populace is to remain solvent, locating responsibility for financial stability at the level of the individual, not the social; see McGlynn (2016).

In reducing the depth of intellectual focus, the contemporary content landscape elevates emotion as a more authentic mode of interaction and expression. The iterations of this affective state range from the mode of outrage in the public sphere and the dominance of Instagram and TikTok to the proliferation of plotless videos featuring cute animals, recursive vines, and ASMR triggers. Similarly, the phrase "all the feels," which scans ungrammatically, privileges a static emotional condition over the active experiencing of it.[13] Feeling frequently replaces sequenced argument or narrative progress; relatedly, Sharae Deckard references "a timeless, homogenous present, mired in the instantaneity of affect" (2017, 5). In post-boom fiction, the deployment of affect substitutes for ratiocination, hypotactic logic, and even linear narration. The absence of diegesis can feel fresh and empowering, but such plotlessness can also serve as a capitulation to powerlessness and a belief that nothing can be changed, which can in turn absolve a culture (or, say, a class of investors, policymakers, or bankers) from responsibility. As no single economic actor can be faulted for a global economic crisis, focus on specific individuals—and even the empathy generated for them—can also work as a means to evade blame. The novels I explore in this book erupt into irrealism and ungrammaticalities in response to our contemporary apotheosis of the personal.

Jeffrey Derksen appears to have been the first to use the term "long neoliberal present" (2009), grounding his analysis in the work of David Harvey and Neil Smith. We see aspects of this new temporal condition in John Urry's references to simultaneity as well as its attendant feeling of inescapability (2007); in Manuel Castell's "timeless time" (1996); in Deckard's sense of "neoliberal temporality" (2017); in Douglas Rushkoff's "present shock"; and in Michael Cronin's "tachyocracy" (2002). There is a similarly extensive critical conversation on a sense of stuckness in the present moment, an

---

13. "Feels" as a noun is nonstandard, an instance of either anthimeria or use of mass noun as a count noun.

"eternal present" or "total homogenization of time-space" (Deckard 2017); moreover, critics debate the extent to which a recognition of such a feeling constitutes capitulation to it. In this vein, Sarah Brouillette, Mathias Nilges, and Emilio Sauri warn against accepting a notion of the instant, one akin to Francis Fukuyama's "end of history" (1992) or Hans Ulrich Gumbrecht's "broad present" (2014). They caution against a mindset in which we read "one global time, an omnipresent instant in which concepts such as change and development no longer have purchase" (Brouillete et al. 2017, xv).

Clearly it is important not to internalize problematic analyses like Fukuyama's, which blithely paper over ongoing unrest and the sorts of combined and uneven development that the WReC so aptly characterizes. Nevertheless, Brouillette et al. construct a straw man in suggesting that theorists of our moment who locate and analyze feelings of disempowerment and entrapment are thereby subscribing to this worldview. To borrow Niklas Luhmann's (1990) terminology: such analysis errs in equating "first-order observation" with second, eliding the distinction. Certainly Gumbrecht situates himself pessimistically when he expresses "fundamental skepticism about the possibility of directing events—or even changing them in part . . . [situations] lie entirely outside what we can hope to control" (2014, xii). But while I disagree with and critique his passivity, it does not negate his observations about our contemporary moment, which resemble those of his critics except in his negativity. Indeed, I imagine Gumbrecht might agree that "forms of non-contemporaneity attach themselves to the logic of class or political beliefs that trouble notions of simple synchronicity" (Brouillette et al., 2017, xviii). To trace the ongoing presence of an oversimplified synchronicity or homogeneous present, and to infer from it such traits as hopelessness and inescapability in texts, is to offer criticism of the worldview whose processes shape our sense of possibility.

Navigating between the ideas of an inescapable present and a heterogeneous contemporary, we can locate a persistent sense of presentness in any number of recent texts; we must test explanations for why this literary trend is pervasive at this moment, acknowledging the emergence of an "aesthetic form consonant with new social relations" (Moretti 1996, 79).[14] In this case, the new social relations are bound to the economic changes set in motion by the rise of neoliberalism. As Christian Kloeckner and Stefanie Mueller write, "Recent decades of intensified financialization have *restructured temporal experience*" (2018, 1, emphasis mine). The varied ways that fiction has made thematic engagements with this turbulent economic and social moment have been well explored by Leigh Claire La Berge, Annie McClanahan, Kloeckner, and others. In the Irish context, most pertinently, Claire Bracken, Pilar Villar-Argáiz, Joe Cleary, and Jason Buchanan have examined the impact of crisis and austerity on literary production—a valuable conversation that I inflect here with sustained attention to aesthetic form. I contend that the concerns about boom, bust, austerity, and precarity in recent Irish fiction are formally generative of different types of fiction than we have seen in earlier eras, even those with similar socioeconomic contours. Proving such a case might suggest the ways in which our neoliberal moment, while part of Giovanni Arrighi's long-wave cycles of capitalism, is also a distinct escalation, one fed by an exacerbation of corporate capitalism and growing inequality, by specific technological innovations, and by an ever-accelerating global climate crisis. Recognition of cycles and resemblances allows us to see meaningful shifts and differences as well.

An earlier cycle offers a useful way to think about the current reconfiguration of perceptions of time. The advent of large-scale mechanization in the first half of the nineteenth century inaugurated major changes within the experience of time. Andreas Huyssen, quoting Anthony Giddens, reminds us of the "'commodification of

---

14. It's important to note that there are long-wave cycles and resonances with other periods here: this sense of a slowing of change or embeddedness in the present is not unique to this moment. One can think, for instance, of the cyclical time of the medieval era, bound by agricultural and ritual repetitions (Gurevich 1985, 98). Elliott (2018) has written about "static time" in American women's fiction dating back to the 1970s.

time-space' during the formative decades of industrial capitalism," adding that "we only need to think of the well-documented changes in the perception and articulation of time and space brought about by railroad travelling, the expansion of the visual field by new photography, the restructuring of city space with the Haussmannization of Paris, and last but not least the increasing imposition of industrial time and space on the human body in schools, factories, and the family" (1986, 18). This brisk list points to a link between technological developments and aesthetic innovation, an idea Hugh Kenner also advances in *The Mechanic Muse* (1987), noting the role of the typewriter in the development of Modernist poetry. The march of technology since the typewriter has continued to inform literary production. In extending this exploration of the intersection of form with its technological amniotic environment, the analysis below connects as well to discussions of actants and the animation of inanimate objects, interweaving attention to temporality (at both formal and thematic levels) with the often-ungrammatical eeriness of seemingly self-powered homes and machines.

Temporality as a formal dimension of irrealist and ungrammatical fiction assumes several main guises: the attention to present tense, the rise in fragmentation, the growth of paratactic logic. These features are not literal reflections of their culture—we must follow Dick Hebdige's injunction not to seek too direct a link or to assert causation. In his discussion of the semiotics of the punk subculture, Hebdige warned against describing "the pogo [dance] as the 'high-rise leap,'" as "such readings are both too literal and too conjectural. They are extrapolations from the subculture's own prodigious rhetoric, and rhetoric is not self-explanatory: it may say what it means but it does not necessarily 'mean' what it 'says'" (1979, 115–16). This line of analysis cautions against a blunt connection of form to environment. For example, in my discussion of ungrammaticality, I will not argue that a novelist's choice to use sentence fragments in her novel means her methods derive from the contemporary cultural default mode of text messaging, any more than I would want to suggest that the use of a literary present tense automatically allies an author with a pessimistic worldview that we are trapped in a neoliberal eternity.[15] Nevertheless, it would seem foolish to ignore the possibility that the rise of instantaneous communications has affected what and how authors write, as well as what texts are selected for publication. It therefore feels like a dodge when Irmtraud Huber declares the scant appearance of "recent communication technology and new media" (2016, 108) in the present-tense novels she analyzes as evidence of the lack of relevance of these developments. Aware of the Scylla of an overliteral reading and the Charybdis of ignoring cultural pressures on the novel form, we must account for the extent to which novels *do* innovate in tandem with their milieu.

Huber usefully distills earlier work on fiction in the present tense by narratologists including Dorrit Cohn, Monika Fludernik, and Gerard Genette to explain how it is that present-tense narration becomes freed from mimetic restraint: "Once the perspective shifted from the fictive situation of narration—which derives its preference for past tense narration from a mimetic commitment to real-life communicative situations—to the perspective of the reader, for which the narrated events share the same present as the moment of narration (the present moment of the reading experience), past-tense narration is exposed as a specific literary convention" (2016, 14).[16] Huber's terms are also helpful: she distinguishes among four discrete manifestations of present tense usage, noting a growth in usage within what she calls "retrospective" narration, in which "the present tense is used to portray past events, whose pastness is firmly established by context and historical markers" and "simultaneous narration,

---

15. Despite her protracted exploration of the role of digital communication in human relationships, Sally Rooney, hailed as the voice of the millennial era, ventures into ungrammaticality substantially less often than the novelists whose works I analyze at length in this book; In her case, the label of irrealism does not apply. Thematic attention does not oblige a particular form.

16. See Banfield's *Unspeakable Sentences* (1982) for a detailed linguistic analysis of the development of tensual indications of consciousness in free indirect discourse.

in which the present tense is used to narrate events which are co-instantaneous with the moment of narration" (17). As commentators often broadly link the present tense with a feeling of heightened affect, Huber makes the case that it is "imprecise" (21) to assert such a connection, building on Cohn's insight that the affective impact is dependent upon a shift between past and present; Fludernik calls this "tensual deviance" and notes it only stands out in its "intermittence" (99, quoted in Huber 2016, 10). Huber further suggests the perception of present tense as indicating emotional or affective intensity fits best with the "interior monologue" type of present tense narration. As I will discuss in connection with a number of texts that overtly deploy present tense as part of the manufacture of amplified affect, intermittence—a break in chronological perception—is indeed key, as is the idea of deviance, which connects temporal shifts to the sorts of departures that I classify as ungrammatical.

The attention throughout the book to Derksen's long neoliberal present yokes together economic conditions of precarity and the structures of feeling that naturalize the triumph of individualization across the cultural landscape. The sense of inescapability is a major feature in the sense of powerlessness that serves the engines of inequality. Analysis of how they are constructed and maintained provides hope that we can move beyond our becalmed, restless state.

2

Americanization and the Naturalization of Risk

Paul Lynch sets his bleak 2013 novel *Red Sky in Morning* in Ireland and Pennsylvania, in 1832, articulating a moral via the final words of Faller, a cold-blooded settler of scores, who speaks philosophically to the unnamed man who has pursued him in order to kill him: "I've come to notice that whatever calculations we make in life are destroyed by accidents or agencies beyond our control. . . . All this nonsense about our destiny being our own. How parochial. Every man, every nation, thinks they have control over a world that throws them about like a high wind. I'll tell you, there's always an agency more powerful than your own. Think about that. The terrible beauty of it. How it lies there unseen waiting for you. Every fate, every life, every story swallowed by forces greater'" (254). Faller's rhetorical flourishes—the anaphora of the recurrent "every" and his postpositive adjective in "forces greater"—give his speech a biblical cadence, a tone of pronouncement and judgment in keeping with its theme. The initial mention of "calculations," which would seem to valorize a quantitative framework, is undercut immediately by a mocking repudiation of the illusion of self-sufficiency, "nonsense." The implication is that the language of self-sufficiency and meaning merely creates the illusion of order in our lives, which actually have no sense, a feeling extended by his meteorological metaphor. The randomness of the high wind naturalizes the role of chance, preparing us for another nature metaphor wherein an undescribed powerful agency hides, a predator that will "swallow" us. Within this context, the parallel of man and nation feels like a jarring move:

How do winds throw nations about? Do nations have predators? The unexpected juxtaposition sets forth an allegorical reading in which a complex macroeconomics consumes the plans and policies of any single sovereign state. The passage annihilates the possibility of meaningful action at both individual and collective levels, subordinating all human efforts of understanding to a capitalist framework that "necessitates that human subjects submit themselves to its higher rationality rather than try to control it with their own" (Staten 2017, n.p.).

While this sentiment would seem to conflict with the ethos of personal responsibility, the contradiction is effaced by the reference to William Butler Yeats's "Easter 1916." By evoking the "terrible beauty," of unknown forces greater, *Red Sky* aestheticizes the randomness of history. Lynch explains in back matter accompanying the American edition of his book that he "had begun writing [it] in the spring of 2009, a time when the world economy was coming apart" (2014, 3). Lynch echoes "The Second Coming" here, though it is not the world, but its economy, that falls apart, once "mere anarchy is loosed upon the world" (Yeats 2008, 200, line 4). Faller speaks nearly a century before Yeats constructs his grand narrative of unleashed violence and widening historical gyres, this moment itself roughly a century before the global economic crisis during which Lynch wrote. The overlay of the three moments enacts a deference to grand narratives, ceding Lynch's characters to a relentless, American narrative of progress. At the same time, the inverted adjective construction and the string of sentence fragments at the end—ungrammaticalities reflective of the novel's linguistic patterns—act as traces of anxiety about the message. The inversions and fragments create a staccato that curtails momentum, creating a passage whose message of progress is undercut by its medium, a tidy analogy for the contradictions of a supposed free market actually buoyed up by monetarist interventions. This dynamic, the push-pull of progress and anxiety, is a metaphor for not only the ways a nation navigates the global economy but also for Ireland's relationship to the United States, a place that serves as an escape, a projection of fantasies, and a model for capital accumulation. The ways that Ireland positions itself in the global system have been shaped by state admiration for US financialization.

An (Irish) American Dream

In 1985, a group of politicians broke away from Ireland's longtime main ruling parties, Fianna Fáil and Fine Gael. Fed up with what it saw as illiberal social and economic policies—including a 60 percent income tax rate and resistance to divorce and contraception—the new party presented itself, and was received, as radical. Its departure from entrenched tradition was symbolized by its name (notably, in English, not Irish) the Progressive Democrats.[1] While they never held a majority in the Dáil Éireann, the Progressive Democrats had an outsize effect via coalition governments, particularly on the economic front. The embrace of social policies considered uncontroversial elsewhere in Europe was less central to the party image than was its free market ideology, including support of lower corporate and income taxes and advocacy for privatization of public goods like telecom companies, airlines, and health insurance. The party's rise coincided neatly with Celtic Tiger Ireland itself—a small entity, conservative at heart, punching above its weight.[2]

The apex of the Progressive Democrats' influence came under the leadership of Mary Harney, who served as Tánaiste (deputy prime minister) in a coalition government from 1997 to 2006, a period during which the Progressive Democrat economic program appeared so successful as to become synonymous with the national agenda, particularly in the goal of attracting foreign investment via low tax rates and other incentives. These years also saw the nation distancing

1. The name does echo the short-lived National Progressive Democrats, 1958–63, who merged with the minor Labour party.

2. The Ireland/Progressive Democrat parallel can be extended, since the party's demise coincided with that of the Celtic Tiger: the PDs were in a practical sense defunct in 2008, dissolving formally in 2009.

itself from the EU in social and economic policies; Adam Kelly reads Ireland's boom years as a time of "rapid globalization and Americanization" (2017, 51). Harney herself would readily agree; in a representative speech in July 2000, she contrasted what she characterized as a European interventionism with the "'American way . . . built on the rugged individualism of the original frontiersmen, an economic model that is heavily based on enterprise and incentive, on individual effort and with limited government intervention'" (quoted in O'Toole 2010, 173).[3] With her tribute to individual agency, Harney affirmed an Irish attachment to what were perceived as American ideologies, complete with a whitewashed, romanticized narrative of radical individualism, westward expansion, and manifest destiny. Her emphasis on enterprise and limited government underscores her investment in a specifically neoliberal America.[4]

Loïc Wacquant asserts that what we call "neoliberalism" stems from the "historical crucible and the planetary spearhead" (2009, xv) of the United States, that America acts as a "Living Laboratory of the Neoliberal Future" (xi). We can see reflections and interpretations in Ireland of an Americanized outlook in the fiscal policies, trade decisions, and tax laws put in place during the Celtic Tiger years, and especially in the debt restructuring and imposition of austerity in the wake of the bust.[5] Even the primacy afforded to economic yardsticks as a way to measure a society's health stems from the United States,

---

3. O'Toole himself is insightful in his discussion of Harney's remarks; for another in-depth, truly excellent analysis, see Kelly (2017).

4. I refer to the United States when speaking about a historical state, reserving the term "America" for the imaginary nation.

5. It is beyond the scope of this project to track the myriad examinations of the encroachment of US policies and ideologies in the social welfare states of Europe; beyond Wacquant, see work by David P. Dolowitz (2000). See also Monica Prasad (2006), who notes, "In retrospect, it is hard not to see the Reagan Revolution as inevitable, a natural outgrowth of the radical individualism and distrust of government that are supposed to be ingrained in the American character" (43). In a specifically Irish context, Seán Ó Riain links 1990s openness to foreign investment to "long-term patterns" (quoted in Kelly 2017, 55).

most visibly in the consumerist glee of the Tiger. Americanization helped to make economics the central organizing principle of public life and a key dimension of cultural production as well. The economic and symbolic investment in distinctly American narratives of radical individualism and meritocracy naturalized cultural beliefs in self-help, social mobility, and rugged individualism, a mindset that fed into the conditions of the bubble and crash.

The mythology of America implicit in Harney's "original frontiersmen" remark activates a long-standing cultural understanding between America and Ireland, involving imaginative projections of each nation by the other, spanning centuries. By the early twentieth century—when, according to the *OED*, the term "American dream" came into circulation—Ireland evoked for the United States an unspoiled rural life of romantic privation that functioned as a counterweight to the potential energy and profits of the streets paved with gold. Historic constructions of the American dream tie it to immigrants who arrive in the United States with only labor and perseverance to offer. While early iterations focus on social and political equality, achievement becomes measured via material accumulation after World War II. Certainly by the time the Irish economy began to grow rapidly in the 1990s, the American dream functioned primarily to signify economic opportunity and success, using social mobility as its gauge but couching its measurements in a fetishized narrative of bootstraps and picket fences.[6]

In an essay about the release of U2's 1988 album *Rattle and Hum*, Fintan O'Toole argues that, despite the band's progressive ideological stances, their success relied on sentimental notions of an American past: "They have re-mythologised America, given new life to images of America that no one other than Reagan has dared to tap in

---

6. I would even argue that post-Watergate disenchantment created a nostalgia for the idea of the American Dream, now frequently referenced alongside assurances that it "still lives." Ta-Nahesi Coates makes a stinging repudiation in *Between the World and Me* (2015) that emphasizes the racialized costs built into the fantasy from its invention.

modern times. . . . [U2] have created a mythic America in a way that is enormously appealing to their largely white, middle-class American audience, and, I believe, enormously destructive for the Irish young" (1994, 76–77). O'Toole recognizes here that the Irish band conveys different messages to its multiple audiences; their songs register with the American audience as affirmations of American good intentions, a view that Reagan is the first to revive after Watergate. Meanwhile, this same America serves for Irish listeners as a superior alternative and convenient escape, "saviour and refuge" (77), from the problems of their own nation. More recently, O'Toole has argued that, during the Tiger years, Ireland embraced "the notion that our authentic social identity is really American" (2002, 5) and the belief that "our identity, culture and traditions lie with American liberalism rather than with European leftism" (6). Given his earlier attention to the arts, O'Toole's focus here on the way that Irish economic interests are served by the affiliation with America accentuates the degree to which the economic has become the focal point of cultural definition. In keeping with the reach of neoliberalism elsewhere, we see in O'Toole's evolution how cultural conversations become overshadowed by the economic, such that shared cultural values are read as economic mindsets, with the elevation of ideologies of efficiency, expediency, and optimized rationality. This predominance of financial and economic concerns is a hallmark of the rise of neoliberalism globally; as Wendy Brown frames it, "neoliberalism governs as sophisticated common sense, as reality principle remaking institutions and human beings everywhere" (2015, 35). Neoliberalism's inflection in Ireland features the redefining of purported national characteristics as intrinsically pro-market, a move that reifies regressive views of nation.[7]

In autopsies of the Irish economy following the economic crisis of 2008–9, observers cited the year of Harney's declaration, 2000,

7. In tandem with the economic mimicry by the Irish, we see social parallels in moves restricting immigration and progressive social policies. See O'Toole (2002) on ways that Ireland defines itself against the rest of Europe.

as the point when the boom tipped into a bubble. Seán Ó Riain characterizes this "orthodox" view as an argument that wage competitiveness, low inflation, pursuit of foreign investment, and pro-trade policies in the 1990s were succeeded by a "departure from these fundamentals. Spending increased, wage competitiveness and export performance declined, and the economy was allowed to overheat, in particular through the creation of a credit and property bubble . . . due to the weakness of even simple prudential regulation" (2014, 8). Large swaths of the popular press agreed with government statements that affirmed that a period of good and healthy growth had been supplanted by a morally problematic greed that tipped the healthy economy into a state of excess.[8] Such a perspective was evident in the various directions that scapegoating took place. As Micheal O'Flynn, Lee F. Monaghan, and Martin J. Power indicate, a process "protective of powerful interests and the status quo . . . [blamed] myriad targets, ranging from a collective 'we who went a bit mad with borrowing' to more specific groups such as public sector workers, the unemployed, single mothers and immigrants" (2014, 921).

Although this majority view held sway within the media, there were dissenting voices before the crash, voices that grew to a loud chorus in the immediate aftermath. While such critics remain on the margins of the mainstream, their counterview resists narratives that blame common consumers and attends more to what Adam Kelly calls "important continuities between pre- and post-crash Ireland" (2017, 51). Lauding market forces and capitalism for supposedly healthy growth and blaming the subsequent crash on a shift into irrational exuberance ignores the fundamental assumptions that unite both: their debt to an ethos of speculation, risk, and personal choice,

---

8. See Coulter and Nagle (2015) on the "festival of prosperity porn that often passed for journalism during the Celtic Tiger" (11). The bust has not chastened the media: Julian Mercille in 2013 charged that the "Irish mass media are relentless cheerleaders for austerity" (quoted in O'Flynn et al. 2014, 925).

factors that meld in what gets packaged as a "free market" ideology that decries government ownership, regulation, or even taxation.[9]

Indeed, as the economy appeared to thrive, inequalities persisted and grew, with too few media, creative, or scholarly voices lodging concerns (Mercille 2014a, 1). In an excoriation of Irish intellectuals and academics for their failure to critique the Celtic Tiger as it was happening, Colin Coulter reserves some of his harshest words for the Field Day: "It would seem that the Field Day scholars would prefer to dwell on the memory of British imperialism than to confront the actuality of its American successor" (2015, 30).[10] As noted in the introduction, critical assessments of the Celtic Tiger were less absent than many observers would argue, yet Coulter's point about the United States resonates in regards to fiction from major publishing houses.[11] Irish novels skeptical of the Celtic Tiger were present, as Jason Buchanan (2013) has stated. Such domestic critiques can be read alongside another strain of response—the Irish novel of America, often written by an author affiliated with an American university.[12]

9. Adam Kelly's remark about continuities above aligns him with those who see the crash as a logical conclusion of decades of pro-growth policies like generous tax subsidies for corporations. See Kelly (2006); McCabe (2011); Mercille (2014a); and Kerrigan (2009).

Scholars of neoliberalism, most notably Mirowski (2018), but also including Cooper (2017) and Konings (2015), have aptly noted the contradiction between neoliberal rhetoric, which decries government intervention, and neoliberal policy, which seeks certain types of regulation from the government and makes weird contortions in the name of the free market.

10. Coulter convincingly argues for the lack of meaningful distinction between liberal and neoliberal elites, but as a result he fails to note O'Toole's extended critique of Ireland's appropriation of America.

11. See Kirby (2010), as well as the material Coulter himself cites. We can contrast O'Toole's heavily moralistic reading of the crash with Ó Riain's efforts to see it less as a result of individual human failings and more as a structural crisis.

12. Cleary (2018) has written about Joseph O'Neill, Colm Toibin, and Colum McCann in this context, all of whom had novels in press just as the crisis hit in both the United States and Ireland.

Such novels figured America as an alternative to Irish materialism via an embrace of the notion of meritocratic upward mobility, in which an individual's class status is understood as negotiable, and a working-class identity is viewed as best discarded. This faith in the viability of American-facing narratives of progress has clearly been called into question in the crash and the post-boom years by similar economic crises in the Irish and American economies, a fact registered variously by the novels I explore here.

While Ireland's sociocultural debt to America centers on a romantic myth of the individual and a pragmatic insistence on the primacy of economics, Irish literary expression moves beyond a literal, thematic engagement, responding through literary form as well. The relevant formal features in the novels in this chapter center around choices of narrative focalization, and, relatedly, narrative and grammatical agency and unity. Reading the intricacies of focalization choices within the ubiquity of economics reveals how this level of narration can carry mixed ideological valences, both foregrounding and masking—for instance, in working to assimilate to prosperity rhetorics or unearth the ways in which such a macroeconomic lens can obscure counternarratives. Attention to agency, through the choice of grammatical subject in a sentence as well as in the dimensions afforded to that subject, reveals the ways that aesthetic representation helps to constitute and regulate the ideal disinterested (neo) liberal individual. This individual is configured as the right shape and size perform the complex calculus needed to assume personal risk and internalize responsibility.

This chapter links theories of risk and responsibility to modes of framing responsibility for the crisis. In addition to some attention to overt themes of fortune (in both its senses, of luck and finance), I argue that work done by narrative focalization is connected to these contexts of scope and blame, thereby creating an ideologically pervasive form. The American setting and connections in my texts are not casual—they rely upon anachronistic constructions that work to retroactively construct an American back history to Irish cultural attachments to self-help, social mobility, and rugged individualism, rhetorics of classlessness and blame that fed into the conditions of the bubble and crash.[13] I read first a pair of multivocal novels: Joseph O'Connor's *Redemption Falls* (2007) and Colum McCann's *Let the Great World Spin* (2009). Both deploy a wealth of narrative perspectives, yet their focalizations delineate an American social order that locates success within the purview of the individual, elevating an Americanized neoliberal meritocracy that venerates the emergence of a few hybrid voices. While the heady exuberance of the global economic market opened space for critique of this model, even revealing it as faulty at its core, these novels nevertheless double down on the faith in social mobility. My next section returns to *Red Sky in Morning*, which uses discourses of the American westward expansion and manifest destiny to trace how ideas about luck and chance actually place responsibility on individuals, a message advanced in part through the novel's choices in syntax and tense. Extending my attention to the ideological implications of such techniques, I redouble focus on risk and luck via comparison of two novels: Sebastian Barry's *On Canaan's Side* (2011) and another McCann novel, *Transatlantic* (2013), both of which feature American migration stories that span lifetimes. Via formal choices that amplify affective responses to adversity, both novels misconstrue the extent of individual responsibility in troubling ways that normalize an austerity mindset.

In all of these novels, particularly those since the crash, ungrammatical textual configurations (e.g., incongruous tense shifts, distorted sentences) and ideologically weighted decisions about focalization create a context of inevitability for economically constructed

---

13. The texts that engage most overtly with "America" tend also to be set in the past. The exception to this axiom in recent Irish fiction is in the thriller genre, which happily demonizes American capitalists; see Alan Glyn's *Winterland* series in particular. Relatedly, as McClanahan notes in a footnote, recent realist 'credit crisis' "novels ultimately and intentionally produce sympathy for rather than antipathy toward their protagonists . . . This arguably distinguished these realist novels from the 'financial thriller' genre that also boomed in the wake of the crash: thrillers are perfectly willing to render bankers as 'evildoers'" (2018, 206n38).

neoliberal subjects that naturalizes risk, undercuts the efficacy of action, and silences the losers on the global stage. Paradoxically, the ungrammatical constructions can sometimes act as traces of the unworkability of the meritocratic worldview. In response to the failures of the global markets and their flagrantly bogus rhetorical linkage of pluck and prosperity, these novels seek new narrative means to articulate a competitive and individualist perspective, a move that requires some temporal displacement of narrative voices as well as some sentences that evade logical scrutiny.

Risk and Responsibility

As Susan Mizruchi characterizes it, "Risk differs from the neighboring concepts of 'chance' or 'danger' in its exclusive reference to adverse outcomes and in its focus on human agency" (2009, 111). Elements of human choice determine risk, meaning people bear responsibility for it: "these are potential catastrophes we have brought upon ourselves" (111). A flood is a danger; living on a floodplain is a risk. And, indeed, discussion of risk often focuses on human interaction with the environment. The 1970s and 1980s witnessed many environmental crises resulting from industrial negligence and accident—disasters such as those in Three Mile Island, Bhopal, and Chernobyl. Concurrent to these instances of human failure with ecological implications, of risks gone wrong, was the rise of the derivative era of financial speculation, a form of risk through price volatility. These environmental and economic circumstances converge to shape an era for which Ulrich Beck coined the term "risk society" (1986).

Scholars of risk society read it as both a period and a cultural condition, making the case that the sorts of risks that humans experience have "fundamentally mutated over time" (Mythen 2018, 3). Beck contrasts a premodern era of natural hazards—say, floods or fires—with a "first modernity" during which industrial society faced risks like factory accidents and other threats that result from human errors. In first modernity, fire and flood hazards become risks when they are amplified by human structures, as when the South Fork

Dam failed in an 1889 flood in Johnstown, Pennsylvania, or in the Triangle Shirtwaist Factory Fire in New York City in 1911. For Beck, first modernity is succeeded by a second modernity in which such accidents persist but are "superseded" in magnitude, frequency, and scale by a new category of "manufactured risks that stem from developmental goals of modernization and are socially rather than naturally produced" (Mythen 2018 3). Disasters are no longer the result of bad luck or an angry deity but, to echo Mizruchi, self-inflicted. Beck refers to both persistent pollutants like DDT and to discrete events, such disasters as the Union Carbide Bhopal chemical leak or the nuclear catastrophes at Chernobyl and Fukushima, which instantiate the sort of crises that "los[e] their latency and become globalized" (Beck 1992, 154); focus is less on a specific instance or a particular human error and instead on a system that cannot function except precariously.[14] The expectation of crises has in turn spawned an ever-growing scientific-industrial complex to manage and contain them. As Scott Lash's 1992 introduction to the English translation of Beck's *Risk Society* memorably states, "The axial principle of industrial society is the distribution of goods, while that of the risk society is the distributions of 'bads' or dangers" (3).

This historical narrative locates risk society temporally, seeing it as a successor to first modernity's industrial society, an era that had culminated in a midcentury Fordist system that, for all its problems, represented the height of unionized collective power.[15] During the

14. A recent example of a built-in systemic precarity can be seen in the goods shortages of the COVID pandemic, which arose largely due to a "just in time" supply chain model that developed to increase efficiency and keep costs low, essentially betting against disruptions to the pipeline.

15. See Konings (2015) for a (corrective) discussion of how some recent characterizations of a postwar utopia misread the extent to which this time was itself predicated on speculative markets and fictitious value: "Not only do such perspectives miss the fact that financial expansion is deeply imbricated with the restructuring of work and subjectivity; they are also formulated against the background of a highly nostalgic (and in many respects misleading) image of the early postwar era as an order that served to suppress the role of speculation and finance" (19–20).

subsequent decline of a society so grounded in industrial production, "the unstable unity of shared life experiences mediated by the
market and shaped by status, which Max Weber brought together in
the concept of social class, began to break apart" (Beck 1992, 95).[16]
This shift in social organization is central to Beck's argument about
risk society as cultural condition, which extends his analysis beyond
the technological and environmental to include economic and social
risks. In fact, he spends less time discussing specific environmental
threats than underscoring how integrated risk is within the structure of a contemporary everyday life in which the measurement of
risk is calculable. In this, Beck focuses at length on what he sees as
the obsolescence of discourses of class, arguing that their dissolution
gives rise to what he terms "reflexive modernity," in which individual
choice in identification replaces class solidarity.[17] Skirting declara-
tions about whether the move to reflexive modernity is a positive or
negative for individuals, the argument is largely descriptive as to the
ways increased choice and responsibility are both bugs and features
of an era in which the individual supersedes the collective as our
frame of reference: we see the dissolution of "the traditional param-
eters of industrial society: class culture and consciousness, gender
and family roles . . . These detraditionalizations happen in a *social
surge of individualization*" (87).[18]

Beck's argument rests on the supplanting of the discourse of class
with examination of the life of the individual in reflexive modernity.
Before arguing for the value of Beck's terminology despite my certainty
of the ongoing relevance of class, I will introduce two final concepts

---

16. It's worth noting the word "unstable" here—Beck does not privilege or
romanticize this earlier era in this portion of his argument.

17. While second modernity and reflexive modernity are often treated inter-
changeably by scholars writing about Beck, the former seems to me to fit better
within Beck's historical framework and the latter within the cultural descriptions.

18. Cooper has offered a modification to the idea of the neoliberal individual,
arguing that a more apt framework is one sanctifying the family as the site of
private dependence and accumulation: "private family responsibility" (2017, 21).

about the individual arising from Beck's ideas: the non-linear individual and the bricolage biography. These are terms Lash develops in his commentary on Beck's work with Elizabeth Beck-Gernsheim on individualization: "Second-modernity individuals haven't sufficient reflective distance on themselves to construct linear and narrative biographies. They must be content, as Ronald Hitzler has noted, with *Bastelbiographen*, with bricolage-biographies in Levi-Strauss's sense. The non-linear individual may wish to be reflective but has neither the time nor the space to reflect. He is a combinard. He puts together networks, constructs alliances, makes deals. He must live, is forced to live in an atmosphere of risk in which knowledge and life-changes are precarious" (Lash 2001, ix). "Non-linear" refers both to time and to space in Lash's formulation, echoing the ways modernity has itself been described by others, not to mention the techniques associated with modernism as a literary movement. Such fragmentation is tied, importantly, directly to risk and precarity.[19]

While the attention to risk and precarity is welcome, critics of Beck dislike his refusal to acknowledge the persistence of class. Moreover, his interest in the massive environmental catastrophes he foresaw—which still increase in number and severity with each passing year—downplayed the ways they would be borne by a social system still steeped in inequality. His taunt that "poverty is hierarchic; smog is democratic" (1992, 36) and accompanying contention that the earth "no longer recognizes any distinctions between rich and poor, black and white, north and south or east and west" (39) grossly

---

19. For a different but related analysis, see Boltanski and Chiapello (2005), which similarly traces successive phases, though its periodizations see nineteenth-century industrial capitalism as a phase balancing risk and stability, with a mid-century version being marked by hierarchies and meritocracy; both succeeded, and here we see the greatest overlap with Beck, by a contemporary moment in which nomadic individuals operate via networks on projects that help them to build personal capital. Their analysis of the networked dimension of contemporary capitalism also resonates with Lash's deal-making networker, the disruptive innovator so much the darling of our current moment.

misreads the extent to which the plutocratic elite insulates itself from the consequences of its consumption.[20] At the same time, I'd argue that Beck is knowingly polemical, making a provocation meant to incite action. In the same section of *Risk Society* as his smog quip, he acknowledges that "wealth accumulates at the top, risks at the bottom" (35), a clear admission that dangers tend to accrue more among those of lesser means, who in turn have less of an ability to mitigate their effects. As Jennifer Wenzel so vividly writes, "To understand vulnerability to environmental harm as unevenly universal is to recognize its inflection by histories of unequal relation to both capital and carbon accumulation, in which economic and ecological models of harm intersect. To focus on the universality of vulnerability at the expense of the unevenness—to move too quickly to ideas of the human as species, or community as planetary—is . . . a gentrification of the imagination" (2019, 33).

Beck's interest in turning our attention away from class is thus about his sense of environmental urgency and the increasing impossibility of accurate calculation of risk, but it foreshadows as well a principle I would call "vengeful democracy," in which we are gleefully informed that we reap what we sow. The current Republican regime in the United States has no interest in distributing social goods, but it certainly takes perverse delight in asserting that social "bads" belong to us all, whether they be the burdens of tariffs, the wages of gun culture, or the supposedly inevitable climate events attributed to a vindictive god.[21] While Beck himself does not state it

---

20. Beck himself in 2013 called "smog is democratic" "a metaphor" and suggested class was too "soft" a category to account for "the transnational, cosmopolitical explosiveness of social inequality in world risk society" (4). His *World at Risk* in 2009 is substantially more attentive to inequality as well, though across his career he remains committed to his arguments as to the limitations of class as an explanatory category.

21. In 2020, the politicization of mask-wearing during a pandemic led to statements like "If God wants me to get COVID, I'll get COVID. And if God doesn't want

this way, his discussion of risk society is descriptive and aligns quite nicely with an American aversion to discourses of class and the sort of atomizations that Annie McClanahan (2018) notes are central to the practices girding the credit economy. Indeed, it suits the mon-eyed interests to hear that class is no longer an operative concept. Discourses of shared prosperity ironically had their apex during the height of the Cold War. The reorientation away from such a mindset dovetails with the rising dominance of US cultural imperialism, sup-pressing class-based analyses and policies in Ireland and elsewhere.

Risk Society was published in German in 1986, during a surge of the neoliberal ethos. This cultural dimension of risk society succeeds the collectivism, protest, and student movements of the 1960s and installs in their place a rhetoric of personal responsibility and indi-viduality. As Margaret Thatcher, one of the chief proponents of such radical individualism, famously said, "There is no such thing as soci-ety. There are individual men and women, and there are families" (1987, 29–30).[22] Walter Benn Michaels (2009) contends that literary genres have compliantly accommodated this neoliberal turn; he ties, for instance, the rise in the popularity of memoir, a personal

---

me to get COVID, I won't" (Conger 2020) and "If it is God's will that I get corona-virus, that is the will of the Almighty," as said by Robert Montanelli, a resident of a Tulsa suburb who chose not to wear a mask. "I will not live in fear" (Shear 2020). The resistance to vaccination in 2021 bore similar traits. Such statements of powerlessness in the face of uncontrollable forces speak to the disaffection and per-ceived lack of agency their speakers feel. The restriction of choice to assertions of individual control in place of larger collective action underscores the way in which the burden of all risk has devolved to individuals.

22. Thatcher's quote may be famous, but it is also somewhat misremembered. What she actually said in the *Woman's Own* interview in 1987 usually cited as the origin is "Who is society? There is no such thing! There are individual men and women and there are families and no government can do anything except through people and people look to themselves first." Thatcher does, later in the interview, repeat "there is no such thing as society" (30), but the earlier phrasing is important in that it aligns her with the focus on the family identified by Cooper (2017).

narrative, to the heyday of Thatcherite antisociety rhetoric.[23] For Michaels, attention to the individual is one way "make the reality of our social arrangements invisible" (n.p.). In a social configuration that focuses on the individual, presumes autonomy and accountability, and places the onus of risk upon each of us, what becomes invisible is the extent to which individual risks have social roots and individual problems have institutional causes.

Dovetailing Mizruchi's suggestion that the very discourse of risk carries within it the implication that we have brought our problems upon ourselves with Beck's attention to the individual, I want to extend Michaels's ideas to argue that the invisibility of institutional responsibility very much sculpts a society in which one's home in a floodplain or one's subprime mortgage comes to be read as a *personal choice*. Certainly the Irish economic crisis was swiftly perceived this way, most infamously in a remark by Brian Lenihan that "we [the Irish people] all partied." This thumbnail analysis made the highly dubious case that "the crushing liabilities of six private banks . . . approximately €400 billion in leveraged loans" (McCabe 2011, 169) was somehow the aggregation of personal greediness on the part of Irish consumers, roughly 73 percent of whom had annual incomes below €38,000.[24] Conor McCabe (2015) further offers concrete evidence of the eagerness of the Irish government to see the risky choices of individuals as precipitating the crisis: "Despite the fact that commercial property was the crucial element in the collapse of these banks [AIB, Bank of Ireland, and Irish Life and

---

23. This suggestion seems plausible in part because an interest in memoir is accompanied by an interest in other individualisms like the Walkman and then the iPod and the "personal savior" iteration of fundamentalist Christianity.

24. O'Flynn et al. argue that "Minister Lenihan's somewhat defensive remarks . . . even came to pass as 'common-sense'" (2014, 926). See McClanahan (2018) for discussion of the demonization of individual bankers as vectors of risk who brought down the economy (but were never prosecuted). See also Coulter and Nagle: "Some two thirds of the workforce in Ireland were drawing salaries of €38,000 or less" (2015, 11).

Permanent], mortgage-holders were routinely listed as the root cause of the problem" (59).

Such willingness to locate blame with individuals is itself an indication of the extent to which an Americanized mindset held sway in Ireland.[25] As Rosemary Meade contends, "narratives of blame" rely upon "that most pervasive of ideological devices, the fetishisation of individual choice . . . [assuming] that individual citizens— be they ordinary consumers, politicians or employees of financial institutions—can be disassociated from their economic and social habitus and thus hold sovereign responsibility for their risky choices in the market place" (2011, 33). To see risk as an expected feature of the landscape, and to frame economic crisis to privilege the individual over the collective is, as Michaels also argues, to obscure late capitalism's contradictions (Meade 2012, 33).[26] Contradictions like these expressed themselves overtly in the global crises of 2008, as in the transfer of responsibility from corporate bodies to taxpayers.[27] In the cases of subprime mortgages in the United States, overleveraged developers in Ireland, and the European and American banks trading mortgage-backed securities and deploying other financial

25. Ó Riain cites "increasingly close financial integration" between the US and Ireland as a factor in the Irish crisis, adding, "This financial integration itself has been closely linked to a broader project of economic liberalization, most clearly since the 1990s" (2017, 28). See Connor, Flavin, and Kelly (2012) for examination of the similarities and divergences in the two national economic crises; they conclude that "irrational exuberance" among market actors, a "capital bonanza," and failures of regulation and "moral hazard" link the two crises.

26. See Curran (2013) for an effort to reconcile Beck's strident—and, most would argue, mistaken—rejection of class with attention to ongoing economic inequalities.

27. Harvey (2015) quotes Marx as arguing that "world trade crises must be regarded as the . . . forcible adjustment of all the contradictions of bourgeois economy. [This adjustment] manifests itself as crises, *violent fusion of disconnected factors operating independently of one another yet correlated*" (n.p., his emphasis). The continuing recovery without growth in Ireland and the United States suggests the accumulation of new contradictions for a future crash.

instruments that fed bubbles in both nations, private, for-profit companies held speculative positions. Had the windfalls that helped produce the bubbles continued, the returns would have remained in the business sector. But when risks taken in global finance failed to yield dividends, the responsibility for debts was spread across society, leading to massive spending cuts in the public sector in both countries.[28] Given the original concentration of risk within the banking industry compared to its eventual dispersed impact—which in both nations was seen to affect the poor disproportionately—it's interesting to note the contradictions by which the cultural imaginary focuses on the individual for the assumptions of risk but speaks in terms of society in the dispersal of blame.

Indeed, we can see here an oscillation between a discourse that locates choices and risks at the level of the individual and a critique of attention to the individual as limiting or distorting our perspectives. McClanahan argues that fiction and credit both rely upon "a balance of specificity and generality" (2018, 60) in their "imaginative calculus of typification" (61), a metonymic elision of individual and collective. Credit scoring "insist[s] on a new kind of individualized granularity, . . . assum[ing] that economic society is not a complex totality of social classes but merely an aggregate of autonomous individuals" (66). McClanahan notes that this relationship is more "fluid and temporary" (66) than earlier configurations of class, a reconciliation of sorts between Meade's ideas and Beck's that allows me to argue for the ongoing necessity to consider class while retaining from Beck's arguments several key ideas: first of all, we see the reduction of the semantic centrality of what had seemed to be naturalized and conventional class distinctions. With the increasing gap between a super-wealthy plutocracy and an ever-more-precarious

---

28. Ireland's austerity measures included tax increases and public spending cuts equaling $20 billion (over €15 billion) and high-interest loans and funds withdrawn from its pension plan (Faiola 2010). The US austerity plan used blunt, across-the-board sequesters in discretionary spending, originally projected to save $1.1 trillion over ten years (CBO 2011).

everyone else, the tripartite structure of upper, middle, and lower classes has come to be read as dated. In place of this group solidarity and agency, Beck predicted—and we can very much see—the rise of the individual as nomad, responsible for more, laden with and liberated by choices.

In keeping with a society where more and more choices rest upon us, we can be seen to be—we can feel—in control of outcomes, as though good results arise from our own hard work, grit, and foresight. Conversely, we can believe and feel as though bad outcomes are consequent to our own shortcomings. This sort of attribution frequently extends to literary characters as well, shaped by narrative perspective. "Narrative focalization," Gerard Genette's term for the perspectival and interpretative lens through which we perceive a story, gives authors the ability to voice their narratives monologically, dialogically, from below, in critique. Narratological perspective affords access to a broader swath of voices; one of the strengths of the crash and crisis fiction has been its extension of narrative subjects and viewpoints to those on the margins. A nonjudgmental narrator can operate outside the realm of the sort of "privilege" that Wayne Booth equated with omniscience, a powerful and controlling single perspective. The focalization choice can affirm or displace the centrality of subjective experience. This is not the only ideological work done by narrative focalization: as Divya Dwivedi, Henrik Skov Nielsen, and Richard Walsh note, "It is a crucial vehicle for foregrounding, or masking ideological questions. . . . Focalization is often more importantly about the socially constructed aspects of political situations than the idiosyncrasies of individual subjectivity; it provides for the irreducible role played by beliefs, allegiances, and historical and ideological positionality in the unfolding of social and political struggles" (2018, 20–21).

Meritocracy Gospel

Focalization in Irish novels about America serves in the era of the Celtic Tiger to naturalize a veneration of the individual that simultaneously undercuts the efficacy of action.[29] Examining two novels whose production precedes the global economic crisis, this section demonstrates the narratological allegiance of their authors to a vision of Americanized neoliberal meritocracy that celebrates the triumph of a few hybrid voices. Boom-era novels by Colum McCann and Joseph O'Connor give voice to marginalized groups via textual heterogeneity, but in each case, this platform is summarily retracted by novel's end.

McCann has remarked that he sees *Let the Great World Spin* as a post–9/11 novel; its 2009 publication date locates it as well as a novel of economic expansion. The novel is set in New York City in 1974, during the week that Nixon resigns and Philippe Petit walks between the World Trade Towers on a tightrope. To offer a complex portrait of this moment in cultural and political history, McCann shifts narrative perspectives frequently, with each section narrated by someone different. Petit's performance and a car crash on the same day function as the twin axes around which the novel revolves, with the two characters who die in the collision on the FDR East River Drive in turn figured as twin towers themselves. In a novel related to us by twelve narrators, largely in first person, the characters who die, Corrigan and Jazzlyn, are narrative subjects—they do not speak outside of quotation marks, nor do they ever serve as focalizers.[30]

A chapter featuring an adolescent Puerto Rican photographer, Fernando Yunqué Marcano, opens on the subway, his ride offering an analogy to the novel's narrative method: "At times he gets dizzy just anticipating the next corner. That speed. . . . Control and oblivion. Sometimes it feels like he's the one driving" (167). McCann's focalization, here a third person free indirect discourse, is voiced in a slang-filled, neologistic Spanglish that creates the illusion that Fernando controls the text; at the same time, the section bears

29. For a longer version of this discussion, see McGlynn (2014).

30. McCann opts to depict dialogue in some of his sections with quotation marks, while other narrators use dashes.

hallmarks of McCann's own characteristic style, the vivid, ungrammatical sentence fragments serving as a reminder that Fernando is not the one driving; rather, McCann's tightly constructed novel pairs him with Petit, another outsider and artist. Fernando photographs graffiti, which served as a venue and voice in New York in the 1970s, framing it and presenting it to an audience who would not see it—or not see it as art—otherwise. Like the aerialist Petit, the young photographer incorporates the twin towers in his own artistic expression, one infused with physicality. Both redefine beauty as something intimately linked to, even arising from, everyday places and events, a message in keeping with the novel's own aesthetic. The use of some third-person narrative past narration for both further parallels the artists.[31] McCann presents both characters as engaged in precarious balancing acts, their risks paying off in a novel where most characters experience very bad luck.[32]

Fernando's brief section—the novel's shortest—ends when he realizes the police he spots are not about to ticket him for riding atop the subway with his camera, and he decides to follow them through the turnstiles at the Wall Street stop of the #5 train. The photograph he presumably then takes—of Petit high above on the wire, a plane flying by—appears between two later narratives, a copyright logo affixed to it. We do not witness his act of creation, only the product, a move by McCann that invests his character with autonomy beyond

31. Narrative perspective is complicated in *LTGWS*: about half of the novel's sections, even some by peripheral characters, are narrated in first person; some sections are narrated in present tense. Claire and her husband are also third-person focalizers, as is Jaslyn; Sam, Adelita, Tillie, Claire, and Jaslyn are all in present tense. Tallies: seven of thirteen sections in third person, six of twelve voices use present tense. Another set of variations without clear pattern come in the choice of tense: Claire, Fernando, Sam, Tillie, Adelita, and Jaslyn use a narrative present, while the other sections are mostly or entirely in narrative past.

32. McCann's bad luck does seem disproportionately to affect his female characters, who suffer recurrently across his opus. Most painfully, many of them, including Tillie here and multiple women in *TransAtlantic*, lose their children.

the bounds of the words on the page. In this, McCann depicts the boy not as a narrative subject but as an artist himself.[33] (A doorman at the *New York Times* even jokes that Fernando is "Horatio José Alger" (172), allying him with the authorship of narratives of upward mobility rather than with Alger's characters.) Fernando's creative gesture presumably brings him the fame he craves, at the same time as his disappearance from the novel indicates how peripheral he is to the storyline—we hear no more about him. The photograph, art and journalism at once, tells the story of another, simultaneous sidelining of the Hispanic character and a freeing of him from an objectifying gaze.

Fernando doesn't know or interact with any of the other characters; rather, McCann uses him as representative of New York's Hispanic population, along with Adelita, Corrigan's beloved. Adelita comes to New York with dreams of becoming a doctor, an ambition that distinguishes her class status from that of the prostitutes or even Gloria, a college graduate whose working life is not foundational to her identity. Together with Adelita, Fernando is emblematic of the migration patterns shaping New York City in 1974; alongside Adelita's work ethic, Fernando's photography—a step distinct from graffiti, mediating it for consumption as art—sketches a portrait of immigrant striving. Via the inclusion of words in Spanish in the sections focalized through these two characters, McCann marks both characters with a bilingual identity; he does not seek to assimilate them into a monolithic culture so much as to show them successfully entering into a vibrant diversity.

Despite the Spanish terms, however, the novel's voice remains remarkably consistent. Adelita remarks that Corrigan's efforts to use the occasional Spanish phrase "sound like stones in his mouth"

---

33. Fernando's melding of artistic inspiration and photojournalistic reportage stands in rebuke of the esoteric, distanced, ultimately pretentious paintings and performance pieces created in the book's previous section by Lara and Blaine, trust fund babies who seek fame and an artistic outlet in rejecting the present and painting with the style and technological limitations of the 1920s.

(278), a perception that readers might share. Similarly, reviews have noted that the voice of Tillie, the uneducated prostitute who narrates in something of a dialect (studded with "aks" and "ain't"), is unconvincing. Despite the gestures to mark the speech of several nonwhite characters, McCann's powerful stylistic signatures, from his imagistic parataxis to his knack for the mundane sublime, mean that all the sections share pretty much the same voice. Partly for this reason, the novel's final section, "Roaring Seaward, and I Go," feels like a completion as it tells us the outcomes of various characters in the thirty-four years since Petit walked his tightrope. The retrospective vantage opens space for a moral, offered somewhat explicitly, on the novel's final page: we "find in others the ongoing of ourselves" (349).[34] This last section also imposes a present lens on the past, filtering out the characters whose narratives, with hindsight, we can now see offered local color or atmosphere to the nuclear events.

Gone, without comment, are *all* the Hispanic characters. We hear no more of Fernando, for instance, but, more troublingly, neither do we know what becomes of Adelita and her children. Adelita's national origin becomes muddy in the memory of Ciaran, Corrigan's brother, who spent time with her: "From South America—I can't remember where, Columbia or Nicaragua" (349). The conflation of Central and South America in Ciaran's mental map, along with the utter erasure of her actual country of origin, Guatemala, which gets replaced by nations viewed as sensationalistically violent, eliminates any "ongoingness" for Adelita and renders New York as a black and white and cosmopolitan city, not noticeably Hispanic at all. Instead, Hispanic identity becomes something distant and

---

34. The section title (like the novel's title) comes from the final line of Tennyson's "Locksley Hall," which many have read as thinly veiled autobiography. Its hero, like Jaslyn, is an orphan. Christopher Ricks sees the ending of the poem to be one of "vigorous vacuity" (1989, 153), arguing that the light versification is unfit for the heavy themes. I'd suggest that McCann's attraction to the poem might arise from precisely that tension of tone and heft, a juxtaposition descriptive of his own projects.

hazy, associated with political upheaval and the drug trade. Adelita is vanished and silent.

At the same time, Adelita has narrated a portion of the novel, and her ambivalent class status speaks to complexities of identity that Ciaran's callous geography overrides. The fact that she narrates her own section invests her with the same immediacy as the other first-person narrators, Ciaran, Lara, Tillie, and Sam (a.k.a. the Kid). Moreover, with her aspirations and drive, Adelita is a precursor to Jaslyn, Jazzlyn's daughter, who focalizes the novel's final section, which presents a view of twenty-first-century America as a place with racist mindsets still intact but social mobility possible for certain smart strivers. Jaslyn has a degree from Yale and a not-for-profit job helping victims of natural disasters navigate the bureaucracy, a combination that signals her membership in a politically progressive meritocracy, the end point of the dreaming we see from Adelita and Fernando.

For despite the complexities that erase and silence Hispanic characters in the novel, its presentation of them also invests them with creativity and ambition. It is telling that Adelita's reproductions, her children, do not factor in the 2006 narrative, but Fernando's reproduction, the photograph, does: McCann does not quite trust his story to have an impact without a present-day coda, and the work of art and Jazzlyn's child together bring the past into the present. Their spinning world suggests both stasis and movement, acknowledging that, while time does pass, memory and reproduction posit alternative endings: "The intrusion of time and history. The collision point of stories. We wait for the explosion but it never occurs. The plane passes, the tightrope walker gets to the end of the wire. Things don't fall apart" (325). Although this section has a different narrator than Fernando's, the parataxis and sentence fragments emphasize their shared voice and worldview shaped by the nouns that have no accompanying verbs: linearity, in the form of time and history, would be an *intrusion*.

As Jaslyn stares at the photograph taken the day her mother died— the picture clearly the same one credited to Fernando earlier—her thoughts suggest a multitude of other stories, most poignantly the one in which other planes pass the towers. Jaslyn melds the world without a terrorist attack and the one in which her mother survives, undermining Yeats's widening gyres of history. The only part of her imaginary world that did happen is that Petit did get to the end of the wire; the real man separates here from his symbol of a risk gone horribly wrong. McCann sets his final chapter at a moment of economic optimism, the year that construction was begun on One World Trade, the new tower. Petit's caper thereby suggests a risk that has paid off, an economy that has overcome adversity to grow again. The focus on the individual here (one, incidentally, whose sideline is sleight of hand and theft), like the focus on Jaslyn herself, allows readers to see exemplars rather than the mass for whom the years 1974–2006 saw a decline in real earnings despite a record GDP. Extraordinary individuals merit our attention, while ordinary masses don't register, an endorsement of meritocracy resonant with the novel's US setting.

The novel's final line is "The world spinning" (349), a fragment whose gerund evokes an unfinished feeling underlined by the recurrent nature of spinning itself. This moment of ungrammaticality fits with a narrative view of "the intrusion of time and history" as well as within a larger cultural tendency toward irresolution. In their analysis of increased evasion of responsibility in recent World Bank reports, Franco Moretti and Dominique Pestre argue that the use of a gerund leaves "an action's completion undefined, thus depriving it of any definite contour" (99). In McCann's novel, the gerund likewise creates a "blurred, slightly amorphous temporality" (Moretti and Pestre 99), wherein the static nature of a photograph (or a novel) becomes a refuge from time and history, a fantastic, even irreal, space. The open-ended, indefinite conclusion of *Let the Great World Spin* collaborates with other formal choices by McCann, including the other affect-generating sentence fragments throughout and the structuring of the novel's narration via a sequence of individual voices. This latter move—forging multiple voices into one story—enacts the ongoingness of others in themselves, as the novel's moral would have it. Such combination of the various structures of ongoingness calls to mind Lash's nomadic, deal-making combinards, suggesting that *Let the Great World Spin*'s narrative structure is a reflection of its environment, with no possibility of a self that is coherent enough to sustain an entire linear narrative. The idea of a minimalist narrator able to focalize a whole novel is sidelined in risk society; in place of such a centralizing and organizing perspective, Lash's non-linear individual who "has neither the time nor the space to reflect" must instead be "content" with bricolage.[35]

O'Connor's 2007 novel *Redemption Falls* relies upon a similar bricolage construction, time structure, and final twist beneath its multitude of archival records, narrative voices, and pre– and post–Civil War plotlines. The novel interweaves the stories of a traumatized, mute Confederate drummer boy, Jeddo; an Irish revolutionary and Union soldier, O'Keefe; and a New York intellectual, Lucia, whose lives intertwine in a fictionalized Western territory much like Montana. Their tortured efforts to form a family intersect with the tangled stories of, among others, a burn victim who loves Lucia, Jeddo's illiterate older sister Eliza, a bandit who cares for her, and a formerly enslaved woman who keeps the house. We begin the journey with Eliza, an Irish-born focalizer, walking from Louisiana north and west in search of Jeddo, in the waning days of the Civil War. The novel then moves through a mélange of other American voices, only to end in the 1930s with a hybridized voice of unknown paternity who has, via adoption, become of elevated socioeconomic status, looking back seventy years and offering a meaningful frame for what has come before.

---

35. This is not to say that a story told from a series of narrators is new; we see multiple narrative focalizers in *The Moonstone*, *Ulysses*, and *As I Lay Dying*, to name a few canonical English-language texts. Nevertheless, the proliferation in recent decades of multiple-perspective films like *Eternal Sunshine of the Spotless Mind*, *Babel*, and *Intermission*, and novels such as *Cloud Atlas*, *Trainspotting*, and *The Pleasures of Eliza Lynch* (along with many other Enright novels), does suggest the increasing relevance of the non-linear individual.

O'Connor's novel, like McCann's, offers a sensual and intelligent Hispanic protagonista who furnishes fleeting comfort to a picturesque, idealistic, Irish-born man who lives in the United States but is not allowed to survive his novel. Lucia-Cruz Rodriguez Y Ortega McClelland O'Keefe, whose ungainly name attests to her hybridity, is given far more of a voice than Adelita; we read her poems, a short narrative, letters, and journal entries. We also receive first-person testimony about her life from our narrator-archivist; the omissions of details are presented not as the hidden fires of an exoticized other but as facts excised for the narrator's own "private reasons" (451). Part of the hybridizing O'Connor effects in American culture comes in the class status of Lucia's family, the McClellands, who are wealthy New Yorkers. Lucia embodies an idealized version of an America in which the Civil War acts as a predictor of the suffragette movement, multiculturalism, and massive social mobility. The novel is clear that both Lucia and O'Keefe are hybrids—her mother is Nicaraguan, of Castilian blood, her father a "Republican" and "skeptical Presbyterian" (146, 147). O'Keefe "had Italian blood from his mother" (146). Her willingness to marry O'Keefe, educated but not pedigreed, communicates an acceptance of social mobility that the novel sees as emergent in the postwar years.

Indeed, the central narrative arc of the story traces the path of Jeddo Mooney, child of an Irish peasant and an unknown (perhaps Mexican) father, to a professorship emeritus and swanky Fifth Avenue address. Jeddo's progress stands in for the American dream itself, and the mute subaltern emerges as the puppeteer manipulating all the strings in this massive, complex narrative dance. The novel's final emotional payoff comes in our realization that abject poverty, premature exposure to the violence of war, and early lack of opportunity cannot stop the intelligence and pluck coursing through the immigrant's veins, that the intellectual elite is the same as the huddled masses—a moving conclusion that nonetheless may deliver a troubling ideological message to a Celtic Tiger readership looking for a social system suited to their new affluence. The repeated triumphs over adversity enacted in O'Keefe's dramatic escapes from, first, the noose and then Tasmania are replicated and reflected in Jeddo's flight from destitution. Both characters are cast as diamonds in the rough, possessing both intellect and drive to make something of themselves. Their ascensions are not entirely parallel—O'Keefe is known for his rhetorical grace in public speaking, while Jeddo is speechless for much of the novel—but both men navigate the American class system in ways which make it seem permeable. As in other cultural spheres, here the United States provides Irish writers with a model for an emergent middle-class identity as well as offers a model of social meritocracy; *Redemption Falls* suggests that, upon the elimination of the inequities of slavery, the United States becomes the storied land of opportunity, freedom, and justice for all. The streets are paved with luck.

Jeddo is the vector by which we can track this message. As the novel nears its close, he is cleared by a court of wrongdoing in O'Keefe's death and comes to New York. Jeddo avails himself of the exceptional prospects laid before him and ascends to social respectability and acclaim, able to cast off entirely the unsightly identity he inhabited before. The novel's message is that class status is negotiable, and that a working-class identity is one to be discarded. Advancement within the class system is the responsibility of the individual, on whom the task of overcoming hardship rests. Professor (Emeritus) J. Daniel McClelland has Irish servants in his house whom he claims to find inefficient and perhaps corrupt; he is not seeking equality for all, just equality of opportunity.

Celtic Tiger euphoria promised that there was enough money for all to enrich themselves, and Ireland en masse disowned its own poorer past, embarrassed by its thrift and economy. An ethic of consumption prevailed, one critiqued by novels decrying materialism. (McCann's Ciaran is a model of Celtic Tiger prosperity, complaining about real estate prices in his million-euro house, a bit of an ass with his Internet startup smugness; his marriage to Lara, an heiress, stands in nicely for the way American capital fueled the Irish bubble.) Ironically, however, these novels from the late phase of the boom offer the United States as an alternative to such materialism via an endorsement of a competitive individualism. The erasure of the Hispanic characters in both—via the absence of Adelita and her children in the 2006 part of *Let the Great World Spin*, and the fact that Lucia has no genetic offspring—acts as a trace of the unworkability of meritocracy, of the fact that it tends to work to replicate the ruling class. The rulers are no longer an Anglo-Irish aristocracy or a class of moneyed robber barons but rather a credentialed intellectual elite. The social mobility hereby created and endorsed could only arise in risk society's vision of personal responsibility; its disavowal of class echoes American discourses that serve as guide to a recently prosperous Ireland.

What happens, then, when both nations experience an economic crash that shows that perhaps the fundamentals were not so sound after all? In the next sections I examine the ways that Irish novels since the crisis have narrated the American dream. Risk and precarity more explicitly revealed when novelistic focalization calls attention to scope; moreover, the shifts toward more ungrammatical and irreal textual markers suggest that the bricolage biographies of the boom years can no longer support the ideological apparatus of meritocracy and mobility.

Remote Fish and Bovines Insensitive

Paul Lynch draws his novel *Red Sky in Morning*, set in Ireland and the United States in the 1832, from a recovered historical event, expanded and fictionalized. Lynch's story begins in the Inishowen region of the countryside of Donegal, where Coll Coyle faces eviction by his landlord, Hamilton, for reasons that are not laid out until the novel's end.[36] Coyle is baited into attacking the drunken, sneering landlord, who, reeling from Coyle's punch, hits his head

---

36. The protagonist's name suggests recurrence and circularity, in the evocation of coils by both first and surnames, whose similarity creates a further feeling of repetition.

against a nearby stone wall and dies. Following this moment of very bad luck, the novel traces Coyle's flight from home, out of Ireland, pursued by the malevolent John Faller, overseer of Hamilton's estate (and perhaps also Hamilton's biological father), a tireless juggernaut who leads a diminishing band of hunters on Coyle's trail throughout the novel. After attempting evasive maneuvers en route to Derry, at his first opportunity Coyle boards a ship, by chance headed to Philadelphia, and gets a job filling a valley for the Pennsylvania Railroad. The foreman, Duffy, tells recruits, "You men will be pioneers and you will build your fortune just like me. I am giving you your start" (170). This classic rhetoric of opportunity by an Irish immigrant yokes individualism to profit, grossly misrepresenting the menial submission in which the men become trapped; it also echoes Mary Harney's views of the United States as the land of opportunity. Despite Duffy's promises of a fresh new narrative, Coyle's pursuit by Faller continues, revenant-like, so persistently and effectively that those around the latter man see his abilities as "supernatural." Ultimately, however, both Faller and Coyle are killed by unknown gunmen working for unnamed forces. Coyle and his coworkers, first left for dead as cholera ravages through their work camp, are shot down following an attempted escape (and it is this historical fact that served as Lynch's inspiration).[37] We don't learn why Faller himself is hunted while he hunts except that he has been "upsetting folk in Philadelphia" (252) with his single-minded lawlessness. Each man is returned to the earth—Faller fed to pigs and Coyle dumped in a mass grave as the novel's language waxes naturalistic: "The earth corrupt . . . and filled with violence" (267).

37. The contemporary proliferation of stories of individuals who refuse to give up in the face of extraordinary physical privation speaks to a cultural itch being scratched: *The Revenant* itself, from 2015, stands as perhaps the pinnacle of the genre, but *127 Hours* (2010), *Wild* (2014), *Everest* (2015), and *Jungle* (2017) are relatively successful iterations as well. Even the resurgence of "lost in space" narratives, from *Gravity* (2013) to *The Martian* (2015) can be seen as an outgrowth of the austerity-driven push toward grit and self-reliance.

Lynch has said that his attention to dispossession, eviction, and deprivation speaks to the novel's era of composition, when austerity measures in Ireland were at their most punitive: "Coll was having similar problems to people around me, for I had begun writing the book in the spring of 2009, a time when the world economy was coming apart" ("Story of *Red Sky in Morning*" 3). The first phase of austerity in Ireland, 2008–10, before the arrival of the IMF-ECB-EC Troika, saw internally imposed "sacrifices" by the Irish people: "Adjustments amounting to almost 15 billion euros or 10 percent of GDP were achieved" (Roche et al. 5); at the same time, long-term unemployment "rose from 1.4 percent in 2007 to 9.5 percent in 2010 . . . The burden of rising unemployment and growing long-term joblessness fell mainly on men. Young people were particularly badly affected and have remained so" (15). Even Coll's emigration had a modern-day analogue, given that "610,000 people left Ireland between 2008 and 2015" (15).[38] Coll's status as fortune's fool and his debt to forces larger than himself work as allegories for a populace whose bad timing and relatively small mistakes had catastrophic consequences.

Throughout *Red Sky*, Lynch underscores the human lack of control with heavy persistence, starting with the involuntary nature of the manslaughter of the landlord. Hamilton has callously threatened to evict not just Coyle but his brother and has further promised to rape Coyle's wife and kill his child. Lynch depicts Coyle's reaction through topographic metaphors: "Coyle's head clouded . . . and his hand bouldered" (15). In classical rhetorical terminology, the rendering of a noun as a verb is known as *anthimeria* (more broadly, anthimeria is the use of one part of speech for another). This ungrammaticality renders Coyle inanimate, further distancing him from agency by separating Coyle from the acts of his own head and hand. Coyle flees Ireland since he feels he has no choice, no chance

---

38. See David Monahan's compelling photographic series "Leaving Dublin," featuring eighty-four portraits made between 2010 and 2013 as a "direct response to the re establishment of Irelands Migrant culture" [*sic*].

of justice. Chance again shapes the story prominently in the randomness of Philadelphia as Coyle's destination, a formal enactment of the way fate is seen to loom larger than self-determination. The railroad job on offer serves the goals of manifest destiny, a force beyond Coyle's comprehension or control. The final disappearance of Coyle and Faller both, consumed by a trajectory of development even more indefatigable than Faller himself, concludes the novel's argument as to human impotence. The small vendetta Faller advances into the United States is too minor and parochial to be allowed to have an effect on inexorable growth. We can map an easy allegory for other eras of imported labor and technological advances: the protagonist is a victim of arbitrary economic decisions; the economic machine is too big to control; and local or personal disputes have no impact on the giant wheels of capital and the unrelenting narrative of progress.

For an individual character trapped within the momentum of capital at work, many moments and events can feel arbitrary; the novel's recurrent use of randomness to propel the plots frames such occurrences as coincidence or (bad) luck. The culmination of the feeling of arbitrariness comes in one of the short interludes narrated by Coll's wife, Sarah, who learns after he is gone that Hamilton's choice to evict has come because *"Hamilton said he had passed Coll on the road that same day and Coll did not doff his hat"* (269, italics in original). Coll's infraction here is his failure to perform his subordination to the other man. The novel is clear in its critique of the social system that supports such hierarchy, depicting Hamilton as in no way worthy of deference and showing his legal father to be decrepit and demented. The suggestion that Faller is Hamilton's biological father can also be seen as critique, linking the arbitrary and cruel treatment of both men to the accident of birth itself and further affirming that Hamilton's elevated status is in no way earned or deserved, that there is no biological justification for class differences. It's also important that Coll does not recall this moment or have any idea how he has caused the other man to turn on him: again, there is no sense of deserving or asking for one's fate. Rather, good is rare, and bad is distributed without a sense of what is deserved, a backward extension of the ethos of risk society.

Recurrently, Lynch reminds his readers that individuals are mere dots on the earth's surface. However, at the macroeconomic level, the need for labor creates conditions into which individuals are propelled; what feels random to a character assumes a logic, even a politics, from a broader perspective. As Annie McClanahan has suggested in her analysis of recent American novels about credit and crisis, it is the focus on the individual which distorts our understanding of the forces in play: "Dependent on behavioral economic accounts of individual action and formally trapped in their own first person or focalized narrative, credit-crisis realist novels struggle to formalize the relationship between individual actors and the broader social field these actors occupy and shape" (32). If novels tend to focus on a protagonist or a handful of characters, this presents a problem of moving between scales, of assessing an individual's ability to determine her own course of action and the larger context that creates and limits possible outcomes. For *Red Sky*, this problem is resolved, or at least effaced, by recursion to the generic norms of naturalism. The novel's deference to laws of nature and the idea that such laws restrict human agency give rise to its fatalistic worldview.

Lynch's minute formal choices buttress such a reading: his stylized, self-consciously literary prose ventures frequently into distortion and ungrammaticality, foregoing verbs, using one part of speech for another, and disrupting standard syntax. While working for Duffy, Coyle and his fellow conscripts "begin to work not like men but beasts" (173), an image Lynch offers in mordant rebuke to the men's eager one-upsmanship as to what animals they envision buying with their wages to eat. "For sups of water they hardly stopped and the stock was better soused and when they did stop for something Duffy's eyes were on them and he made warning to keep working or they would not be paid for the day, for time was not their own and they learned to watch who was watching and when they stopped to eat they took no more time than was necessary" (175). The sense of "hardly stopping" is enacted by the ongoingness of the sentence, which extends multiple times via polysyndeton—the repeated use of "and." Its eight independent clauses recreate the ceaseless labor of the work camp. The inverted syntax in the opening phrase further dehumanizes the thirsty men, displacing them from grammatical prominence in the sentence, a subject position that the stock is granted, along with more water.[39]

Syntax also works mimetically to fix Lynch's characters in their disempowerment. As Faller and his associate Macken pursue Coyle, they are shot at: "They reached the far side of the valley where trees stood thin and it was there that Macken heard not the sound of the gun being fired or if he did he heard it only as something indistinct, an approaching murmur" (219). The inversion in "heard not" gives the sentence a scriptural rhythm that reinforces the feeling of allegory in the novel, but, more pertinently, it replicates the shot itself. To say that Macken "did not hear" would be to depict not hearing as an active process, whereas "hearing not" retains Macken's lack of agency. The end of the sentence, which unfixes the action further, concedes that "if he did he heard it only as something indistinct." In this moment, hearing is conditional, imprecise, futile. Lynch's narrative focalization here, while godlike in its intonations, is limited in its powers; it acknowledges the impossibility of knowing whether or not a dying man has heard the bullet that hit him. This choice can be seen to stress how little it matters whether a human is conscious in his final seconds, but it also reinforces the novel's own attention and deference to larger scales than those within which it seems to work.

As readers, we are trained by the novel itself to accept such grammatical irregularities and their semantic implications. In a recurrent move so common as to be a distinguishing trait of the novel, Lynch

39. Rhetorically, Lynch's inverted syntax can be seen as anastrophe or hyperbaton. "Anastrophe is most often a synonym for hyperbaton, but is occasionally referred to as a more specific instance of hyperbaton: the changing of the position of only a single word" (http://rhetoric.byu.edu/Figures/A/anastrophe.htm, accessed 31 May 2022).

links a fragment to a main clause with "and": "A gibbous moon winking at him through the trees and the forest began to thin" (28); "pain pulsing in Faller's leg and he chomped down on his teeth" (222); "to the north a house isolate and they rode towards it" (104). This final sentence—just to choose one—begins with its prepositional phrase, in a mode comprehensible but uncommon in English. Given that "isolate" is a more lyrical, far less common, adjective than "isolated," the passage can be seen to substitute one part of speech as another, a further example of Lynch's *anthimeria*, and its opening clause is, as noted, a fragment. In a pattern Lynch uses upward of fifty times in the novel, a fragment-plus-main clause sentence begins with the accumulation of rhetorical and syntactic ungrammaticalities and then is succeeded by a prosaic, simple sentence with a standard English SVO syntax. The initial fragment frequently serves to create a mood, offering a poetic description without motion or argument. This preliminary sensation of timelessness or suspension functions as a semantic immobility into which the main clause then injects action. Even in the phrase "pain pulsing" above, the use of a gerund again leaves "an action's completion undefined" (Moretti and Pestre 2015, 99); the pain is a state of being that pervades.[40] The gerund creates this sense of ubiquity, one to which pain itself is especially well suited. William Davies, in *Nervous States: How Feeling Took Over the World*, argues that the contemporary understanding of pain creates an "acute absence of narrative" (2018, 109). Without moral or religious meaning to provide narrative sequence, feeling dominates; the overall sensation is to prioritize ambience, substituting mood for motion. In Lynch's gerunds, the effect is the creation of a feeling of ongoingness that gives the events of 1832 resonance nearly two hundred years later, mapping the novel's painful plot onto contemporary narratives of dispossession, emigration, and deprivation. The difference between past and present is diminished, and the novel signals

---

40. Imagine if Lynch had instead written "Pain pulsed in Faller's leg and he chomped down on his teeth," which creates a feeling of causality and even sequence.

its embeddedness in what John Urry (2007) refers to as simultaneity and Sharae Deckard (2017) calls "neoliberal temporality."

Other stylistic features reinforce this state of suspension, as when "house isolate" inverts its adjective and noun, another textual inclination that recurs throughout the narrative voice of the novel— "strength supernatural" (Lynch 2013, 142); "bovines insensitive" (181); "shape indistinct" (220); "fields rufous" (241). Frequently, such postpositive adjectives (a subset of the rhetorical device of anastrophe) are less concrete than the more tangible nouns that precede them. The sequential disruption coils each construction back in on itself, obliging the reader to reread and reorder, slowing and even reversing linear, temporal progression. Such movement recalls the non-linear combinards of Lash and Beck, as well as Moretti and Pestre's argument that the process of nominalization of verbs "take[s] 'actions and processes' and turn[s] them into 'abstract objects' . . . where temporality is abolished" (90).[41] Placing the noun first similarly creates this sort of stasis or simultaneity. As with the fragments, the reader's attention remains with the alienating ungrammaticality. Its echoes of Irish syntax give the narrative voice a ponderous, archaic sensibility.[42] Lynch's overlay of techniques blurs the line between prose and poetry, emphasizing stasis and also, importantly, affect. The lyrical style operates in a gray palette of moods, a displacement of sentimentality in favor of a more generalized feeling of doom and looming peril that pervades the novel. In part through its pervasive affect, which insinuates itself by assuming a guise of

41. See Lanham, *Analyzing Prose*, where he contends that "a style based on verbs, on *action*" can be contrasted to "a style based on nouns, on *stasis*" (2003, 11, emphasis his). Like Moretti and Pestre, Lanham sees the value of such stasis to a bureaucracy: "The noun style dominates workaday prose in our time" (28).

42. While Latinate languages, and, significantly, Irish, use postpositive adjectives as a default, the normative reliance in English on prepositive attributive adjectives means that these phrases stand out to speakers of standard English. The construction may at some level reinscribe the Irish language into a novel from which its near-total absence feels historically anomalous.

"always and everywhere," the novel capitulates to a logic congruent with neoliberalism, rhetorical consent sought and obtained via a rhythm that recurrently characterizes subjects as caught in a tangle that it then normalizes.

Formally, Lynch's circumvolutions at the level of word, sentence, and even scene assume ideological significance in that they enact the lack of agency affecting his characters. Coll's nonexistent agency is overdetermined: stalked by Faller, he is also refused his wages and next forced by local farmers to remain at the camp in the throes of a cholera epidemic, only then to be shot. The novel makes clear that Coll never stands a chance; the naturalistic fatalism of the novel produces a sense of acceptance of this outcome. As Joe Cleary has explained naturalism, its "assumption that the laws of heredity and social environment . . . allowed for only a very constricted sense of human agency" (114). Beck might classify a cholera epidemic as a risk of first modernity, where human errors amplify natural hazards, but Lynch's narration from a risk-society perspective, with its sheen of inevitability, lends the events a sense of normality: the loss of fifty-seven Irish immigrants on a segment of the Pennsylvania Railroad is a cost of doing business. The sense of limited options that Cleary argues is a hallmark of naturalism here merges with a more contemporary neoliberal ethos that tells us There Is No Alternative, a mindset in which economic imperative eclipses all else.

The imperatives of business provide the only forward momentum in the novel: Faller, having pursued Coyle from Inishowen to Donegal to Philadelphia, tracks him to the railway work camp. Alone and in pain, both conditions a result of gunfire from unknown pursuers the day before, Faller approaches a work site and searches among its workers: "He took appraisal of the dig, watched the men slam and slice the earth. He took in their faces, their complexions dark and their eyes unlooking and he saw that many of them were Chinese working free of the sun under wide-brimmed coolie hats. Nobody noticed him and if they did they paid no attention to him and he walked to where a sheet of rock lay exposed like they were unearthing the preserved remains of some remote fish upon a prehistoric seabed" (244–45). The polysyndeton, inverted syntax, and contra-dictory conditional clause work in this passage as elsewhere in the novel to instill an atmosphere of inevitability. The episode ends when Faller heads back in the direction he came from, telling the man with whom he spoke that he needs supplies.

Given that the scene ends with its plot trajectory turned back on itself, the historical accuracy of the inclusion of a Chinese labor camp along the Pennsylvania railway dig seems arbitrarily imposed on a novel. As in other twenty-first-century Irish novels narrating American westward expansion, *Red Sky* here links its Irish immi-grants to other imported workers and to racial others. The narrator defers mention of race during Faller's approach to the supervisor and even during his initial imperial gaze that twice "takes in" what is before it. Lynch's postpositive adjectives, with their references to dark complexions and unreadable eyes, clearly traffic in stereotypes of inscrutable Asians. The episode provides the Chinese characters with no agency or interiority, touching on them en route to its grand scale reference to epochal time.[43] From a perspective that encom-passes prehistory, racial differences do not seem to matter at all: the question arises as to what end is served by the single sentence that makes reference to the Chinese workers and their "coolie hats." McClanahan cites Colleen Lye's argument that "'the Asiatic' has been a particularly significant figure for portentous economic anxi-eties" (quoted in McClanahan 2018, 136), in keeping with Lynch's parallels of modern austerity Ireland with the 1830s. The failure of the Irish work camp to complete its job, and its complete erasure from the rail line are juxtaposed to a twenty-first-century economy in which China did not experience the 2008 crash and subsequent crisis to the same extent as other global economies. The heady years of the Celtic Tiger behind it, Ireland's downfall appears inevitable, foretold, its economic ruin tied to an Irish failure to navigate the

---

43. The metaphor of the excavation of fish metafictively prefigures the burial of Coll and the others, with the idea that their remains have been preserved through an act of storytelling.

American economy successfully, something the Chinese are here seen to accomplish, past and present. Indeed, even Faller's departure from the site, back where he came from, signals the inability of the Irish to advance, linking the scene's construction to many of Lynch's other formal choices. While the Irish in the novel recurrently fold back in on themselves, whether via postpositive adjectives, fragments, and gerunds, or thematic and narrative coils, the railroad will and does proceed onward, and the Chinese are figured as the trajectory by which the American economy moves forward, leaving the Irish behind.[44]

Thus the sentence-level lack of action and linearity fails to override the novel's larger tragic trajectory. Coll's death on the site can in this context be read as the consumption of Irish bodies by a hungry American machine hell-bent on westward expansion, and the novel certainly supports this macroeconomic message. But its formal choices insist on the relevance of Coll's failure to doff his hat; like the massacre at the dig, this scene reinforces the idea of an uncaring and arbitrary universe while also insisting on the importance of the class hierarchy in the distribution of brute luck, contrasting its prevalence / pervasive force in Ireland with an idealized America where personal agency could matter more.[45] The persistent belief in Irish failure and downfall is contrasted to the (admittedly false) promise of an America where hard work can advance a man. Coll's death is thus not about the cruelty of the universe but rather a consequence of his failure to achieve the escape velocity needed to move beyond the downward pull of Irish inevitability. Even the dingy ribbon belonging to his daughter that Coll carries throughout the novel—a clunky bit of sentiment that Lynch might better have avoided—represents the

---

44. The construction of Irish immigrants, past and recent, as doomed, conforms partially at best to a historical reality in which Irish Americans have leveraged their status as white English speakers to become as a demographic far more economically secure than the US population in general.

45. Dworkin (2000) distinguishes between brute luck, which is about situations we do not choose, and option luck, where we willingly and wittingly gamble.

restraints of Irishness and family, entangling nets that Coll fails to fly by. His flaw is his recurrent thought to return to family rather than achieve a full-fledged American individualism. The novel's recursive structures act as traces of the unsuitability of the Americanized narratives of progress for its Irish protagonist.

By contrast, the American blacksmith, who is the only character spared at the dig, finds the ribbon as he digs a mass grave for the others; he "holds it for a moment in wondering and then he lets it go, taken off his hand by the breeze. The day is then done under a soundless sky and he looks up and sees red sky of evening" (274). The blacksmith, not tied by sentiment, easily allows the ribbon to be subject to the forces of nature. The morning red sky of the novel's opening page, which in the old adage portends calamity, has been replaced by the evening red sky that is the sailor's "delight," foretelling good things for blacksmith, railroad, and American economy alike. Indeed, the paragraph is overfull of positive meteorological foreshadowing: the blacksmith burns the camp, while "the west festooned with coming night and rain clouds thick and waiting . . . the return of autumn. The land steps into the shadow" (274). The burning, the cleansing, the forward progress of the seasons, and the animation of the land so that it can actively step forward serve as a reflection of the opening paragraph of the novel, but Lynch has moved from narrative past to present tense, and thus the American setting advances beyond the tragedy into which the novel launches the Irish landscape on page one. Indeed, we know in 1832 that the Great Hunger lies ahead for Donegal; the novel's one-paragraph epilogue, in which Coll moves into a dream of home that he has had while in the camp, returns to narrative past, locating him—and any happiness of the novel—into a parallel universe in which time does not advance (or intrude, as McCann would have it).

Thus the novel's ungrammaticalities fold back in on themselves and deny Irish agency, in contrast to an America figured as linear and making progress, from the continuation of the railroad to the survival of the only American at the camp. The lack of accountability for the Americans who murder the Irish also allows the narrative of

American innocence to advance. The novel absorbs from its American setting the suggestion that some people are deserving and some are undeserving, but this vision, itself obviously problematic, is nevertheless smothered under a larger preexisting Irish ambience of inevitability. Although Lynch locates fault with an archaic Irish class system, which is critiqued as inherited, unworkable, and arbitrary, its power still affects the entire course of the novel. The parallel of past and present in Ireland is juxtaposed with the linear progression figured as possible for the Americans and the Chinese, a move that by extension absolves a contemporary Irish elite of bankers, politicians, and developers by ascribing the crash to an inescapable Irish condition.

Things Unexploded

2013 seems to have been a bumper year for postpositive adjectives in Irish novels about human agency in the United States and Ireland; my subheading comes from the prelude of Colum McCann's *Trans-Atlantic*. The novel begins with a focus on animation of the inanimate: "The cottage sat at the edge of the lough. She could hear the wind and rain whipping across the expanse of open water; it hit the trees and muscled its way into the grass" (3). McCann ungrammatically merges wind and rain into one whole, "it," which is embodied, given muscles. The brief opening overture concludes with a metafictive raising of the curtain: "Soon the rooms began to stir, the opening of windows, cupboards and doors, the wind off the lough moving through the house" (4). Like the wind and rain, the house itself appears alive. The sentence moves without human force, again skirting ungrammaticality with the participles in its final absolute phrases.

Inside this "house worth listening to" (3) an unnamed woman hears sounds she cannot at first decipher—they turn out to be oyster shells, dropped upon the roof by gulls seeking to open them. A shell does not always crack upon hitting the slate: "If it dropped sideways through the sky it wouldn't break; it lay there like a thing unexploded" (3). With the indefinite word "thing" and the slide from shells that break to one that might explode, McCann evokes an undetonated bomb and its coiled-up potential for violence, an image that gains haunting resonance throughout the stories of the women in the novel, for whom daily life is a series of chance happenings, some of which detonate, wreaking destruction. The sentence's syntax also embeds the potential for violence via its anastrophe; the shell is a "thing unexploded," its postpositive adjective deferring mention of the explosion as long as possible. Once they have fed on the oysters, the gulls depart "in squadrons of blue and gray" (4), military terminology linking this moment to the devastation wrought by the American Civil War, extending backward historically and forward narratively. The novel is at this moment itself a thing unexploded.

As noted above, McCann's paratactic style has long tracked multiple story lines in multiple time periods; their convergence usually suggests the inheritance of memory, a sentiment captured in *Trans-Atlantic*'s epigraph, by Uruguayan journalist Eduardo Galeano: "The time that was continues to tick inside the time that is."[46] The novel holds true to McCann's signature patterning, connecting four generations of women and two of the three male historical protagonists via an unopened letter. As an act of communication that never reaches its intended recipient, the letter also functions as a ticking thing unexploded, but it does not complete the novel: "I wasn't interested in getting to the endpoint, if there was any" (285), says its final owner. In its refusal of an ending, disruption of a single linear narrative, and presentation instead of seven discrete sections that are neither synchronic nor diachronic, neither following chronological time nor developing sequentially in the novel, *TransAtlantic* enacts precisely the sort of timeless time that I discussed in the introduction and that characterizes the condition of the non-linear individual in contemporary risk society.

---

46. Galeano's "ticking" is bomblike—the past threatens to explode in the present.

McCann's text directly addresses the economic crisis, bookending its 167 years of narrative with recent scenes at the loughside house—the cottage's historical provenance, its mid-twentieth-century modernization and expansion, and its twenty-first-century debt and foreclosure recapitulate in miniature the property boom and bust.[47] Likewise, Sebastian Barry's *On Canaan's Side* begins and ends in a little house on a shore, telling a story with some striking similarities. Both novels take the Irish relationship with America as central to Ireland's economic development, with particular attention to racial dynamics. Each narrative centers on the experiences and descendants of an Irish immigrant to the United States, each named Lily/Lilly. Each woman has a short-lived alliance with an immigrant Irish man, raising a son on her own, a boy later lost to war. Both women make second marriages to men of hybrid backgrounds. Both novels show the senseless deaths of a family's final generation, due to political conflicts in which they have no personal investment. Contrasting the lives of great men and small women, each novel lauds the immigrant work ethic yet distrusts its worth in the contemporary era, hedging their faith in the American dream and casting escape from a life of endless striving as pure good luck.

The novels are punctuated with reflections on the nature of risk that privilege effort and pluck but view bad luck as nevertheless inescapable, a contradictory response to cultural conventions that prize social mobility and naturalize economic inequity. In each novel, the attention to individual grit and equality of opportunity is linked, psychically and rhetorically, to the United States, a nation figured

---

47. The cottage is in Northern Ireland, complicating analysis of the economic crash in the Republic of Ireland. Nevertheless, Antoin Murphy notes that "Northern Ireland has suffered many of the consequences of the Republic's financial crisis most notably in banking because of the problems that have arisen for AIB, Bank of Ireland, Northern Bank and Ulster Bank" (2014, n.p.). In McCann's novel, the bank manager forcing the property's sale has "a southern accent laced with some London, all our troubles in one voice" (2013, 258), embodying the interwoven economies.

as created and sustained by the physical labor of immigrants and people of color, in particular. Echoing ideas from Beck and Lash about the relationship of the individual to the collective, they depict lives shaped by transnational migrations and buffeted by the vagaries of chance. Effort and accomplishment are seen as the province of the individual, as are setbacks; "luck" is the cognitive process through which risk is made personal and understandable. These thematic preoccupations seem ideologically suggestive of the era of their novels' publication, a time in which nearly two decades of prosperity narratives in the Global North quite abruptly cease to be operative, obliging a reconsideration of the assumptions that had burnished them.

Still, the two novels have overt, pronounced differences in style that translate to different ideological orientations. While Barry's Lilly narrates a continuous narrative spanning most of the twentieth century, McCann's Lily is the focal character of only one section in a novel traversing centuries and generations and coming to its concluding emotional climax in the narration of Lily's great-granddaughter, Hannah. The formal differences in narration and focalization are paralleled at the sentence level—Barry expresses heightened emotion via run-on sentences, while McCann tends toward sentence fragments. Each shuns normal syntactic connections, using such ungrammaticality as a formal technique. Each narrative form bears ideological weight, raising questions as to whether their thematic similarities override the surface differences in form. Such formal analysis reveals how *TransAtlantic* and *Canaan* advance sophisticated reassessments of economic agency and the potential for social mobility in the wake of the Irish economic crash. In their constellated constructions of risk, luck, hazard, and misfortune, Barry and McCann indict the narratives of progress of which the American dream is emblematic. Nevertheless, in working through their inherently neoliberal narratives of risk, both to varying degrees forswear agency and accede to a contemporary feeling of impotence.

In constructing their cultural responses to the crisis, McCann and Barry extend the Irish imaginative engagement with Ireland's global economic partners, reexamining the American dream and attendant rhetoric of opportunity and locating the ethos of hard work within immigrant and nonwhite populations in particular. McCann's Lily offers a microcosm of the immigrant story, landing in New York and working her way westward, serving as a nurse in the Civil War. She then marries another immigrant, and they build a business and a family, passing on enough wealth that her children's educational attainments and employment prospects outstrip her own. McCann juxtaposes her story to that of Frederick Douglass, the renowned writer born in slavery, who travels to Ireland to sell copies of his book and raise funds for the abolitionist movement. Despite tragedies—Douglass witnesses the horror of the Irish Famine, while Lily endures the death of three sons—*TransAtlantic* presents a largely positive view of the American dream in these early sections, suffused with gratifying images of its extension to the formerly disenfranchised and laying the groundwork for later sections in which an American of immigrant stock, George Mitchell, will reflect on his humble Irish and Lebanese working-class origins and succeed in bringing about peace in Northern Ireland.

In a like vein, Barry's protagonist moves from Ireland to New York, moving on through Chicago, Cleveland, and then Washington, DC, before coming to rest in the Hamptons, an American odyssey directed by her work as domestic help. Just as McCann's Lily came into contact with Douglass while a servant in a Dublin house where he stayed, Lilly meets Martin Luther King Jr. when he asks to thank her and her son at the end of his meal in the fine home where Lilly cooks. King pronounces Ed "a fine boy. . . . He could do anything he wants." (190). As Lilly reflects later, "He was just a cook's child maybe, but in America, a cook's child might do anything." (205). While the reservations coiled within "maybe" and "might" come to be prophetic, Lilly's sentiment echoes King's in its capacious "anything," crediting America with expansive possibility and embracing the active idea of doing, rather than a passive, inherited state of being.

Barry's novel makes an even more overt endorsement of the rhetoric of opportunity via the family of Lilly's employer, Mrs Wolohan. As Elizabeth Butler Cullingford notes, Lilly's job ties her to "white Irish America . . . a family based on the Kennedys" (2014, 75). As stand-ins for the clan that most vividly embodies the ascension of Irish immigrants to wealth and power, the Wolohan family represents transcendence of humble origins and the ideology said to enable it. Lilly works first for her current employer's mother, worshipfully telling us that "once upon a time one of the richest women in America was also one of the nicest" (183). The fairy-tale phrase and subsequent superlatives render this family matriarch fictional, fantastic. Mrs Wolohan's mother hires Lilly out of a belief in "Fairness with a capital F, and people making their way, and the principle of the Helping Hand" (182). Lilly adopts the locutions of her employer, internalizing the ideology of self-sufficiency by capitalizing "Helping Hand" so that it is equated, textually, with fairness, despite the implicit recognition of inequality in "help." Such contradictions within paternalist industrial capitalism underlie Lilly's hire and her half-century of interactions with the family.

Although Lilly is the beneficiary of the family's recurrent kindness and charity, she is never promoted and does not advance in her career. Rather, the chance for improvement is displaced onto subsequent generations. "Mrs Wolohan . . . said she would be happy to help with [Bill's] college fees," Barry writes. "She said it would be her privilege. This is her way of doing a great favor without attaching any burden to it" (232). The Helping Hand is in action here to help Bill to make his way. In the final sentence, Barry's rare stylistic move to present-tense narration renders Mrs Wolohan's patent generosity as part of an ongoing pattern, which in turn naturalizes the discrepancy in privilege. Indeed, the word "privilege" cuts two ways: Barry signals the modesty and sensitivity of the wealthy woman, but we see also the implication and acceptance of social inequality that the present tense underscores. Bill is lucky to have a patron, but to see it thus accepts that college is a privilege rather than a right.

Both novels thereby set forth—initially—a version of the United States conforming to popular conceptions of the American dream. But this vision comes under scrutiny as the historical conditions under which this national narrative was able to flourish are placed under global pressures.

Neoliberal Risk and Reward

TransAtlantic begins in proper with an act of overt risk: Teddy Brown and Jack Alcock reconfigure a Vickers Vimy bomber for transatlantic flight, becoming, in 1919, the first men to complete such a journey. In a chapter laden with the sort of techno-historical research McCann delights in, we learn of gadgets and odd details, as well as of the genuine peril comprising the flight, including freezing temperatures and the lack of any sight lines or sense of the horizon during flight in a cloud. The trip is emblematic of Beck's industrial modernity, with both risks and solutions a combination of natural and technological. The element of chance that dictates this section lays out the philosophy governing the lives detailed in the rest of the novel. This ethos is articulated most explicitly when the plane is mired in a massive cloud, and the airspeed meter stops working; the men settle upon a plan to put the plane in a spin and spiral dive beneath the cloud: "We'll take our chances now. . . . The only way out is to maintain speed in a spin. To have control and lose it, too" (34). The passage relies on a paratactic rhythm devoid of coordinating conjunctions that would establish for the reader the relationship between the ideas presented.[48] Rather, they are "short on verbs and shorter on connectives and causalities," (Cleary 2015, 67), a technique that McCann

---

48. Lanham refers to parataxis as "syntactic democracy" (2003, 29), in reference to both the equal footing of a sentence's elements and deference to a reader's ability to establish relationships. See Mieszkowski (2019) for an extended reading of Whitman's "sprawling paratactic formations that wreak havoc with conventional grammatical relationships. . . . The result may be an egalitarian—or as Whitman himself would have it, 'democratic'—discourse of nonhierarchical sentences or simply an a-syntactic maelstrom in which there are no longer any sentences at all" (36).

has long liked to use, though never to such an extent as in *TransAtlantic*.[49] The sentence fragments, which signal heightened tension in the novel, are McCann's own way of having control and losing it, too, as they free the text of syntax and mechanical rules, releasing an ungrammaticality that feels like a signature style of the era of memes and text messages.[50] Such ungrammaticality designates a mode of non-linear language that dovetails with the non-linear collage of stories and the catachrestic ideas about the individual they imply in an era of intersectional precarities.

On Canaan's Side enacts the unequal distribution of risk via the sacrifice of three generations of Bere men to global conflicts. None is killed on home soil or in direct defense of his nation. Lilly's brother Willie dies fighting in France for the British army during World War I. Her son Ed gets drafted to serve in Vietnam, returning a broken man: "Ed died clearing landmines in Vietnam, I mean, he did not die, [but] Specialist First Class Ed Bere as good as died, or at least did not come home, or ever could find his way" (207). Just as this sentence makes a declaration and then qualifies it multiple times, the novel balances upon the tension between praise for the promise of America and the tragic realization of the limits and price of that promise. Lilly's grandson Bill also returns from war (the first Gulf War) physically intact, only to hang himself just months afterward. The mounting tragedies that structure the novel function as prime examples of Lilly's stunningly bad luck, which also encompasses the loss of her first husband to an IRA retaliation and the second to racial anxiety (he fears disclosure of his passing as white). Nevertheless, Barry shows these stricken soldiers as byproducts of unjust wars; as Elizabeth Butler Cullingford

49. Before this book, instances of McCann's fragmentary style occur sporadically, even in such early works as *Songdogs* and *This Side of Brightness*. But the technique emerges in its most recurrent and pronounced manner at the end of *Let the Great World Spin*, another novel that reflects at length on the vagaries of chance and the particularly difficult consequences of risk society for the poor and disenfranchised. 2020's *Apeirogon* represents the apogee of the technique.

50. We can also hear an echo of Fernando's sense that he is the one driving.

observes, "If a novel in which father and son both suffer from post-traumatic stress disorder stretches credibility, so do current veteran suicide statistics" (2014, 76–77).

For while Beck positions the contemporary individual as an agent invested with choice, risks borne in trenches and minefields are painfully undemocratic, increasingly so when military service is concentrated in low-income sectors of society. Despite such privatization of risk, *Canaan* treats enlistment as a noble good: "Willie went out to the Great War . . . and he was very happy to go" (29). While the novel deploys the words "happy" and "happiness" recurrently (fifteen and seventeen times, respectively, more than three times the number of "sad"/"sadness" mentions), the sentiment can feel misaligned with the novel's events. Barry delights in the idea of characters happy despite their circumstances; as he mentions in interviews (Cargill 2011), his model for Lilly was "a woman in an American print dress, in the summer, full of life, the happiest person I ever remember seeing as a child." Each character goes to war willingly, leaving Lilly to suffer; men are figured as risking their lives and women as enduring tragedy. The repetition of this pattern across three generations makes it seem inevitable, obscuring the difference between voluntary enlistment and the draft. The actual reasons behind the conflicts—to preserve geopolitical stability and economic control, (i.e., to fight communism and maintain cheap oil prices)—are eclipsed by the presentation of risk as personal, reinforcing an image of America as affording free choice while concealing how selectively the state guarantees freedom.

Barry's privatization of risk expresses itself through ungrammaticality. "Four killing wars, with all those sons milled into them. . . . And I have felt all that, for those that went out for the good of America, for the love of her. Oh, and I knew what safety and haven was America to me, so how could I not understand that something had to be given up for her? Something so close in me, it was really part of me. Oh, Bill" (29). Lilly equates four wars that personally affected her, focusing for the remainder of the paragraph on how America processes its male bodies. The image of America as refuge—Lilly first lands in New Haven when fleeing Ireland—retains a belief in American exceptionalism. The phrase "given up" echoes the biblical cadences coursing through the novel, evoking here the Last Supper, Christ's body "given up for you," a rhetoric of sacrifice connoting not only surrender but also, in this passage, despair. The vagueness of "all that," a gestural relative pronoun whose referent is not resolved in the passage, points to asymmetries and confusions underlying the whole passage—does Lilly mean that she felt the milling? Or that she felt for those who "went out"? There is a principle of exchange implied—freedom for bodies—but the syntax of the paragraph declines to resolve this into a logical equation. Instead it dissolves movingly into affective overwhelm, paralleling McCann's uptick in fragments at fraught moments in his novel. In both cases, the implication is that risk is beyond even linguistic control, utterable only ungrammatically.

Such ungrammatical constructions mark instances of heightened emotion throughout *Canaan*, most noticeably in Barry's use of extraordinarily long sentences. These syntactic spreads, extending sometimes beyond a page, venture to account for both intense stress and epiphanic joy. Generally, such moments accompany risk, as on a roller coaster ride:

> We poised, three beating hearts, three souls with all their stories so far in the course of ordinary lives, three mere pilgrims . . . Cassie and me and Joe, here we are, so high, so high, oh paradise of Cleveland, oh suffering America, long story of suffering and glory, and our own little stories, without importance, all offered to heaven, to the sky and the river, to . . . the passing decades, the worrisome future . . . two minutes of falling and weeping, and I knew everything that had happened to me was just, because it led to this, and this was my reward, the infinite friendship of my Cassie (119–20).

I quote here only a small fraction of the whole sentence, which lasts nearly two pages—the two minutes of the ride. Barry links America to suffering and to story. Yet Lilly minimizes her own pain, as well as that of her friend Cassie, whom she knows is regularly raped by their boss. The passage conflates time and space, offering up stories to both physical places and the "passing decades." The sentence both references the future and slips into the present tense itself: "Here we are." Past, present, and future coexist in a passage which figures the roller coaster ride as emblematic of Barry's America, where risk is a cost and joy is a "reward." The motif of having control and losing it, too, which structured Alcock and Brown's dive, applies aptly to a roller-coaster ride, in which danger is palpable and met with a frightened yet ecstatic embrace of the intensity of life.

It's crucial that the three passengers, an immigrant and two characters of color, are labeled "pilgrims," emphasizing their lack of rootedness while imbuing their working lives with an image of religious journey. Such a conflation of messianic destiny with the United States—throughout the novel romanticized as "America"—apotheosizes the American dream and effaces the negative. The reduction effected in talking about the "mere," "little stories" of these characters atomizes their experiences and their suffering, rendering them smaller even in aggregate than those of great men. These small individuals and their tiny, difficult pilgrimages represent the American dream as something precarious, present tense, and ungrammatical. Let us turn to the implications of this neoliberal construction of minimized selves and privatized risk.

The Non-Linear Individual in Non-Linear Time

While no novel in this chapter is written exclusively in present tense, all of them turn to the present in evoking moments of particular immediacy, to privilege feeling over logic. Recalling the way that Raymond Williams characterizes "structures of feeling" as opposed to the "conversion of experience into finished products;" noting that "In most description and analysis, culture and society are expressed in an habitual past tense" (1977, 128), Williams seeks a way to study culture without resorting to abstractions or fixed definitions, ways to talk about culture as a living process. Part of his goal is to separate the analytical from affective experience, which he sees as a real-time sensation. This connection between feeling and the present tense is key to understanding the bind in which neoliberalism places non-linear individuals.

McCann concludes each of the three books comprising *Transatlantic* in present tense—his first two, the historically based George Mitchell chapter and the fictional narrative of Lottie Tuttle, are in present tense throughout, while the final chapter, Hannah Carson's narrative, moves between past tense and present frequently, its final paragraph containing one sentence of each. It would at first look like McCann opts for past tense for the more distant narratives, switching to present to indicate moments closest to the reader's historical present, but this pattern is belied by inconsistent present tenses—like the shift to present tense in Alcock and Brown's chapter once the plane is aloft, and the fact that the novel's chronologically most recent section is in past tense. Rather, the present tense appears to serve as an index of risk: Mitchell delicately negotiates a tenuous Good Friday agreement; Lottie narrates her largely happy life through the lens of her grandson Tomas's random murder by paramilitaries; and Hannah considers the role of chance in her life in a present tense that comes to seem like a metafictive authoring of her story "when I strike the nib of my pen against the page" (261) and, perhaps, given the consistency of voice throughout the novel, of the whole book. The risk of the present emerges starkly when the narrator reports in a gut punch of a phrase that "Tomas is shot dead" (247). McCann's present tense creates an ongoing sense of instantaneity, rendering the violence as endlessly recurrent.

While the entire novel is blanketed by chance occurrences—coincidental meetings, horrific acts of God, elegant literary parallels—the present-tense sections reflect most overtly on the role of randomness. Moments before we learn of Tomas's shooting, Lottie recalls their final conversation: "It strikes Lottie how very odd it is to be abandoned by language, how the future demands what should have been asked in the past. . . . Was it just one of those random things, slipshod, unasked for, another element in the grand disorder of things?" (246). Similarly, Hannah reflects on "what chance, what accidents, what curiosities" attend the unopened letter, which retains "its preservation of possibility" (253). And Mitchell, whose quest to achieve peace in Northern Ireland is motivated in part by deaths like Tomas's, concludes his section with "There is always room for at least two truths" (152). Knowledge is precarious, unfixed. Thus the novel is rife at formal and thematic levels with non-linearities: Emily Ehrlich's famous "odd tangents" (17) in her journalism; the repeated crossings of the Atlantic in denial of uniform patterns of immigration; the insistence on the inevitable fictionality of any historical record; the refusal of the logical progression of a grammatical sentence. As a group, these non-linearities belie the likelihood of relentlessly upward economic trajectories and cast doubt upon all narratives of progress.

Barry's novel also relies on non-linear constructions to deny notions of development, suggesting that America embodies both past and future. When Lilly and her first love, Tadg, flee to America, she reflects that "even before we got there, I was experiencing a sort of nostalgia for the land, I do not know how other to describe it. As if I had been there before, had left it, and was returning after a long voyage" (58). Lilly calls attention to her own status and limitations as author as she grapples for words. As seen in the roller-coaster sentence, the nation is built on stories. While the trope of nation as imaginative construct is well worn, it has particular resonance in a novel so keen to meditate on its own composition, leading us to read metafictive moments as reflections on the creation of America itself and its connections to innovation and development. As Lilly and Tadg travel westward to Chicago, she "had the oddest sense that America was being built in great haste all in front of us, being invented for us as we went" (60). In writing her story, Lilly assumes responsibility for the hazards she faces, while Barry's non-linearity makes them inescapable, part of the past and the future.

The final link among America, fiction, and unbearable amounts of risk comes when Lilly's dear friend Mr Nolan confesses on his deathbed that he had carried out Tadg's assassination some seventy years before. His choice to unburden himself to Lilly before he dies reveals a horrific dimension of American invention: "'In America,' he said, 'everything is possible. Everything is both true and untrue in the same breath' (240)." In an articulation reminiscent of McCann's Mitchell, Nolan depicts the rhetoric of opportunity so central to the American identity entirely as an act of creativity, suggesting that his own bricolage-biography, as an Irish American serving the IRA and a loyal friend who brought Bill to live with Lilly, can be resolved into a sensible story via the denial of a central, dominant narrative. Lilly's furious reaction exonerates America—in two extended, ungrammatical run-on sentences—imagining the "letter of shamrocks and harps" (246) instructing Nolan to kill Tadg. She relents slightly upon considering how much her love for him has been akin to her love for Tadg and her husband, Joe, a blurring of distinctions not only mirrored by the simultaneous truth and untruth of American stories but also, graphically, by the ravages of pancreatic cancer assaulting Nolan: "My heart . . . bled for him, as his own body bled. . . . The borders between his intestine and upper body had so broken down that he had endured little bouts of faecal vomiting, a very terrifying and monstrous betrayal of the body" (244). Lilly and Nolan merge; likewise, Nolan's digestive and excretory systems run in reverse, a chimerical confusion of space and time that leaves aside the joy of the roller coaster and instead emphasizes the toxic fatality of life as a combinard.

And it is here that we see the divergence in ideologies that ultimately separates Barry's worldview from McCann's. Nolan's "little bouts" of vomit recall the "little stories" of "mere pilgrims." As she does elsewhere throughout her narrative, Lilly uses diminutives about herself and her story: "Many great souls were killed in the sixties, and my small soul would not have registered, for sure" (206). Such diminutions counterbalance recurrent pairings of the wealthy with largeness, from the "American mansion" (183) where Lilly works to Mrs Wolohan's "own Himalaya of grief" (206) when her brother, a "great soul," is shot. At this tragic moment, Lilly reports that "I never, even in my own life, saw anything so sad" (204), elevating the patrician woman's pain over her own. In stark contradiction of ideals of American equality, *Canaan* is riven with hierarchies of race, region, and, most prominently, class. Rather than linking the magnanimity of her employers to their wealth, Lilly unquestioningly accepts and naturalizes the difference in scale between their lives and hers. Where McCann asserts an essential equality, Barry venerates the plutocracy.

In reflecting on the good fortune that brought her into the employ of Mrs Wolohan's family, Lily marvels, "I don't know where I had earned the luck for that" (182), a phrase whose contradictions reveal the unfairness built into the American system. Lilly does not feel entitled to credit for her own efforts, seeing her position rather as a gift from the privileged. While Mrs Wolohan's family suffers deeply, losing sons to war and assassination, the novel elevates the lives and suffering of this plutocracy above the experiences of the manual laborers told to feel lucky for what they earn, to accept risk as integral to their existence. Their lives are the resource through which the wealth is amassed and maintained, their bodies the sacrifice offered up to sustain the system.

TransAtlantic embraces a far more widespread notion of risk than *Canaan*, distributing hazard not only to the unlucky poor but also among an increasingly unlucky middle class. As Beck has it, "Endemic uncertainty" will "mark the lifeworld and the basic existence of most people—including the apparently affluent middle classes—in the years that lie ahead" (quoted in Heise 2008, 147). The growing flexibility that late modernity appears to afford is better seen as a decline in security; the cruel optimism of our contemporary moment has increased exposure to risk without delivering the promised increase in mobility. While both novels bemoan a world in which individuals are subject to the whims of transnational geopolitical unrest, only McCann critiques the global financial system. *TransAtlantic*'s unopened letter suggests the positive potential of creativity. When it is finally opened, in Hannah's desperate hope that it will be of sufficient financial value to mitigate her debts, it turns out to be a simple expression of gratitude with no market value. It contains more value unopened, as potential, as a gamble for an investor. Opening the letter deflates risk society, offering an escape via acts of reading and writing from a society in which decisions are made based on finances alone. On the other hand, Barry's novel does not question the impossibility of upward social mobility, instead valorizing happy have-nots content with their lot. In locating his critiques at the level of individual responsibility, Barry accepts a model of reflexive modernity that acts as a penumbra for the undiminished power of the very rich, directing attention away from the structures and institutions that could reduce the heavy toll of each crisis upon the most vulnerable.

Both Barry and McCann generate an affective ungrammaticality that I have argued emerges as a symptom of risk society; emotion is offered instead of solution. But they take divergent directions in their responses to that risk—Barry's response to risk isolates and privatizes it, diminishing his critique of risk society and the American dream. The recurrent contraction of the lives and experiences of working-class characters does not advocate for a resurgence of class-based critiques but rather adjusts its frame to accede to the dominance of the rich.

McCann disperses risk across a collective in space and time, contracting formally and generating a fragmentary novel focusing on myriad characters, with stories as incontrovertibly multiple. The circular narrative, which ends months before the opening scene takes place, brings the social trajectory of the American dream to an end, Hannah as dependent upon wealthy Dubliners as Lily was, nearly two hundred years before. Yet its brief final paragraph, with one sentence in past tense, the other in present, affirms a shaky optimism via the fact that Hannah outlives her narrative: "We have to admire the world for not ending on us" (300). The grammaticality, collective pronoun, and present tense unify fiction with its readers, offering solidarity in the midst of risk, a clear contrast to *On Canaan's Side*, which culminates in Lilly's joyous death, an act of mystification and ungrammatical, intensified emotion: "The darkness enfolded on itself, like a fog made miniature, it turned and turned and advanced, and framed suddenly in great clarity and lovely simplicity, a creature dancing, dancing slowly, its collar studded with glass jewels, glinting darkly, dancing, dancing, the long, loose-limbed figure of a bear" (256). Connecting via the bear to the first run-ons in the novel, this sentence also recalls Barry's repeated diminutions and, through its glass jewels, the false promise of abundance. The challenge to readers of McCann's novel is open ended, inviting and requiring an active effort to imagine what will happen to the things unexploded; Barry's final, dazzling explosion enfolds on itself, denying to afford us that agency.

The World Not Ending on Us

Throughout the post-crash period, Irish public intellectuals and artists decried the passivity of the populace in the face of autocratic economic decisions, austerity cuts, and ongoing privation. The few moments in which uprisings swelled were met with encouragement and celebration; most prominent among these was the water rates protest that I will address in the next chapter. But the staid, forbearing resignation with which the Irish people plodded on puzzled the commentariat. As the argument here shows, a mode of personal responsibility and initiative translates into self-blame and impotence. The ways that all the novels I consider play with time and movement, both on a thematic level and via syntactic choices, suggest a belief in narratives of progress and a conviction that Ireland's story is incompatible with them.

Within this mindset is nestled a paradox, between the agency of personal responsibility and the determinism of impotence. Faced with the tension between what Jane Elliott has called "a conception of agency as a quality that inheres in the sheer fact of human choice" (2018, 8) and a feeling of inescapability that Stephen Dedalus once characterized in quipping that "history is the nightmare from which I am trying to awake" (Joyce 1990, 28), these novels seek textual solutions, irreal and ungrammatical ones, to real-world contradictions.

This chapter has argued that ungrammatical constructions can underscore a feeling of inescapability for economically constructed neoliberal subjects. Such entrapment relies on ideas about luck to naturalize risk; it destabilizes the faith in action; and it reduces mobility and choice for the precariat. The estrangement evinced by such ungrammaticalities can serve as a trace of the unworkability of these underlying ideologies. In the context of the failure of global capitalism and its girding gospels of bootstraps and prosperity, these novels consider what paths remain for Ireland. While their nostalgia is profound, their answer is bleak.

3

Post-Boom Infrastructure

Jobstown—a village whose name (as written, if not pronounced!) seems misleadingly cruel, given how hard this part of Co. Dublin was hit by the post-2008 recession and austerity—became the site of a small but highly contentious protest against the installation of water meters in November 2014. At that time, the unemployment rate for men in Jobstown was 49 percent, making the proposed plan to charge households for water on a usage basis yet another expense to worry about.[1] To clarify: the Irish people were already funding the water through general taxation; the change to metered billing was motivated by both austerity budgeting and clever bookkeeping. One condition of the 2010 bailout from the EU troika was the establishment of a commercial semi–state corporation, Irish Water (Uisce Éireann). Patrick Bresnihan (2015) explains that its formation in 2013 was a strategy to move this expense off the government's books and create a means to raise external capital from global investors, a financialization of a formerly state-run entity. To protesters, the idea of a private entity charging for a natural resource was jarring, particularly during lean times. A demonstration formed outside a local education center, where Tánaiste Joan Burton was scheduled to attend a graduation ceremony; as the day wore on, she was trapped in a succession of vehicles for three hours before finally securing safe departure from the site (Keena 2017).

---

1. This is the percentage given by Brennan (2019).

For many covering the crisis, a brick hurled at a Garda vehicle late in the protest provided evidence that civil disobedience can never remain civil, that the people are always a scarcely contained mob who cannot be trusted to gather peacefully and by extension ought not be given autonomy. The brick did not injure anyone; nevertheless, it offered a diversion for those seeking to discredit and delegitimize the protests.[2] As Martin Power, Eoin Devereux, and Amanda Haynes unearth in their analysis, coverage in the Irish media of the demonstrations was in keeping with long-standing "protest paradigm" patterns in that it "undermined their legitimacy [and] presented the actions of dissenters as violent and subversive" (2018, 30), a tactic that divides and thereby minimizes "appropriate" opposition. Commentators on Newstalk FM, as well as in the *Examiner*, the *Irish Times*, and the *Independent* fretted that thugs and fascists threatened the very fabric of democracy. Here was evidence that Ireland was broken, but, for the commentariat, the fault lay with protestors, not the elites who had pushed them to the breaking point.

While the press coverage frequently reflected an establishment frustration with the Irish Water demonstrations, activists and academics tended to read the uprisings around the nation as proof of collective spirit in a population worn down by austerity and heretofore largely compliant in bearing a tax burden that shifted private debts onto public ledgers. The symbolic role of water and nature more generally in Irish culture also factored in the reactions of the protestors. The establishment of Irish Water consolidated thirty-one separate regional water authorities, a conversion of a fully public utility funded by taxpayers into a private, semi–state company seeking to raise revenue from both household rates and market investors. Communal ownership by the Irish people was removed via

---

2. See, for example, O'Byrnes (2014), who argued that the pretests were an "anarchic campaign being fomented by extreme left-wing factions across the country to undermine democratic politics." Bielenberg (2014) titled his article for the *Irish Independent* "A Brick Too Far."

what Patrick Bresnihan has labeled a "biofinancialization" that put in place a new relationship "between the flows of water in Irish taps and the flows of money in global financial markets" (2015, n.p.).

This redistribution of the flow of capital also tapped into a sense of water's symbolic importance, reflected as well in the EU's Water Framework Directive (WFD), from the year 2000, which declares that "water is not a commercial product like any other but, rather, a heritage which must be protected, defended and treated as such" (quoted in Melo Zurita et al. 2015, 170). In their examination of the framing of water in the neoliberal era, Maria de Lourdes Melo Zurita et al. identify the perverse logic in this characterization, which at root solidifies the notion of water as a *product*: "The WFD definition . . . removes the definitive preclusion that water is *not* a commercial product and asserts heritage value rather than (EU-wide) communal ownership rights" (173). Michael Rubenstein (2018) makes a similar point in his attention to the slippery terminology with which Peter Brabeck-Letmathe, of Nestlé, categorizes water as alternately raw material, foodstuff, and market value. Such tensions between some notion of a common good or national trust and a contemporary zeal to extract as much value as possible from natural resources expose just how deeply the neoliberal project has embedded itself in water dynamics globally and in Irish public policy in particular.[3] It is into this context that the plan to install water meters in each residence was advanced, converting a shared national resource into a commodity for personal purchase. The brick narrative focused national attention away from the maneuvers by which resources are privatized and debt is borne by the public, instead defining the "real" problem as

3. Beyond Irish water, we can think about the opening of Irish farmlands to industrial development, not to mention the rhetorics of human capital in the marketing of Ireland as tourist destination and tax haven. A related effort can be seen in the campaign "investNI," which encourages direct foreign investment in Northern Ireland in part by touting a young, English-speaking labor force, low costs, and the sorts of flexible labor practices that retain power in the hands of employers. See O'Rourke (2003).

individual acts seen as extreme or antisocial.[4] Such emphasis deflects discussion away from issues of economic precarity, instead spotlighting personal choice.

Chapter 2 explored the perils of valorizing the rugged individual, examining discourses of individual grit within narratives of global migration and national identity, in texts that stretched backward into the twentieth century and before. Turning to novels set in the present and future, chapter 3 will think about community configurations by attending to networks within Ireland, particularly those that function on the level of the county, city, town, or village. With a backdrop of the ongoing, accelerating global ecological crisis, examined within the scope of local infrastructure—via analysis of the postapocalyptic steampunk power in the imagined *City of Bohane* (2011) by Kevin Barry, and the water-treatment plants in Mike McCormack's *Solar Bones* (2016)—this chapter argues that such fixtures operate as sites of concrete, real, and shared social endeavor as well as communal environmental hazards. As such, they reveal anxieties and ambivalences about collective enterprise and cooperative projects like nations and the relationship of such projects to economics. While, historically, infrastructure has forged social bonds, Barry and McCormack both envision irreal situations to conduct thought experiments about the role of infrastructure in the twenty-first century in solidifying the dominance of neoliberal capitalism, augmenting attention to biofinancialization with a recognition of the affective leverage that attaches to ideas of the natural. Hannah Boast's formulation is useful here: "The making of water legible as a fact of 'Nature' is what allows us to conceive of it as a resource existing in quantities independent of human intervention which we might discover, access, exploit or improve" (2020, 20).

4. This is a tendency reflected in coverage of Black Lives Matter marches in the United States following the murder of George Floyd in the summer of 2020, with ongoing efforts to define some protestors as legitimate and others as looters, as well as in related protests and counterprotests in the United Kingdom, such as those following the removal in Bristol of a statue of slave trader Edward Colston.

Infrastructure is the mechanism by which such access, exploitation, and improvement takes place. Water lines, power grids, roads: these sorts of ever-present but largely unseen structures formed part of the social contract that took shape in the first half of the twentieth century. Certainly such public works have been at best imperfect means of providing for basic physical needs and knitting a social fabric.[5] Nevertheless, the neoliberal compact that took shape in the mid-to-late twentieth century has sought to diminish their role, this attack forming part of the larger effort to dismantle, privatize, and monetize the social welfare state, a project with American and British origins but effects, as I've argued in the last chapter, traceable in Ireland as well. Paying attention to how novels of austerity represent infrastructure, both thematically and formally, offers one way of looking at the status of the collective project since the economic crisis. Contemporary novels engage both the ways that infrastructure offers a metaphor for social networks and connectivity as well as anxiety about the current status and future fate of the social in the face of environmental and economic threats. Moreover, as gestured to in Boast's line of argument, the networks themselves function as posthuman or extrahuman structures, actants operating outside of human control and perhaps even working to limit human possibilities. While my final chapter focuses on such animacies and actants, here they are important as aspects of a larger infrastructure. Seeking to account for the shift in temporality from the America-facing novels examined in chapter 2, my discussion of infrastructure will touch as well on the ways that human time differs from environmental and other temporal frameworks.

The textual component of this interest in connection arises via grammatical connectors like conjunctions and related rhetorical techniques such as polysyndeton, parataxis, and hypotaxis, as well as through syntactic choices and narrative perspective. Coordinating

---

5. The terminology of public works here acknowledges in particular the groundbreaking work of Rubenstein (2010) in his book of that name, which functions as a backdrop and inspiration to this chapter.

and subordinating conjunctions create different logical, and, by extension, ideological relationships among ideas. Textual disruptions of time and space further create an ungrammatical environment that is reflected in thematic and narratological irrealism. The irrealism of these novels, as well as their formal brokenness, lay out visions of, and concerns about, an Irish society that does not function as a public, mounting "a powerful implicit negative critique . . . indirectly, through the idealized images of a different, nonexistent reality" (Löwy 2007, 196). Yet, despite their shared challenge to the era of austerity, only McCormack, with his single-sentence novel, offers even the slightest hope for a cohesive social identity.

Fantasmic Depletion

While precise numbers are not easy to calculate, in the EU over 90 percent of waste is industrial, not municipal, much less personal.[6] However, individuals are repeatedly enjoined to recycle, creating a perception that environmental degradation is largely a problem of wasteful households. The focus on an individual rather than a corporate and industrial scope badly distorts our sense of how to approach reform. Just as the scale of efforts is influenced by constructions of personal responsibility, the rate of change is misaligned with human understanding. As Vivasvan Soni explains, "This calamity [of human self-destruction]" is taking place in "slow motion beyond the human scale of time" (2017, 132).[7] While some of the environmental degradation we are inflicting is becoming increasingly observable even within our lifespans and temporal measurements, the perception of

---

6. See "Waste Management in the EU" (2020).

7. Soni does not overtly reference, but certainly writes informed by, Nixon's 2011 *Slow Violence and the Environmentalism of the Poor*, which highlights "a violence that occurs gradually and out of sight, a violence of delayed destruction that is dispersed across time and space, an attritional violence that it typically not viewed as violence at all . . . incremental and accretive" and erecting "formidable representational obstacles" (2).

the rate of passage of time that Soni refers to provides a way of connecting temporality to the collective: "By bringing energy into cultural awareness, we might be able to fashion forms of collective life
and patterns of energy consumption that avert" disaster (132). The
focus on community solutions is a particularly important rejoinder
to the devolving of ecological responsibility onto individuals. The
dilemma of how to enact change persists.

For now, Soni's attention to the collective dimension and relatively slow unspooling of environmental calamity can provide a point
of entry to Kevin Barry's 2011 novel, *City of Bohane*. Its formal features, thematic interests, and dystopian steampunk future roughly
forty years hence open space for analysis of the novel as irrealist and
ungrammatical. Bohane, an imaginary city on the west coast of Ireland, relies on technologies considered outmoded and even archaic
in the early twenty-first century. The digital and industrial achieve-
ments of the era of the novel's publication seem to have given way to
those of an earlier moment, one reflected as well in the fashions of
2053, another dimension of the novel's obsessive temporal recursion.
Bohane's citizens wax nostalgic for what the novel calls the "lost-
time," a period of indefinite era signaled by such emblems of 1950s
and 1960s fashion as crombies and creepers; the novel's highly traditional gender roles and smoky old-man pubs hail from that epoch
as well.[8] These rural pubs are found in an area known as the Big
Nothin', a landscape of bogs, massifs, and sandy terrain; further east
is the Nation Beyond, an entity largely irrelevant to the lives of those
in and around Bohane. Even if the novel's place-names draw from a
recognizable Irish history, Barry's geography is unrecognizably distorted by some unnarrated catastrophe: Bohane in 2053 is a place

---

8. To write about the lost-time during the COVID-19 quarantine, in a cultural
moment so aware of its own "beforetimes," is to see reality catch up to what Ben
Zimmer traces in the *Wall Street Journal* (2020) as the sci-fi visions of *Star Trek*
and its *South Park* parody. Barry's own term is prescient about the adaptability of
neoliberal culture to nostalgia for a vaguely periodized sense of something better
than right now, less Proust than retro reboot.

with a warm, tropical climate on a river that empties into the Atlantic.[9] The novel declines to define or even to reference overtly the technological wreckage and climate changes, though traces of devastation are part of how, as Annie Galvin puts it, "the novel makes legible certain processes of slow violence at work in our current world" (2018, 584). For instance, we learn in the opening lines that "whatever's wrong with us is coming in off that river. No argument: the taint of badness on the city's air is a taint off that river. This is the Bohane River we're talking about. A blackwater surge, malevolent, it roars in off the Big Nothin' wastes and the city was spawned by it and was named for it: city of Bohane" (Barry 2011, 3). The opening diagnosis performs several jobs, positioning narrator and readers as a collective first-person plural subject to an environmental pollution with a moral facet. Indeed, this passage and the remainder of the novel's opening pages act as an instruction manual for the reading of the book, alerting the reader to a number of its stylistic predilections: its use of second-person plural, its casual voice, its reliance on present tense, its occasional omission of articles and pronouns, its neologisms, its polysyndeton, and its inversions of syntax.

In this context, it is worth noting that "blackwater" has different meanings in ecology (a river, often tropical, poor in nutrients), in mining, and in public sanitation; the phrasing welcomes multiple inferences in an ungrammatical torrent that itself surges and swirls, recursively explaining that the title is itself a reference to the river. Beyond this mini-etymology, Barry never tells readers what has

9. While the phrase doesn't appear in the novel, a map in one edition of the book calls it the "Black Atlantic," a name not only in keeping with the novel's attention to the blackness of the river waters but also evocative of that term's use by Paul Gilroy and others in reference to the disconnect of culture from a specific national or regional identity that was forced upon enslaved people, Black movements, and Black individuals both during and after slavery. The term makes identity specifically transnational; Barry works to depict a city-state with a multicultural flair and open lines of trade and communication with Lisbon in particular. The Bohane love of calypso music provides another connection to Gilroy's Black Atlantic.

happened to give rise to the postapocalyptic hellhole of his setting, although the origin of the unexplained disaster can be deduced to coincide with the austerity era of the novel's publication. We learn that, in the novel's present, Bohane is "powered largely on its turf, and the bog had been cut away and reefed everywhere . . . its body left scarred, its wounds open" (116). In the era of the novel's composition, turf production and use in Ireland were both in decline, due to (belated) recognition of the destructive environmental impact of turf.[10] Barry's reference to turf from an overtapped source thereby evokes an earlier, specific stage in Irish history: the twentieth-century period during which turf was harvested on an industrial scale.[11] During this era, first the Free State and then the Republic were born, both committed to achieving independence from foreign energy and cultivating economic self-sufficiency via the development of domestic industry. As a tangible link of the young nation to its soil, turf was not just energy but heritage in the form of fuel, as evidenced by the figuring of bog as national body. The distinctive smell of a turf fire bears nostalgic associations and draws the Bohane of 2053 back to an era before the Celtic Tiger.

Meanwhile, the city is littered with the now-disused and deteriorating energy technologies of the intervening period, including "ancient pylons" (97) and "dead cables" (181)—about which more later. When Barry doesn't call the pylons "ancient," their descriptive adjective is "dead," of a piece with the larger ambience of utter decrepitude. Particularly in its evocation of poorer communities, Barry's text

10. Turf as an energy source is even higher in carbon emissions than coal and, as an added financial disincentive, more expensive to extract than natural gas or wind.

11. Galvin's excellent article argues that the "image of the overexploited bog also mobilizes lines of connectivity between the novel's local context . . . and the global flows of capital that drive the market for fossil fuels like peat" (2018, 584). Of related interest is the fact that the troika sought to require the Electricity Supply Board (ESB) to sell off some of its turf-driven power plants during the austerity period, though this diktat came after the novel's publication.

delights in squalor and ruin, the author's manner recalling a literary naturalism associated with the long tradition of working-class urban depiction as well as its somewhat hyperbolic extension into Dublin's "dirty realism" in the 1980s and 1990s.[12] The novel's prose revels in set-piece deterioration, describing one neighborhood, the Northside Rises, as a "bleak, forlorn place, and violently windy . . . on either side of the avenues, the flatblocks were arranged in desolate crescent circles, the odd child leapt from a dead pylon, and dogs roamed in skittish packs" (25–26). Such relentless attention to what is ugly and broken serves as a repeated motif throughout the novel, a tendency reflected in its gleeful breaches of decorum. Characters behave without concern for manners or sensibilities, spitting, cursing, and seeking physical pleasure: "Was a bottle of Phoenix ale on the counter and he raised it and sucked deep on it and burped a cloud of kebab breath (mutton flavour) and he placed the bottle down again, wiped his mouth and smacked his greasy lips and a wee lizardy tongue emerged and tickled the air; see the searching tip of it" (190). This long sentence begins without naming the police officer who is its primary grammatical subject, a displacement that foregrounds the body over the person. The mouth functions as a Rabelaisian orifice, gorging, disgorging, uncontained, its tongue animalistic. This corporeal extravagance is underscored by Barry's choice to conjoin multiple grammatically complete clauses with "and," an act of polysyndeton that reflects the officer's own immoderation.[13] Here, as throughout, both in carnivalesque indulgence and in acts of graphic violence, Barry elevates the bodily excess that Mikhail Bakhtin characterizes as the grotesque.

The same gleeful wallowing in squalor that marks the physical descriptions of setting and character also attends the linguistic. A

---

12. As Jimmy Rabbitte says in the film version of *The Commitments* (1991), "I'm not after a bleedin' postcard; I'm after urban decay" (1:13:10).

13. Fans of the Oxford/serial comma might see its absence here, with the syntactic confusion that ensues, as a further hallmark of the absence of discipline or containment.

supplemental study guide labels the novel's lingua franca "a unique jargon to represent the slangy streetwise speech" (282); this "invented" language is aggressively present on every page. Both the narrator and the characters delight in ribald terms, referring to sex, for instance, via the metonymic "knee-trembler" (70ff). The language manages to be both explicit and allusive, vulgar and coy, abundant and bounded. One unfortunate character bears the name Fucker Burke, though the word "fuck" is never used as a verb. Characters refer freely to excretion, masturbation, and various forms of intoxication in an elaborate, purple argot, the linguistic excess a seeming compensation for the poverty of the setting. A name is seldom used when a nickname can do, whether for an object ("joe" appears more often than "coffee") or a person—the aforementioned Fucker serves as a key lieutenant for a gang leader named Logan Hartnett, who is more frequently known as the Albino, Mr. H, or the Long Fella, this final nickname containing within it a further familiar abbreviation.[14] This sort of linguistic substitution forms a logical extension of a Hiberno-English tendency toward avoidance of specificity. In this context, the terminology of "lost-time" for the period that makes characters pine so ferociously feels akin to the historic labels of the Emergency or the Troubles, a euphemistic reluctance that delicately papers over something unpleasant. The jarring irony of such demurral in a novel laced with profanity and bodily explicitness points up a long-standing contradiction in Irish expression. Like the peat that powers Bohane and the fashions both anachronistic and portmanteau, the novel's language pushes at its limits, overfished and macaronic, an apt counterpart to a city pocked by ruins and depleting its natural resources.

The circumlocutory terminology extends to geography. The novel makes very few explicit references to Ireland, but Bohane is clearly an Irish city, if a speculative one, and the text refers multiple times to the ongoing existence of nations. Oblique mentions of commerce

14. De Valera was known as the Long Fellow, another of Barry's sly nods to his interest in the midcentury ambience.

with England, Portugal, and Tangiers indicate in passing the still-interconnected global community; even more allusive evocations of Ireland underscore Bohane's isolation and self-rule. The word Ireland is used just once, geographically: "It is all as bleak as only the West of Ireland can be" (7). As a sovereign state it is only ever referred to, like so many things in Bohane, by an abbreviation of a nickname: the NB, for Nation Beyond. This state is discussed exclusively in an econopolitical context as a disapproving body whose release of aid is seen to hinge on the ability of the local government, the Bohane Authority, to offer an appearance of control. The dependency on external income is described by multiple speakers in the novel in a familiar metaphor for the welfare state, that of the lactating breast: "NB tight enough with the aul' tit this year . . . The Authority wishes for the calm to persist . . . until such time as the NB tit has been successfully massaged" (40). In this exchange between the gang leader Hartnett and a newspaper editor, Big Dominick Gleeson, both men evoke a withholding mother who needs to be pleased before she grants sustenance. Such imagery activates enduring constructions of the "Mother Ireland" trope that Gerardine Meaney characterizes as "the structural interdependence of gender and national identities" (2013, 125), crossed here with a dismissive reference to the dependence of Bohane upon a welfare state figured as a teat to be sucked.

The Irish national mother who does not nurture has roots in the famine.[15] As Margaret Kelleher notes in *The Feminization of Famine*, "Depictions of maternity . . . reproduce an ambivalence at the very heart of the maternal figure . . . Mother's milk is a central metaphor of the gift of life; her dry breast is thus one of the famine's deepest horrors, expressive of a primal fear" (1997, 29). For this reason, "Depictions of the dry-breasted mother unable to feed her child . . . embody the worst consequences of famine in literary and

15. "I am dying of hunger & cold, mother . . . the Queen has lands and gold, while you are forced to your empty breast a skeleton babe to hold" runs an 1847 poem by Amanda Edmond (1872); the poem was soon set to music and also appeared in elocution texts throughout the nineteenth century.

historical texts" (2). Abby Bender has extended this insight to note that the "trope of the empty breast" creates "a sense that the breast itself seems to be metonymically unwholesome, anxious, and diseased. The famine breast takes on the impoverishment of landscape, diet, and home" (forthcoming). Here, the tight tit yokes Bohane's financial insecurity to the atmosphere of financial austerity during its composition via reference to an earlier moment in which the state failed to feed its citizens.

The novel thus invites the analogy between a famine rarely spoken of directly, operating as a suppressed trauma across the centuries, and a nation not named as such anywhere in the novel. Annie Galvin astutely reads *Bohane* as presenting "a world endlessly disabled by its past, suggesting that we might read austerity not just as economic crisis but rather as humanitarian disaster with deep roots in the historical operations of colonialism and sectarian division" (2018, 579). On a parallel track, Maebh Long argues that *Bohane* emerges in an Ireland long burdened with "failed mourning" not just consequent to the famine but the larger colonial history, a melancholic state: "We see its repetition and failed mourning violently magnified, as [Barry's] Ireland of 2053 retreats ever-further from modernity into a melancholic cycle of abuse. The famine as defining event has been replaced by a global catastrophe whose details are repressed but whose impact is all-encompassing" (2017, 82). Long's interest is in melancholia and its temporal disruptions, but her approach, like Galvin's, is also valuable in its attention to scope. The famine was not, of course, a purely local event; its recurrent, cyclical shortages and hungers form part of the infrastructure by which Britain sustained its regime of accumulation. Nevertheless, the concentration of the famine's ravages in Ireland distinguishes that crisis from the global economic crisis of 2008, which Barry in turn distinguishes from an even more widespread and deep econoenvironmental disaster. As Long points out, everyone we meet in Bohane—with the exception of Jenni Ching, whose assumption to power ends the novel—is beset by attachment to the lost-time, their cultural development thwarted by a nostalgic, melancholic lack. We can read the novel as taking the stance that too much attention to the past and to the personal is problematic; Barry's coronation of Jenni stands as a hopeful note in a text otherwise dour in its predictions—though, as discussed below, it carries troubling implications at the same time.

Mise-en-Scène, Mise en Abyme

The emptiness of spirit in Barry's hollowed-out characters has corollaries in the spatial, temporal, and political dynamics of Bohane. We can trace a steampunk ethos in the novel's approach to these forces. As a general category, steampunk imagines an alternative world in which modernity proceeded along a track that retained the look and technologies of Victorian England, foregrounding the materiality of technology. Barry's iteration of it arrays his setting with analog contraptions, dialing back technological advances of the digital era, warping time and space, and decoupaging an admixture of cultural objects, fashions, and rhetorical tendencies of various eras and fictional genres. This aesthetic montage reveals the stakes in writing a futuristic novel—a project that, in Jennifer Wenzel's vivid construction, can "effect a gentrification of the imagination" if it "serve[s] as an alibi for persistent histories of inequality" (2019, 33).

Wenzel's attention is to the role of "time and futurity" as an "axis of the difference that displaces or disguises the socioeconomic axis of inequality in the present" (2019, 33). That is, a future with inequality built into it can make it seem as though the relevant or significant difference is in temporality, a move that can acclimate readers to contemporary social inequities, depoliticize austerity, or make wealth disparities seem inevitable and built in. This section will explore the ways in which *Bohane*'s setting, including time, might naturalize certain types of dispossession that post-crash Ireland absorbed from earlier cultural forms. We see these internalized discrepancies expressed via a recreation of period costumes and decor and a recalibration of the relationship of past to future. The steampunk aesthetic of the novel intertwines temporalities and forecloses on infrastructure as a space or mechanism for collective possibility.

One way in which Bohane resembles the era of its composition is in the vast gulfs in material well-being within the city and between urban and rural. The city folk call the land outside Bohane the "Big Nothin'," defining its area as a void. This oxymoronic juxtaposition of magnitude and absence captures the reluctant dependence of Bohane upon its rural surroundings, from which, in keeping with urban areas in Ireland of an earlier era, it harvests foodstuffs and police officers. Even more that Bohane itself, Big Nothin' exists in premodern conditions: Gant wears a "buckskin" (2011, 84) and lives by candlelight. The Eight Mile Inn where Hartnett's lieutenants meet with a snitch is lit only by turf fires and populated by old men in flat caps; the rural Ireland being characterized could be 1953 as easily as 2053.[16] The lack of electric infrastructure in Big Nothin' extends to Bohane as well, though diesel-powered generators make for a brighter skyline. The dead pylons and cables mentioned above suggest that the city was once a fully electrified community; in keeping with such aspects of Bohane's crumbled infrastructure, the generators carry symbolic weight, providing power only to the individual structures to which they are attached, a synecdochic gesture toward frayed social bonds. The use of generators makes for a less collective solution, part of the novel's larger portrait of the disintegration of public works and their replacement by retro technologies.

One piece of the technological infrastructure that functions with a bygone feel is Bohane's mass transit. A diesel-powered El runs from beneath the Northside Rises to a terminus everyone calls "Yella Hall." Barry's descriptions emphasize its age, as when the "boxcars" screech on the track, and "elderly heaters juddered like halfwits beneath the slat benches" lit by "yellow lights" (12). Like the "dacent ordinary people" (38) it serves, the El is part of the backdrop and mood more than a key setting or plot element. The "mass" transit that drives the plot is the Beauvista Tram, a proposed development in the leafy, prosperous neighborhood where Bohane's most prominent men live.

16. Rural electrification was begun en masse in 1946 and completed in 1965.

The city's elite are keen to see the tram built, both for their own comfort and for the boon to real estate prices on "every last site for a manse beside it" (80). This dual motive inspires the novel's power brokers—mobsters, newsmen, bureaucrats, and fixers—to conspire in maintenance of a status quo of class divisions and détente. For instance, Dom Gleeson, editor of the *Vindicator*, advocates in print for spending on the El rather than the tram while working covertly with the Bohane Authority and the Hartnett Fancy to secure funding for the tram.[17] Throughout the novel, the free press is in the pocket of the powerful and the elites take self-reinforcing actions to shore up their status. The irony that even publicly funded infrastructure projects are sites for divisive interests to assert themselves bespeaks a perversion of the ethos of mass transit, indicating just how fractured Bohane is in 2053.[18]

While this corruption is at some level tied to the broken moment of the novel's setting, Barry's mise-en-scène links it as well to the earlier eras about which his characters are so nostalgic. The spaces in which Bohane residents gather layer elements of multiple time periods one on another, paying tribute to iconic settings. The Supper Room, "the Bohane power haunt" (8), genuflects in front of golden-age Hollywood, mafia movies, and the Prohibition era: behind a speakeasy-style door, "the edges of the room were lined with red velvet banquettes. . . . Across the fine parquet waited an elegant brass-railed bar" (8–9). The space, in a long-since-converted discotheque, has low lights and ceiling fans that "whirred noirishly against the night" (230) while a barkeep polishes glasses and chips ice. In multiple scenes patrons order oysters; merchants and members of the

17. "Fancy" is the novel's term for a criminal syndicate.

18. The appropriation of public projects for private enrichment is not of course unique to Bohane. The construction of Dublin's light rail system, Luas, was seen at the time to be "developer-driven" in some of its decision-making, and "political interference has left us with two Luas lines that aren't connected in the City Centre" ("Luas" n.d., n.p.), a situation remedied over a decade after the lines began service when a connection was opened in December 2017.

Bohane Authority sit in business suits, covertly craning their necks to look at power brokers. The ambience Barry conjures is that of smoky, dimly lit, luxurious rooms where the fates of many are decided by a powerful few. Unlike the categorical decrepitude that defines most spaces in the novel, the Supper Room, whose name also evokes gracious living in an earlier era, projects opulence of a bygone time, another dimension of the novel's larger construction of nostalgia.

Likewise, a temporal pastiche characterizes the clothing in Bohane and environs. One signature of the novel is its mode for describing outfits, which is frequently structured with the phrase "X wore," followed by a colon and a new paragraph in which the ensemble is detailed in a sentence fragment that lists items in sequence, heavy on the adjectives and inclined toward eclectic juxtapositions. The first of these descriptions is of Logan Hartnett, "a dapper buck in a natty-boy Crombie, the Crombie draped all casual-like over the shoulders of a pale-grey Eyetie suit, mohair. Mouth of teeth on him like a vandalized graveyard but we all have our crosses. It was a pair of hand-stitched Portuguese boots that slapped his footfall, and the stress that fell, the emphasis, was money" (4).[19] This description, like a number of the others that follow for other men, evokes a midcentury look, here of a Teddy Boy with money for high-quality products. The sentence fragment, lack of article, and casually matter-of-fact attitude inflect the time period and class vibe with a noir masculinity, while the inverted syntax in the sentence that follows it places its emphasis on a final noun, in echo of Irish grammar, gestured to as well by the absence of an indefinite article. The disquieting ungrammaticality of boots slapping a footfall subtends the relationship of money to violence.

Indeed, the ideological underpinnings of the style and design preferences adopted by Barry's characters are symptomatic of systems of

19. Galvin, whose arguments are generally persuasive, offers the first half of this quotation as evidence of a "screenplay" quality to the prose, an analysis that accounts for the detailed descriptions far more convincingly than it does the stylistic and tonal dimensions (2018, 580).

social organization at odds with the surface, plot-level affection for the masses. In its embrace of power haunts and peacockery, Bohane venerates forms of male collectivism that organize themselves through hierarchy and physical shows of force. References throughout to pork-pie hats, cravats, and jodhpurs, among other ornamentations, under-score a larger sartorial excess, a culture of dandyism evocative of a number of historical communities that were largely male, whether Old West (boots, waistcoats, gold and silver detailing); Edwardian/ Teddy Boy (ruffled shirts, skinny trousers, velvet collars, top hats); or mod and early skinhead ("an electric blue ska suit with white vinyl brothel-creepers" [148], zoot suits, sleeveless wool jumpers). This hodgepodge of fashions shares only a lack of understatement, a peri-odization evoking the past, and an ethic of consumption. The novel's depictions of economic inequality may be most clearly conveyed by the opulence of some of the getups; at the same time they are sugges-tive of the era of the book's publication, in which the brand of the self is aggressively marketed through image construction.

To be sure, the image construction extends as well to the three female characters who have major plot functions. Girly Hartnett's choices recall the luxury of the starlets of the silver screen, like the "ankle-length" frock with "the ermine trim . . . Lana Turner style" (2011, 269), a combination of wealth and femininity. Maebh Long argues that Jenni's style also activates feminine tropes, in a form of "power dressing," whose "visual symbolism plays on fetishism . . . her tight, vinyl and leather catsuits, boots and steel caps appropriate clichéd elements of the dominatrix" (2017, 94). More importantly, "the violence she offers differs little from the general violence of Bohane" (94), an insight that invites further analysis. At the novel's climax, Barry connects the historic August puck fair with a contem-porary affective outburst of women screaming as Jenni assumes lead-ership of the Fancy, fusing the carnivalesque mass of the former with the gendered collective of the latter. As with other moments of mass action in the novel, we see the orgiastic abandon of sensibility in the face of pure feeling, a depiction of mass action that dehumanizes a crowd's members. Galvin makes a persuasive case for reading the novel as using internecine violence to propel its plot and uncover the environmental and economic forms of slow violence simultaneously in play; she is certainly right to argue that the novel calls attention to "the human and societal fallout of [austerity] politics and, in so doing, provokes us to consider austerity as a modality of violence in and of itself" (2018, 581). Yet the text's relationship to violence bears further consideration, especially in its fetishization of certain modes of masculinized power struggle and its distrust of the masses over which the alpha males rule.

The concluding regime change does not promise a new or different type of society, just a different head of an organization reliant on political intrigue and bloodshed. The bacchanalian excess of the fair yields a hedonistic description that begins with "By midday an air of happy derangement had settled upon the Trace. You could barely walk the wynds for the large and ragged crew that bounced off the walls" (2011, 251), extending through a list of those comprising the throng, including "syphilitic freaks . . . washed up auld hoors . . . and wilding packs of feral teenage sluts . . . any one of this crowd could turn a shkelp in your lung as quick as they'd look at you" (251–52). This passage features the novel's indulgent affection for an unruly populace, a tolerance that expects immoderation and fighting. Barry uses the annual, foreseeable riot as a means to eliminate most of Jenni's possible rivals for control; as dawn breaks, Jenni surveys her realm in an "inaugural" (277) procession, bareback on a palomino—a further link of Bohane to the Old West chronotope. The novel's final fragmented sentence is beautiful and chilling:

> Hung upon the livid air a sequence of whinnies and pleadings, the dogs, and the first taste of the new life came to Jenni
>
> as she rode out the measured beat of her ascension and a bump of fear, too, y'check me
>
> as she searched already the eyes of her own ranks for that yellow light, ambition's pale gleam
>
> as she saw in the brightening sky at a slow fade the lost-time's shimmer pass. (277)

Here we see Jenni seize control, forward-looking, with an undercurrent of apprehension. Galvin reads this final moment as "mak[ing] visible the cyclical, recursive nature of crisis, mapping connections between eighteenth-century colonial oppression and contemporary material deprivation" (2018, 591) and suggests that the value of the past might be recuperated by a forward-looking Jenni. She cites Frederic Jameson on speculative fiction to argue that the novel ends "with a surreal and fantastical vision, a vision that becomes the starting point for . . . 'transforming our present into the determinate past of something yet to come'" (quoted in Galvin 2018, 593), contending that revisualization can enact transformation.

This line of thought casts Barry's ending in a positive light. Much as I share Galvin's trust in the power of the aesthetic, my own reading sees the role of form here in a different valence. The question is in part one of scope, and the passage demands a wider lens. The final paragraph of the novel is only a single clause in a longer, fragmented sentence in which a verb-subject-object syntax strains to resolve grammatically.[20] In beginning with "hung on the air," Barry gives the verb more prominence than the syntactic or semantic subject. The fact that this verb is one of suspension rather than action bespeaks a becalmed stasis. As elsewhere in the novel, the echo in Barry's prose of Irish language grammar affirms at a formal level the connection to the past that Galvin detects on the thematic level; moreover, it charts the intersecting paths of dispossession along linguistic and material axes. The loss enacted by the fragments is not only of a national tongue but also of the possibility of completion in any mode of expression. To parse the novel's final sentence brings to the fore an endlessness in tension with the very sense of resolution—paragraphs break off rather than finish; the sentence is both discontinuous and ongoing. The anaphora of the "as" clauses creates

20. I even find the meaning of the final clause hard to discern—and my analysis differs from Galvin in part because she quotes the final words to be "shimmering past" (592), an adjective and noun, whereas my edition reads "shimmer pass," a noun followed by a verb.

a sense of repetition and recurrence that makes a formal counterpart to the passage's message: that Jenni, having just deposed Logan, is already looking to see who might displace her, a cyclical forward spiral in the novel's emotional impetus that progresses without creating hope or an expectation of change.

To conclude with this gesture toward the continuation of the sorts of machinations and power struggles that have propelled the plot is to naturalize these dynamics. While the novel is deliberate in its depictions of inequality, it romanticizes the social contexts that organized the past: the mafia hits; the vigilante justice of the Old West; the feudal, tribal brotherhoods of the "sand pikeys"; the Fancy; and the Cusack mob, the wheeling and dealing in smoke-filled back rooms. The glorification of these tropes and genres, along with the attendant emulation of the eras of their composition, means that *Bohane* also romanticizes—or at least downplays—their role in bringing the moment to its crisis, particularly via the sorts of hierarchical power structures that the novel leaves uninterrogated. While Barry depicts haves and have-nots, his narrative doesn't challenge capitalist systems of organization, instead lingering on the spectacle of its needier characters as they greedily eye the more affluent—an affirmation, or at least acceptance, of a worldview in which resources are of a fixed quantity, a pie to be squabbled over and divided.

Bohane's standpoint on resources as limited and proprietary affects the ecological and social justice facets of the novel. Through it, Barry validates an individualist mindset, continually depicting corruption and backstabbing in all *Bohane*'s collective enterprises and arguing that power is a universal intoxicant, and that no one acts idealistically. Even Gant's apparent romantic gesture, his return to Bohane to attempt to rekindle his romance with Macu, turns out to be a power play by Logan, who orchestrates the dynamic to test his wife's fidelity; the novel ends with all three characters alone. The framing of human nature as not only brutish but also solitary is a powerful message at a moment in which Ireland's need for austerity is regularly tied to a (misguided) argument that personal consumption and individual risk has generated its crisis and recession. In this worldview, community is not a solution. For a novel with the word "city" in its title, *City of Bohane* is actually not that crazy about groups. Even Barry's presumably well-intentioned gesture toward female empowerment contains, within Jenni's rise to dominance, maintenance of a hierarchical system rather than any sort of democratic alternative. *Bohane*'s women are just as inclined to power grabs and backstabs as its men, and, in the closing words of the book, just as paranoid, just as reasonably. Jenni's triumphal, glorious moment is thus more accurately read as a retrenchment of cynical ideas about how power works and how collectivist infrastructure doesn't.

Postapocalypse as Present

If we accept this premise, then the broken language of the novel mirrors, as I argued above, the brokenness of Bohane's social apparatus—and, in this framework, the limited amount of available power creates a scenario in which conflict is inevitable. The struggle consequent to scarcity extends also to broken infrastructure and competition for resources, the site at which infrastructure and environment meet and the place where the choice of setting in the future becomes significant. Recall Jennifer Wenzel's warnings about the "gentrification of the imagination," and the danger that "the predominant narrative forms for imagining futurity are inadequate for apprehending the challenges of the present" (2019, 32). Her concern is that ecoapocalypse leaves "other futures . . . still unimagined" (32). Barry's forecast of a corruption promulgated by mob and local authorities alike fosters an ongoing dynamic of social competition for resources, unquestioningly accepting the inevitability of both environmental degradations and the persistence of inequities. The futures that remain "unimagined" register a poignant absence, especially when juxtaposed with a novel so many of whose characters remain obsessed with the past, the lost-time.

It is a challenge to discern precisely what "lost-time" refers to—a seemingly deliberate blurring. The generalized concept at various moment appears to apply to two different concepts: first, the moment for which Logan, Macu, and Gant all pine, roughly the year 2028; and, second, the somewhat indistinguishable, unsegmented slurry of time beforehand that inspires the music, fashion, and social configurations Barry creates. Long sees this murkiness as part of the role of longing central to the idea of lost-time: "Of course, the lost-time that is experienced and sought is not necessarily a time that existed, but a fantasy time, a phantasmagoria, the unreal or the absence that causes us to desire" (2017, 84). If the past is not clearly demarcated and explained, Bohane's future seems doomed to repeat it via the undemocratic social configurations discussed above. The fantasmic dimension of the past means that there is no clear understanding of it from which to draw lessons and formulate change. Like the social contract—like the novel's language—time itself is broken, with disastrous implications. The blurring of eras and of real and fictional pasts evades specificity, fomenting an unwillingness to confront past mistakes or link prior actions to present consequences. Nostalgia thereby effaces discussion of environmental and economic collapse, both for Bohane's citizens and Barry's readers. Jennifer Wenzel explains that, "as the narrative expression of a crisis of futurity, eco-apocalypse can misrecognize the present" (2019, 32). The abdication of discussion of what happened in the lost-time, the very vagueness effacing both personal responsibility and a collective social memory, is an outgrowth of Barry's genre choice.

The blurring of the past translates—ironically, for a novel set in the future—into a *loss of futurity*. Wenzel describes this process as one consequent to the abandonment of narratives of progress or development. She explains an idea drawn from James Ferguson, that as colonizers abandon their African conquests "the progress narrative of 'history' reverts to the stasis of 'hierarchy,' 'behind' returns to 'beneath. Inequality endures into an indefinite future longing for infrastructure" (2019, 9). In giving up on progress and giving over to hierarchy, Barry activates the temporal logic by which a people that was behind is located as beneath, the infrastructure denied to them making their spatial inability to progress a corollary to a becalmed time.

The fixation on the past also correlates to a felt loss of agency or control. At moments when "lost-time" refers to a specific point in the past for which one is nostalgic, one balm available to people in Bohane is the chance to watch footage at the Ancient & Historical Bohane Film Society, whose proprietor, whom we eventually learn to be the novel's narrator, has compiled reels of sequences "rescued from the street cameras" (2011, 180)—that is to say, from old CCTV surveillance footage. The feeding of nostalgia for lost-time by this type of video requires some unpacking. The sense of loss is meant, of course, to be for the streetscapes depicted, but access to these views comes through a form of oversight that hints at governments and private entities who are not accountable to the public. The longing to surveil others via technologies of the state and merchant class gives rise to a chilling nostalgia for a social form in which the consent and agency of the public was not sought or valued. Rather, what visitors to the film society would seem to long for is a power that our narrator retains, an omniscient perspective without responsibility. The engagement with the collective is mediated by time—another way of severing responsibility. The means by which visitors to the film society feed their nostalgia reinforce a worldview founded not on community but on separation and control. Even the way that the narrator remains unnamed and separate from his lone patrons, who in turn sit silent and isolated, contrasts markedly to the collective viewing usually associated with cinema. The screening room has only one chair.

Moreover, the name of the organization conjures problematic associations. To begin with, the film society lacks precisely that final component. As Margaret Thatcher might say in this context, "There is no such thing as society." The environment of Bohane has so thoroughly destroyed the social fabric that even the exercise of nostalgia falls into antisocial patterns. The "Ancient" and "Historical" aspects of the society's name need scrutiny as well—the time period for which the archivist is able to provide footage "goes into the Thirties" (2011, 179). CCTV usage by governments and private individuals dates to the 1980s, meaning that no more than fifty years are archived, hardly "ancient" even if we grant that it is historical.

Labeling old video "ancient" severs past from present, unfixing causality. Moreover, the name could be seen to call to mind the Ancient Order of Hibernians (AOH), a Catholic organization with roots in secret societies and affection for conservative and traditional iterations of an Irish identity—a tangential but telling fact, given that the nostalgia for nation exhibited by the AOH can be seen as congruent with the longing for an authoritarian past that I am arguing underlies the novel's narrative perspective.

Indeed, the fact that the unnamed narrator turns out to own the AHBFS demonstrates another problematic choice in the novel's formal structure. *Bohane* reads in general as a third-person omniscient novel, but there are moments in which the first person takes control, in both singular and plural forms. There are even, on several occasions, passages of apostrophe that take the form of direct address, instructing and warning characters. Galvin reads the uses of imperative and first and second person as a means of enclosing readers in the collective solidarity (2011, 591). But where the imperative creates community, it also creates hierarchy. The obscured narrative control of the unscrolling novel is part of a worldview that dictates from above, retaining power, one that corresponds as well to the grammatical choices that displace agency and animacy. The outsider status of the projector who emerges as our narrator may appear to fix the ideological valence in favor of pluralism, but there's an authoritarian dimension to it. His control over CCTV videos parallels his narrative control, both forms of disengaged display. This narrative perspective is reflected thematically in the decision not to interrogate Bohane's power structures and formally in the deployment of the second person.

Like the narrative focalization, the novel's ornate syntax plays with linear progression and personal agency. Barry places his prepositional phrases in unexpected places in his sentence sequences: "The spud-ater swallowed a fresh nip and savoured it and wrinkled *with some delicacy* his nostrils" (2011, 49); "the tout massaged *then slowly with one the other* his Judas palms. Niggled at the decision" (50); "but on the longest night of the winter, on Beauvista, he saw that time had already *from Macu* taken its revenge" (183, emphasis mine throughout). The prepositional phrases would generally follow the objects they modify, but, in these examples, they come first, which renders the language baroque and strange to readers. Foregrounding the preposition displaces the actors, less drivers of action than bystanders. And, ultimately, the coils of syntax evoke the churning blackwater of the opening page, resisting linearity even at this level. Marie Mianowski notes that "the narrative obeys a clear-cut chronology between October 2053 and August 2054" (2017, 101), and Galvin concurs, reading an ekphrastic chapter as a departure from this linearity and a therefore subversive moment of speaking out (2018, 587–92). I am drawn in particular to this latter connection and its ideological orientation, so my argument extends the recognition of the non-linear throughout the novel: Barry disrupts linearity via the fuzziness of lost-time and the gnarled syntax. Mianowski usefully notes the contrast between the "precise time structure at the narrative level" and "the absence of vision and time perspective on the part of the characters" (2017, 101). For now I focus less on the careful structure she discerns in the novel and more on the thematic and formal alinearities that register an ambivalence or lack of faith about teleology, development, and the promise of change, disclosing the novel's complicated feelings about its own futurity. While all critics of the novel—myself included—feel compelled to look at its relationship to the past, we must consider as well its implications for the future, something Mianowski takes on when she writes that "the specific narrative construction of *City of Bohane* points at the failure of language to imagine any possible future" (98). Her analysis usefully traces the way that past and future are equally unnarratable in *Bohane*.

For all the unnarratability, a story does nevertheless get told, through a complex layering of narrative times. The projectionist refers to 2053–54 in narrative past tense several times, suggesting that at least three pasts are in play: the October-to-August span of the novel's events; the early twentieth-century period of the lost-time; and the more distant past of the turntables, peat fires, and sodium lights. As the narrator reflects, "In the Bohane creation, time comes loose, there is a curious fluidity, the past seeps into the future, and the moment itself as it passes is the hardest to grasp" (2011, 60). The effect is of a world without teleology, where violence was in the beginning, is now, and ever shall be unevolving. The juxtaposed eras combine with the recurrent syntactic disruptions to strengthen this impression.

Overall, the novel's lost-time, ambivalence about the future, and general fluidity collaborate with the highly individualized nostalgias as part of a larger atomization that suggests the inability of community to survive. The setting works to infuse contemporary readers with a feeling of powerlessness and isolation. As we see characters long for times that we know are not that great, this in turn suggests to us that we ought to be happy with what we've got, making dissatisfaction into a character flaw, a failure of resilience rather than a space to envision a more egalitarian or fulfilling future. In this worldview, the past is a foreclosure that has already normalized this moment and all moments that are to come.

Recursion and the Rising Spiral

The irreal setting of *City of Bohane* extends the antisocial conditions of austerity forward in time, revealing how a lack of commitment to infrastructure as a collective enterprise contributes to the breakdown of the social contract. Mike McCormack explores similar themes in *Solar Bones*, a 2016 novel with its own irreal dimensions and plotlines touching on infrastructure, construction, and community development. Locating the origin of social breakdown not at the imposition of austerity but during the rampant growth of the Celtic Tiger, McCormack's novel meditates on the structures and contracts that bind communities and families together. In his engagement with such diverse emblems of the collective as birth certificates and water-treatment plants, McCormack's novel considers the function of what Bonnie Honig calls "public things," a category she declines to define but extends to institutions, infrastructure, media, and common spaces. Honig argues that public things not only provide care but also "constitute us, complement us, limit us, thwart us, and interpellate us into democratic citizenship. This is true of sewage treatment plants and railroads" (2017, 5).[21]

The plot of *Solar Bones* hinges on an outbreak of a water-borne parasite, cryptosporidiosis, in Galway, seemingly drawn from a real-life episode that began in the spring of 2007. Liam Leonard begins his discussion of this water-contamination incident by asserting that "one offshoot of the accelerated growth in the Republic of Ireland since the mid-1990s has been an increase in crises related to infrastructural development" (2007, 379). Largely a result of haphazard growth in new construction, poor regulation of the industrial sector, and consequent stress placed on a civic infrastructure that had long been undermaintained, a series of waterborne pathogens in Ireland in the last two decades have infected people via public water systems, notably in Galway and Roscommon. Such outbreaks represent a symbolic inversion of the promise of public works, from a connective, protective social thing into an embodiment of menace. As the crises grew, inadequate and unsatisfactory solutions enacted neoliberalism's disavowal of the commons: local councils in each case outsourced responsibility for safe drinking water onto private individuals (instructing people to boil water) and onto capitalism (advising people to drink bottled water).

The 2007 Galway crisis lasted some five months, during which a round-robin of blame had no organization or body accepting responsibility. Simultaneous and subsequent investigation revealed that a 2005 report had warned the council of "significant risk," a condition that by 2013 applied to "85 percent of water bodies at risk of not meeting the objectives set forth by the EU's WFD" (Leonard 2013, 211). Two dimensions of this issue are troubling and relevant: first, Ireland, a nation known for its lush green landscape and ample

---

21. I am indebted to Michael Rubenstein for introducing me to Honig's *Public Things*, about which he writes insightfully in "Aquacity versus Austerity" (2018); the credit for connecting Honig and McCormack is his.

rain, has built its way into a long-term water crisis; and, second, the slow violence of infrastructural neglect and underfunding is being addressed only when necessary and often with an eye to protecting private interest or investments. The links here to the water-rates protests that arose in Dublin underscore the neoliberal and corporatist orientation of the Irish government leading up to the economic crisis as well as since; even the language of crisis, in both environmental and economic contexts, is often used as an excuse or a premise to justify a neoliberal intervention—the imposition of water rates, say, as a way to "protect" water, or the enactment of state austerity measures as a response to private debt issues. As Sharae Deckard cautions, "The proliferation of neo-Malthusian ideas buttresses neoliberal forms of dispossession and the reduction of civil freedoms in the name of resource securitization. . . . 'Water scarcity' must be understood as socially manufactured, rather than naturally inevitable: the creation of capitalist hydrological regimes" (2019, 110). In both the water-rates and cryptosporidiosis contexts, corporatist and financialized responses lock in place measures that defund public coffers and perpetuate the precarity of the general population.

McCormack's choice of narrator affords readers the opportunity to reflect on these crises and their contexts and implications. Marcus Conway grew up on a farm in Mayo, moving from an early religious vocation into mechanical engineering, these twin system-wide views of the world shaping both what he focuses on as a narrator and how he approaches his subjects, as when he reflects on the Catholic catechism: "the whole world built up from first principles, towering and rigid as any structural engineer might wish" (2016, 82). Among the motifs that Marcus revisits in the novel are various infrastructures and their modalities. While the waterworks in Galway underlie much of the plot, Marcus also ponders many other public works, including wind energy, road and school construction, and the bureaucracy supporting (and complicating) such development. Moreover, his ruminations take in both larger structures, such as digital interconnectivity and global modes of exchange, as well as smaller networks like neural webs and the circulatory system. Marcus's worldview positions readers to consider the interaction of infrastructure and crisis, with Ireland's economic bust frequently the explicit subject or a ready analogy reliant on physical and spatial metaphors of collapse. All these reflections are subject to a cosmological perspective that equates the divine with engineering: "scale and accuracy, mapping and surveying so that the grid of reason and progress could be laid across the earth, gathering its wildness into towns and villages by way of bridges and roads and water schemes and power lines—all the horizontal utilities that drew the world into settlements and community" (92).

Such a spiritual perspective on seemingly mundane matters infuses the novel with a lyricism reflected in its form. While many reviewers note that the novel is a single continuous sentence, McCormack himself has pointed out that it's not a *complete* sentence, but, rather, a fragment, beginning and ending without grammatical markers.[22] Despite this overall ungrammaticality, the prose complies with the major mechanical and syntactic norms, a strategic reflection of an engineer's always-provisional imposition of order onto chaos. At moments, it reads like a poem, with short, discrete lines that rely on repetition and pattern, of a piece with a novel often less linear and plot-driven than a more conventional text. Marcus's worldview and the form of McCormack's novel are congruent in that both acknowledge a world that is disordered and entropic but can be brought to stability—or, at least, legibility—through human intellect.

Solar Bones opens at noon and takes place between 12 and 1 p.m. on November 2, 2009, with the bulk of its flashbacks to a few weeks in March 2008 and the remainder stretching across Marcus's earlier life.[23] While some critics locate the two major time settings as

22. See Treasa De Loughry's interview with McCormack, where he says that "people say the book is one sentence, as far as I understand it the book is an excerpt from a sentence that extends from before the beginning of the book, and after it has closed. It's a few clauses from the middle of the sentence" (2019, 111–12).

23. The Angelus bell begins the novel, meaning it starts at noon; Marcus refers to the passage of the minutes several times, noting that twenty minutes have passed

only eight months apart rather than twenty, a careful examination of the timeline shows that the novel is structured so that Marcus in November 2009 reflects back on the weeks leading up to his heart attack on March 21, 2008, which, that year, was Good Friday.[24] The novel uses the Catholic holy days as markers, their religious resonances carrying meaning in that Marcus, like Jesus, dies on Good Friday, meaning that his narration of the present-tense sections is from beyond the grave.[25] The narration by a restless ghost on All Souls' Day is particularly appropriate, given that Catholic tradition deems it a day to commemorate the dead, specifically those whose souls have not yet been cleansed for entry into heaven.[26] In keeping with the novel's allusive and elliptical narrative modes, we do not actually learn that Marcus is dead until the final pages of the novel.

In both content and form, the novel is interested in webs and interconnections. Marcus creates metaphors juxtaposing the literal and the figurative in a variety of scientific contexts, including

---

at roughly one-third of the way through the book (81), and that the day is "now into the early afternoon, twenty to one by the clock on the wall" (159), roughly another one-third of the way through. McCormack confirms in his interview with DeLoughry that the novel's story-time spans only one hour (2019, 112).

24. Not only does the day of the week point to a 2008 flashback, but a spring 2009 death doesn't leave enough time for the school construction project to take shape. The local politician John Moylette envisions himself "about eighteen months from now . . . holding a big shiny scissors to cut the ribbon which opens the lovely new school behind me" (166), a prediction that comes to pass, in the novel's back-and-forth temporality, a few pages earlier, in a section taking place in November 2009: "this picture in the local paper showing four men in suits standing in front of a new national school . . . holding a length of ribbon between them" (160).

25. Mianowski makes a very convincing reading of the importance of the fact that March 21 is also the vernal equinox: "*Equinox* being the Latin for "equal night," Marcus Conway dies at the moment of perfect balance between night and day" (2019, 4).

26. In some parts of Ireland, people leave out food for their dead relatives on All Souls' Day; it seems "Mairead has laid out some food for me on the table . . . a sandwich on a side plate, covered with a napkin and a glass of milk beside it" (34). I thank Carmel McMahon for this detail.

neuroscience, classical mechanics, fluid-flow dynamics, and wave amplitudes. In each context, Marcus views a scientific principle as creating a rule or pattern by which he can make sense of events in his story. Similarly, the novel takes on an increasingly dense, interwoven shape as it moves back and forth through time, primarily between March 2008 and November 2009, but repeatedly revisiting and building on narratives of earlier important moments, like Marcus's affair and its fallout before the birth of his first child, and the decline and death of his parents. The novel also creates a thematic lattice in its repeated explorations of collapse, of twitching, and of viral spread. Throughout, the prose cuts off and gives way to lists of nouns, free-standing lines on the page that look like poetry, usually in a series of pairs or trios—a minimalist evocation counterbalanced by dense, prosy descriptions, carnivalesque in their rambling excess, as in the lengthy description of a French man with autism who draws a vast, complicated city plan, or the description of a mass gathering and performance art in which Agnes participates to protest Galway's cryptosporidium crisis. These divergent tendencies inject texture and heterogeneity into the monologic narrative voice, their linkages and interconnections providing analogues to the novel's thematic attention to networks.

Posthuman and Other Animacies

Just as *Solar Bones* remains comprehensible despite its single-sentence and non-linear narration, its plotline also obeys all known natural laws. While narrated by a dead man, it otherwise conforms to the precepts of realist fiction in its content. Despite his status, whether acting as character or as narrator, Marcus avoids crediting the spiritual or supernatural world with a verifiable existence, instead restricting reference to it within affective and subjective realms. He makes no truth claims; therefore, his perceptions are not subject to falsification. Akin to the critical irrealism Michael Löwy characterizes as an "oneiric" atmosphere, McCormack's novel is not "conformist in . . . ethical and social values" (2007, 196). Rather, this space of a "flickering sense," rather than any "conviction" (Royle 2003, 1), suggests that this novel is less ghostly than irreal, uncanny. While the heart attack that kills Marcus comes only as the final plot point of the novel, there are suggestions throughout that his narrative present bears a persistent irrealist dimension, as when he describes "this anxious feeling that everything around me has settled into places and patterns unknown to me, things no different or mysterious in themselves but everything off a degree or two, this slight imprecision all around me as if things have shifted out of position" (2016, 147). This near-familiarity, the sensation that things are slightly askew, with its accompanying unease, corresponds to Freud's conception of the uncanny: the familiar surroundings that suddenly become strange and anxiety-producing. Freud's connection of the uncanny to repetition compulsion can also be seen to underlie the narrative structure in *Solar Bones*, as Marcus circles back to reexamine episodes in his life, a pattern that buttresses the novel's dense interconnections. At the same time, the repetitions, never quite the same, reinforce the uncanny sensation, amplifying feelings of déjà vu and attenuating the reassuring familiarity of linear temporality.

Sharae Deckard argues that in an era of globalization and neoliberalism, a deceased narrator can speak to questions of agency as well as the function of time in narration. In discussing Simon Ings's novel *Dead Water*, Deckard observes that "the creation of a supernatural perspective outside the realist narrative conventions elsewhere in the novel" allows for "characters capable of perceiving the whole:" a pair of dead orphans (2017, 96). For Deckard, *Dead Water* is problematic in that "all capacity for subjective understanding is displaced into the magic realist portion of the narrative, the spirit of history compartmentalized within strict generic divides that accentuate the hegemonic perception of an immovable, predetermined present" (97). I want to consider what we can learn if we retain the idea here of death as providing a larger scope for examining capitalist totality while viewing it in the context of a novel that remains consistent within its narrative mode. Marcus's outlook from beyond the grave is not so much a difference in type as in scale, given that he was already thinking in world-systems terms before. What his death allows is a posthuman perspective—literally post-human, as in posthumous: Marcus is no longer an embodied human, and a posthuman perspective in that the ghost of Marcus decenters the human and places it as one aspect in a larger assemblage, one with a role in a local ecology that functions outside human constructions of time.

Solar Bones explores posthumanism via its attention to scope, scale, and incommensurability, as well as in its related engagements with networks, temporality, and questions of agency. Malcom Sen links the tension between the slow violence of the water crisis (or, rather, gradual-then-rapid violence) and the immediate violence of Marcus's death (2019); each, unanticipated and inevitable, shapes the narrative, as does the imperfect parallel of Mairead's illness to the community outbreak. While attentive to these congruencies, the novel rejects easy analogies among its various scales: its macro and micro are not reducible to one another. On the contrary, they contain equally complex constellations, a condition that raises questions about responsibility and comments on the larger economic context, suggesting, for instance, the limits of the simplistic austerity rhetoric that the national purse can be managed like a domestic one.[27]

As Marcus comes to understand the source of his wife's illness, he navigates these questions of interrelations and proportions in a way evocative of Beck's characterization of the individual in risk society. During a phone call with his daughter Agnes, whose Galway gallery show was the occasion of Mairead's infection, Marcus learns that hundreds in Galway share symptoms with his wife. In keeping with Beck's assertion that socioecological risks become harder to avoid in industrial modernity (1992), the social safety net in Galway has failed to prevent or avoid risk. The crisis *response* in Galway is swift: warnings to boil water are circulated, "every channel of communication

---

27. In Niklas Luhmann's systems theory, spheres reduce internal complexity but remain separate and autonomous from one another.

utilised to carry the word to homes and business places, to wherever the city's population might gather in work or worship or entertainment, all angles covered" (2016, 107). While the city was not proactive in preventing the outbreak, Agnes emphasizes the thorough deployment of networks in the blanket notification. The city's configuration is better at dissemination, whether of dangerous protozoa or public health messages, than it is at prevention. The novel's attention to the former rather than the latter can be seen as a form of tacit acceptance of this state of affairs, a capitulation to the reactionary mode characteristic of secondary modernity's risk society.

Agnes moves from her praise of the swift response to a critique that Marcus refers to as "apocalyptic riffing" (2016, 108). She relates a "rumour" in Galway of three to four hundred hospitalized with the illness:

> sweating and shitting themselves into oblivion, as she vividly put it, suffering from cryptosporidiosis, a virus derived from human waste which lodged in the digestive tract, so that, she continued, it was now the case that the citizens were consuming their own shit, the source of their own illness and there was something fatally concentric and self-generating about this, as if the virus had circled back to its source to find its proper home where it settled in for its evolutionary span, rising through degrees of refinement every time it went round the U-bend, gradually gaining on some perfection—hardiness and resistance and so on—with god-knows-what results, probably reaching such a degree of refinement that would become totally resistant to every antidote and we would be host to this new life form. (108)[28]

28. A small point of clarification: cryptosporidium is a single-celled protozoan parasite, not a virus. McCormack's novel uses the term virus and the trope of viral spread frequently. While cryptosporidiosis's eukaryotic protozoa also reproduce rapidly, with basically no role in the public health imaginary they lack the semiotic coding that activates imagery of a quick spread. The metaphor of the parasite also lurks on the margins of this and other passages in the novel.

The passage tacks between words of Latinate and Germanic origins to jarring effect: the high-minded term "citizens" casts the people of Galway in a positive and engaged light, invested in a state to which they have duties and responsibilities. By contrast, Agnes uses visceral Germanic terms for bodily functions, "sweating" and "shitting"; the etymological variation enforces a distinction between the conceptual and the physical. As Agnes leaves aside the literal, her language becomes itself self-generating; she feeds on her own imagery as she spirals into panic over the uncontrolled contamination. The central metaphor, that humans feeding on their own waste thereby set in motion an endogenous cycle of viral growth, parallels imagery Marcus uses elsewhere in talking about the untrammeled economic expansion of the Tiger years. In both cases, human consumption is at the root but humans are rendered peripheral to the ultimate goal of viral reproduction.

Despite Agnes's "reasoned hysterics" (2016, 109)—Marcus uses similar derision elsewhere about his son's elaborate condemnations of the status quo ("Darragh's voice has that note of hysteria to which it is prone whenever he has to grapple with the human slobberiness of the world" [31])—it would be too easy to construe her self-consuming circularity as negatively circumscribed or enclosed. But the movement in this passage shares some features with the novel's repeated "twitching" neural network of waves and electrical impulses.[29] The twitches coincide with episodes in which the boundaries of the human are transgressed, whether by an uncanny sensation ("Something twitchy and indistinct about this day . . . the uncanny feeling of dragging my own after-image with me like an intermittent being" [158–59]) or by a challenge to the idea of discrete, bounded individuals (as in the "twitching cluster of synapses" proving "democracy inheres in our very souls" [96]). The twitch is often accompanied by references to modes of connection, like the synapses, as well as

29. Buchanan has written about *Solar Bones* as a novel of austerity and crisis, analyzing networks as a reflection on the role of digital communications (2019).

in passages that figure the inanimate in animate terms: "The ghost house beneath the paint and fittings asserts itself, flickering like an X-ray with that neurological twitch and spasm which is imbedded in the concrete, in the vertical and horizontal run of all its plumbing and wiring, those systems which make the house a living thing with all its walls and the floors pulsing with oil and water and electricity . . . this web of utilities a tiny part of that greater circumterrestrial grid of services which draws the world into community" (129). In characterizing the house as a living thing, Marcus figures it as self-generating: not only does it take on agency such that it can assert itself but it also comes to life as a result of its own lifelike circulatory networks, which in turn link it to larger networks in an enormous whole.[30] The valences of the passage pull it toward vitality—all that kinesis—as well as destruction, particularly in the fossil fuels mentioned. The reference to a ghost house activates both an uncanny and an economic dimension, as 2008 is the year that so many construction projects were abandoned in Ireland, giving rise to the phenomenon of the "ghost estate." For now, I want to emphasize that Marcus construes living as a porous concept, not restricted to humans or discrete beings. Relatedly, Sen notes that McCormack "expand[s] the ecology of homeliness onto a planetary scale," part of a "tidalectics of contemporary Irish literature" that considers scope and futurity, moving "from the personal to encompass the national and the planetary" (2019, 21).

In contrast to the branching, linear movement of twitching networks, the motion in Agnes's apocalyptic riff is recursive and circular-tidalectic; the novel itself is marked by these competing or coordinating energies, all of which ignore boundaries between people and between animate and inanimate. In a characteristic maneuver, Marcus analyzes the lack of warning before "our recent

30. Hanna's insightful analysis of *Solar Bones* in "Habitations" notes how closely this passage tracks Henri Lefebvre's metaphor in *The Production of Space*, where it is used to undermine the "bourgeois notion of the house as self-contained entity" (2020, 127).

economic collapse" (2016, 13) and recognizes that reasoned discourse is limited:

> no point whatsoever meeting catastrophe with reason when
> what was needed was
>   our prophets deranged
>   and coming towards us wild-eyed and smeared with shit, ringing a bell, seer and sinner at once while speaking some language
> from the edge of reason (14)

The sort of measured approach to problems that Marcus himself prefers is a mode that he simultaneously recognizes as inadequate to moments of crisis, and he praises and grudgingly admires multiple times those operating at the edge of reason who "startle people out of their torpor" (201), from a hunger-striking environmentalist to Agnes herself as visual and performance artist. With each such moment, Marcus acknowledges the limitations of rationality and the bounds of human control; he opens space for the transformative powers of less linear or rational modes of thought, a line of logic that decenters the human and can by extension be seen to justify or account for his narrative position from the afterlife.

This reconfiguration of perspective extends to the questionable parallel of Mairead's illness to the public health crisis in Galway in order to underscore both the ways that the correspondence works and how a "civic hazard" (2016, 124) is different not just in degree but in type to a personal one. This theme, in which the collective most definitely is *not* the individual writ large, plays out in other subplots as well—namely, Marcus's own struggles at work, where he battles repeatedly with pushy and irresponsible developers, contractors, and politicians who create dangers larger than their own greed intends. This set of narrative satellites work to suggest that systemic problems are sometimes less the fruition of malign ambitions by evil actors than problematic ramifications of the complex web of society, of the fact that we are both many and one simultaneously, as in this characterization of Galway as it weathers the crypto outbreak: "A story that appeared to linger on so that the city itself now seemed becalmed in its own unmoving filth, stagnant as the algae cloud which thickened in the rising temperatures of those days, a toxic bloom under the sun which swarmed through the city's nervous system and the digestive tracts of its inhabitants, shifting responsibility for the crisis onto the city itself, or more accurately onto the rapid expansion of the city over the past decade" (196).

McCormack's description, like the cryptosporidium itself, is not easily contained. This excerpt uses the idea of the algae bloom as a metaphor for the uncontained economic and urban growth that is the larger target of this subsection of the novel.[31] A wealth of human-amplified environmental menaces comprises the passage: the toxic blooms are a product of still water and excess fertilizer; the increased heat can be traced to global temperature changes due to human pollution; humans then can spread the disease one to another. The locus of these threats is obscured by visceral language evoking revulsion and by their inanimacy: as Mel Chen puts it, "Toxicity incontrovertibly meddles with the relations of subject and object" (2012, 195). Chen explores the cultural production of toxicity through the lens of the linguistic category of animacy: "If language normally and habitually distinguishes human and inhuman, live and dead, but then in certain circumstances wholly fails to do so, what might this tell us about the porosity of biopolitical logics themselves?" (7). In the current example, the hierarchy by which the "more animate" retain grammatical and agential power over the "less animate" is subverted by the algae cloud. Marcus notes the inanimate actors cited as causes of the toxic bloom and connects them to a "shift of responsibility" away from any specific human, via a construction that edges toward the affixing of agency to inanimate bodies, a tendency Marcus displays throughout the novel. Chen's discussion tracks the "role of metaphor in biopolitics" and "the ambiguous subject-object relations of

---

31. Such bacterial blooms are not actually vectors for cryptosporidiosis but have similar causes and pathologies to the protist parasites.

toxicity" (2012, 190): in the "basic semantic schema for toxicity . . . two bodies are proximate; the first body, living or abstract, is under threat by the second; the second has the effect of poisoning, and altering, the first, *causing* a degree of damage, disability, or even death" (191, emphasis mine). The toxic bloom that swarms is given animacy and, by extension, agency, grammatically responsible for the act of transferring culpability off of itself and onto an abstraction: Galway's growth during the Celtic Tiger era.

In framing accountability through the semantics of the toxin, Marcus connects the individual and the collective via an apt ungrammaticality: "bloom" is a singular term used here with a verb that evokes a collective, "swarm."[32] The conflation/confusion here of number marks the importance of a societal perspective, one that sees cryptosporidiosis as a public health issue and not a problem for an individual. A second ungrammaticality arises in this light, a syllepsis in which the bloom swarms in both the shared nervous system of Galway and in the individual digestive tracts of its citizens.[33] The incongruity of an algal bloom that is conscious and able to invade a metaphorical network and a physical organ system is mirrored by the attaching of blame not to the city but to the abstract idea of city expansion. While the former is a recognizable social actor, assigning responsibility to the second requires a reconfiguration of the ideas of animacy and accountability, as I will discuss below. For now, I want to stress the way that McCormack and his narrator create dissonance in assigning blame, a disjunction echoed by the passage's paragraph break, this final ungrammaticality ending a paragraph with a preposition that always requires an object. Here that object is

32. This particular construction is not unique to McCormack; ladybugs and phytoplankton in particular can be referred to as blooms that swarm.

33. Chen also speaks to the interdependence of a body's organ systems, contesting the "idea that each organ has a discrete function" (2012, 251). While Chen does not make the connection, there is an echo here of Derrida's assertion in "White Mythology" that "we have ideas of an object as superior to ideas of relations, and correlatively the superiority of the substantive" (1974, 36).

curtailed visually as well as semantically, a choice that—particularly in conjunction with the disintegration of agency—hints at the problematics of accountability that the novel explores. In creating a posthuman scale in which people are not dominant actors, McCormack risks absolving us of the destruction we have wrought.

The consequences of the choice to write only one sentence are particularly evident in such moments of the novel, as the impulse to assigning responsibility finds itself in conflict with patterns of grammatical abstraction. The nouns we discern as the grammatical subjects of this part of *Solar Bones*'s long, clausal fragment, in the paragraph that follows the one just quoted, are nouns without human referents and of varying degrees of abstraction: expansion, its (acting as a pronoun referent for "lake"), flow, cryptosporidium. In Chen's schema, abstractions register low on the animacy hierarchy, which means that what Chen calls the "'ambivalent grammaticalities'" (2012, 30) that allow them control here reveal a "leakage" that can illuminate the overlay of multiple discourses: "nature" and "science." The Latinate terminology, Linnaean genus and all, again conjures abstraction and distance from an unidealized body, a body here made invisible.

Marcus's ruminations become momentarily concrete in tracing the lake levels and fertilizer runoff through Galway's pipes, but they resume an ambivalent grammaticality as he reverts to causation:

> when
> the civic authorities sought to locate the exact origin of the disaster it found that it could not be pinpointed to one specific cause, human or environmental, but that its primary source was in the convergence of adverse circumstances—decrepit technology and torrential rains, overdevelopment and agricultural slurry—which smudged and spread responsibility for the crisis in such a way as to make the whole idea of accountability a murky realm in which there was little willingness on the part of the authorities to point the finger at farmers or engineers or those planners and developers who had allowed the city to grow beyond its ability to keep itself supplied with potable water so that with

no blame or responsibility gathering anywhere
the story hung through the city's ambience as a kind of rolling
fog which, with each passing day, thickened to a whitewash over
the whole crisis in which it became clear that no one would be
blamed nor held responsible (2016, 196–97)

The subject/pronoun agreement between "authorities" and "it found" extend the conflation of singular with collective in the bloom swarm, paralleling the authorities to the mass of single-celled organisms. These authorities begin the paragraph with grammatical agency, an enactment of the hope that they will in turn assign accountability to other humans, only to revert immediately to a further series of nonhuman actors in the subject positions: disaster, circumstances, idea, realm, willingness, the city, blame or responsibility, story, it. The significance here is twofold: first, these nouns are again abstractions, which lays the groundwork for the second point, that the possible actors here who created the problem—engineers, developers, farmers—are objects of a preposition, grammatically incapable of agency and instead acted upon, a syntactic demonstration of a systemic evasion of responsibility. Even the despairing recognition that there is "no blame or responsibility gathering anywhere" decenters those humans who could affix the onus upon someone. McCormack's style would seem to have backed itself into an untenable position in which, in order to represent the scope of environmental devastation, the form shrinks human agency toward an exoneration, and its interest in circular and networked energy would seem to becalm it and render motion impossible; as with the stagnant story that lingers, narrative here seems to assume control only to be passive. If we read the crypto epidemic in particular as analogous to Beck's analysis of risk society's dispersal of risk across a populace (1992), whether environmental or economic, *Solar Bones* reflects on the degree to which the 2008 economic collapse in Ireland functions like the public health crisis, dispersing blame to the point of meaninglessness.

Syntax and Complexity

Is *Solar Bones*, like *City of Bohane*, a novel that finds itself out-maneuvered by neoliberalism's slow violence and temporal suspension? McCormack structures the temporality of his novel so that it comments on the various frameworks—human, environmental, economic—by which time is measured. It is in this context that the syntax of the novel becomes important. I use the term "syntax" in part as a gesture to McCormack's stylistic decision to contain his narrative within a single sentence fragment, as well as to draw upon the affordances of the idea of syntax, both in terms of the linearity that syntax creates and the possibilities for innovation it opens up.

One of the key distinguishing features of human language is in the principle of linguistic recursion. Recursion allows for the embedding of phrases, clauses, or other linguistic units within one another. Linguists often give examples that use identical such units, of which the Irish folk song "The Rattlin' Bog" can serve in this case: "The feather on the wing, and the wing on the bird, and the bird on the nest, and the nest on the twig, and the twig on the branch, and the branch on the tree, and the tree in the bog, And the bog down in the valley-o." The song relies on coordinating conjunctions—all "and," in this case—to extend its single sentence. Recursion can build ever-longer sentences not just with coordinating conjunctions but subordinating ones, creating clauses within clauses within clauses: "She said that he said that we said that she knew that the dog that ate the cat that ate the bird that ate the mouse that ate the cheese . . ." As Jan Mieszkowski explains, "There is no clear limit to the number of units that can be embedded within a given sentence . . . the vision of an infinite sentence takes the notion of building an utterance out of words to the extreme, as the construction, ostensibly intended to be a 'complete' thought, becomes an interminable unit, a linguistic unit beyond units, a syntax that in virtue of its constitutively incomplete form threatens to turn against its own organizing hierarchy" (2019, 27–28). McCormack's aesthetic partakes of this thought experiment, using both types of conjunction to form a massive recursive sentence, tying it to a phi-losophy that is simultaneously cautionary and hopeful on both struc-tural and thematic planes.

Recursion in these examples takes place via conjunctions; which conjunctions are used determines the structure of the sentence and the relationship of its parts. As discussed in chapter 2, polysyndeton (the use of the same conjunction multiple times in rapid succession) can create a feeling of atemporality, of endlessness and inevitability; it is an ungrammaticality or rhetorical excess that relies upon coor-dinating conjunctions and the paratactic equality that results. While we cannot say that grammatical choices have inevitable ideologi-cal implications, I want to consider the proposition that this sort of parataxis is the ideal ungrammaticality for the neoliberal era. Ironi-cally, the democracy of parataxis, the equal sign of the coordinating conjunction "and"—even the positive connotations of both the word coordinate and conjunction, which conjure up collectivism and col-laboration—reveal the limits of equality of opportunity and leave language without context, independent clauses that act as if they do not need one another. They deny causality and, thus, responsibility.

In contrast to this version of parataxis, so prevalent in many of the novels under discussion in this book, hypotaxis is a structure of subordination. Subordination, versus coordination, creates both spatial and temporal axes: "sub-" is a spatial term, placing some-thing under something else, while the linearity of ordering on a page creates a temporal sequence. Given the human power hierarchies the notion of subordination evokes, we could replace it with a synony-mous term, the dependent clause. Not that this language is without its own connotative burdens: dependency was, of course, demonized in the apotheosis of the individual that marks American ideology as well as the rise of Thatcherism and neoliberalism in the latter half of the twentieth century.[34] Yet the term underscores connection,

---

34. The *OED* has a "draft addition" to its entry for dependency that defines "dependency culture" as "*n.* chiefly *British Politics* a social or political environ-ment characterized by dependency on the State (as through benefits or services) or

contingency, causality. While the sentence fragment comprising *Solar Bones* uses both types of conjunction, McCormack's choice to connect so many of his clauses via grammatically subordinate/dependent terms becomes a stylistic recognition and acceptance of the sorts of substantial interconnections that he explores thematically throughout.

Prepositions also do much of the labor in making the extended fragment a workable novelistic form, and, again, their success derives from their purpose—to express spatial or temporal relations—in such a way as to shape the novel's ethos. Throughout *Solar Bones*, several words reappear frequently as the final word in a paragraph, the last word before the sentence breaks off or turns in a new direction. Among the most common is the preposition "with," perhaps the word that best embodies the principle of connection, concordance, and association that stands as the opposite of an independent, free-standing action. A surprisingly complex word with myriad definitions, "with" fosters connection in a novel that is attentive to attachment at many levels—human interactions within family and community as well as in larger national and universal senses; the fixtures that hold together the various machines that fascinate Marcus and his father; the networks of synapses, the Internet, and things that "twitch." In each context, the relational properties of prepositions affirm the principle of interconnection.

Interconnection and dependence emphasize that those in a community are all responsible for one another, and McCormack's extended sentence, which subordinates endlessly, affirms this mutuality and interdependence. To return to the passage about blame for the water contamination, we can see this sort of embedded subordination enacting precisely the interconnection that those responsible ("farmers or engineers or those planners and developers") would

---

other external support rather than individual enterprise." The ideological assumptions connoted by "enterprise" in particular bespeak a commitment to the commercial and a particularly capitalist mindset.

foreswear: "so that with no blame or responsibility gathering any-where the story hung through the city's ambience as a kind of rolling fog which, with each passing day, thickened to a whitewash over the whole crisis in which it became clear that no one would be blamed nor held responsible" (2016, 196–97; I quote here without McCor-mack's visual line breaks on the page). First let us note that the list of responsible parties is given to us with excess coordinating conjunc-tions, a mode that underscores their equality as units in the sentence, with an implication of interchangeability in questions of culpability as well. In contrast to this paratactic gesture, the rest of the passage is rife with subordination. In a passage that thematically addresses issues of accountability, McCormack creates subordinate clauses that perform interconnection. The oxymoron of a whitewashing that "makes clear" that no one will be blamed is reflected in the movement from the abstract nouns of "blame and responsibility" to the concrete verbs of "blamed" and "held responsible," subordi-nating the latter to the former, grammatically negating both while it demonstrates, through the imagery of the thickening story, that dependent clauses can make connections but don't have the force to enact accountability. Nevertheless, in making tangible the spatial and temporal relationships of narrative language—and specifically the "story" of the origin of the cryptosporidiosis in Galway—the hypotactic logic of grammatical subordination and the prepositions here reinsert responsibility by their insistence on the interconnected-ness of actors and consequences.

McCormack's embedded, unspooling sentence also comments on the very nature of complexity itself. A complex sentence is defined grammatically as one that has at least one subordinate clause; Mc-Cormack extends such complexity through his recursive, endless sub-ordination. Such an embrace of complexity represents one response to the proliferation of systems too numerous and complicated for any single human to fully manage. The development of complexity the-ory throughout the twentieth century shows many thinkers engaged in articulating the relationship of humans to complexity. Niklas Luh-mann (1990) in particular saw the social as a means of containing complexity so that action is possible, a stance that contrasts with the dismissive position developed by Friedrich Hayek, who evinced "uninhibited contempt for intellectuals" (Mirowski 2019, 7), capitulating to ignorance and deriding efforts to understand or control such features of modern life as capitalist markets. Hayek's iteration of neoliberal thought elevated what he memorably labeled "men's necessary ignorance," usefully framed by Douglas Spencer thus: "The proposition that human individuals can have little knowledge of the world in which they live is fundamental to neoliberalism. The world is too complex and the perspective of the individual too limited to grasp its workings, let alone presume to direct these" (2016, 17). Spencer goes on to explain that, in Hayek's conception, "logically and ethically disqualified from presuming to grasp the totality of the social order, humans are supposed to submit to the superior organizational capacities of the market, to individual competition rather than to collective solidarity, as the guarantor of their liberty" (18). In short, economic rationality presumes unknowability of the totality.

Spencer further suggests that this version of neoliberalism is more interested in governmentality than in subjugation, and that it operates in part through constitution of a subject whose critical faculties are cast aside in favor of immediate sensory experiences. "The turn to affect," he writes, "is premised on the belief that there is nothing to interpret, no moment of cognition, only a feeling for matter [and] immediacy of perception. . . . [S]ensory affect . . . liberates the subject from the unnecessary labor of cognition" (2016, 10). McCormack's novel engages expressly with the underlying logics of such subordination of the individual to unknowable complexity, offering as counterargument a protagonist who thinks at the level of systems theory. We see the embrace of complexity, from Marcus and the novel both, in a subplot that concerns the pouring of concrete for the foundation upon which a new national school is to be built, a story the narrative launches with one of the most disjunctive moments in its sentence fragment. As Marcus describes the physical care with which he tended Mairead through her illness in March 2008, he breaks off because he sees a picture in the newspaper in front of him in November 2009, of the opening of the new school. The abrupt change of topic in a novel attentive to smooth transitions and embedded clauses makes textual sense, since the new topic is itself about the value placed on various levels of continuity and totality.

Marcus's flashback is to a phone call he received not long before Mairead got sick, from a local politician, John Moylette, represented as speaking in long, uninterrupted paragraphs. Anxious to see construction completed on the school he has promised his constituents, he calls Marcus to demand a signature on a clearance certification for the building's foundation. Marcus explains to Moylette that he cannot sign off since the foundation was poured from different batches of concrete, from different suppliers: "the problem comes from the fact that there are three different foundation slabs locked into each other, three different pours of concrete and the danger comes in the next hot or cold spell when they have to expand and contract which, because of their different compositions, they will do so at different speeds and different pressures . . . when that foundation begins to crack—as it surely will—doors hanging off their hinges will be the least of your problems because any building raised on those slabs will tear itself apart in three different directions whenever the temperature goes through a sudden change" (2016, 164–65). Moylette's response to this is to speak to the political expediencies, remind Marcus of the craftspeople awaiting work, and downplay the risks, pointing out that "this is a national school we're talking about, not a fucking nuclear reactor, what's the worst that can happen" (165). Here Moylette voices what Adam Hanna has neatly identified as the "grimly literal shaky foundations of Irish prosperity" (2020, 124), his disregard for craftsmanship an index of how of "shoddy building work and defective values are brought into stark alignment" (126). In contending that Marcus is being too careful, Moylette rejects complexity and devalues the expertise that Marcus brings, denying that Marcus has a wide enough perspective of the situation. Moylette mocks Marcus's care as excessive to the needs of the situation, of a piece with jabs the politician makes throughout their confrontation that display his view that Marcus is a nerdy bureaucrat with "engineer's scruples" (167) whose paperwork is an emasculating obstacle to the important manual labor he is preventing. For Marcus, the question is also partly about scope, but his is chronological rather than spatial: "the difference between a politician and an engineer, your decisions only have to hold up for four or five years—one electoral cycle and you are acclaimed a hero—but my decisions need a longer lifespan than that" (2016, 167). The logic of immediacy that Moylette demands—in keeping with the sort of timeless time characteristic of the neoliberal moment—is at odds with the more measured care that Marcus feels he must take, a temporal disjunction in which the frameworks of the political and the infrastructural are at odds, as if themselves poured from different batches.

When he turns to the day of the actual laying of the foundation, Marcus begins with a highly technical paragraph that details the exact steps for pouring concrete, a moment of tribute to complexity, care, and proper method. Then Marcus (as usual) turns metaphysical: "and even though

> I've seen it done umpteen times before, there is still something to wonder at in the pouring of a concrete foundation, the way it draws so many skills and strengths together, the timing and cooperation needed and the way the rising and spreading tide of concrete itself demarks, as no other stage in the building process can, the actual from the theoretical, makes the whole thing real in a way that site-clearing or the digging out of the foundation itself can never do, all these are definite staging posts in any structure's transition from the abstract but none of them separate so clearly the ideal realm of plans and paperwork from the physical world than the pouring of concrete, the building at last beginning its rise out of the ground and seeing it for so many years on so many public buildings—libraries, water-purifying plants and so on—twenty years of this still had not taken the excitement out of it for me, that uncanny sense of a building beginning to take on mass and shape in the blue light of the world where so many things can go wrong between this first pour and that ceremonial occasion when
> the building is finally dedicated to its civic purpose (2016, 173)

Marcus treats the concrete pour as beautiful, both for the collectivism that it requires and results in, and for the way it brings time's progress, for him, into sharp focus. In contrast to the feeling of impasse created by becalmed stories and stagnant waters, the pour of concrete is about passages, from abstract to real. The passage circles around this idea, articulating it several times, none quite the same—the prior state he calls theoretical, abstract, ideal, with its counterpoint the real, the actual, the physical. Ironically, of course, concrete quickly hardens, making it a curious vehicle for the embrace of progression and change; its fixity stands in for both the beauty of Marcus's civic vocation and the immovable logics of expediency. Expediency privileges economic growth over a place-based commitment. In this vein, Sharae Deckard reads Marcus's life's work as "intended for a collective good . . . the opposite of a property bubble driven by a logic of profit and financialization rather than use or design" (2016, n.p.).

The progression of the passage is accomplished in part via its moves from ideal to real, from abstract to concrete. While it also advances through its subordinating conjunctions—"though" and "when"—in keeping with the larger interconnections of the novel, what stands out here are the appositive phrases. Marcus in these moments reconceives what he has just said, as here: "twenty years of this still had not taken the excitement out of it for me, that uncanny sense of a building beginning to take on mass and shape in the blue light of the world." Such appositives highlight complexity through their naming of the various elements and connections that comprise the pour. Like the not-quite-interchangeable articulations of the move from abstract to concrete, the appositives make restatements with a slight difference, thereby enacting the uncanniness of repetition that Marcus feels in watching a building transform from a concept to a physical entity with body and animacy. The momentary collapse of temporality connects the uncanny to infrastructure, the irrealism drawing a parallel to the ghost house he describes earlier, which also served as a pathway to reflections on collective civic goals.

This series of steps follows the path laid out by Bonnie Honig in her discussion of public things. Honig begins with the object-relations theory of D. W. Winnicott, "in which objects have seemingly magic powers of integration and adhesion" (2017, 2), juxtaposing it with Hannah Arendt's faith in things to bring "durability and permanence" to "the contingency and flux of the human world of action and to the endless repetition . . . characteristic of the natural world" (2). Honig strives to "think about specifically *public* and *political* things in democratic contexts . . . and to ask whether democracy might be constitutively dependent on *public* things" (3). McCormack's choice of not just profession but venue for Marcus is congruent with Honig's vision, as he works to realize notions of community through the enchantments of shared infrastructure. The concrete pour itself is a particularly pronounced example of the sort of "stability, adhesion, attachment, resilience, concern, and care" (3) that Honig sees enacted through public things; concern and care in particular stand as the nexus of an affective engagement with the principles of democracy and a conscious engagement with complicated ideas.

In order to remain stable, an entire foundation needs to have an identical composition. McCormack's single sentence is analogous to this composite mixture, serving as a stable foundation for the rest of the novel. As Michael Rubenstein has noted about "The Dead," in using gaslight, Joyce "casts as a narrative medium that which is in fact an infrastructural medium" (2010, 85). Similarly, McCormack here deploys an infrastructural metaphor for his narrative medium, insisting on a consistency of medium as a binder for the varied materials he discusses. Marcus embraces what is complicated, the implication being that a moral responsibility for all the possible outcomes rests with him, with us. The novel's apparent leapfrogging of the period of the global financial crisis is actually a scathing critique of human failure to be as careful as Marcus, to defer, delay, be patient, minimize ambitions. In crediting human intelligence with the ability to see big pictures—and this is a recurrent motif, a fascination Marcus evidences in his extended attention to the French planner of the imagined city, for instance—McCormack excoriates us for not having managed to pay that sort of attention ourselves. McCormack elevates continuity to a virtue, a sentence poured from a single source of concrete, an ongoing refusal to separate the individual from the collective.

That Vast Unbroken Commonage

This is not to say that the novel is mistily utopian. It is neither pessimistic nor optimistic, futurist nor nostalgic. When Marcus's father is able to use traditional methods of navigation via triangulation to match the accuracy of a new sonar-reliant plotter in his friend Joe Needham's trawler, Marcus feels that

> I, with all my schooling and instruments, could never lay claim
> to such an accurate sense of myself in anything whatsoever, not
> even as
> an engineer, whose life and works
> concerned itself with scale and accuracy, mapping and survey-
> ing so that the grid of reason and progress could be laid across
> the earth, gathering its wildness into towns and villages by way
> of bridges and roads and water schemes and power lines—all the
> horizontal utilities that drew the world into settlements and com-
> munity . . . instead it seemed that all my circumstances had gath-
> ered to a point where they were unwilling to present themselves as
> a clear account, but settled instead into a giddy series of doubts, an
> unstable lattice of questions (2016, 92)

As with so many of McCormack's dense passages, this section weaves several anecdotes together and moves among five different time periods, a thickness that itself stymies notions of linear progression at the same time as it persistently nudges its way forward in the narrative. Marcus uses the trawler story and some other narrative satellites to demonstrate his father's sense of emplacement and his own lack of that quality. Equating his training as an engineer to the modern instruments that equip the trawler, Marcus finds he must conclude that the technological advances do not ensure any clearer an existential perspective; rather, like the ever-increasingly-complex networks that support modern Ireland, his own grasp of reason, scale, and accuracy might knit his world into a sense of community, but it leaves him without answers. The "unstable lattice of questions" he retains parallels the schema he mentions just before, undercutting and ironizing the "grid of reason and progress" as well as the teleology suggested in the opening pages.

McCormack thereby submits that complexity and technological advance do not automatically constitute an improvement. The novel could run with this direction, noting the ways that society plunges further into an era of manufactured risks with its overdevelopment and continuous precarity; the cryptosporidiosis outbreak is easy to read through this lens. As Honig states, "When infrastructure *crumbles*, it is not only infrastructure that crumbles but its constitutive gifts of (de)stabilization, integration, and adhesion" (2017, 6, emphasis in original); the attention by McCormack (and Barry) to what happens when we cannot depend on public things underscores the direct link between shared things and community relations, as well as the way that infrastructure can fall short. Even McCormack's title, drawn from a passage about a disarticulated wind turbine, speaks to a wistful recognition of "a clear instance of the world forfeiting one of its better ideas . . . the world had given up on some precious dream of itself, one of its better destinies" (2016, 27). The wind energy that is being set aside here is connected later in the novel to

> all those human rhythms that bind us together and draw the
> word into a community, those daily
>   rites, rhythms and rituals
>   upholding the world like solar bones, that rarefied amalgam of
> time and light whose extension through every minute of the day is
> visible from the moment I get up in the morning (76)

This is another passage that relies upon appositives: Marcus here reads human repetition as a version of progress and credits it with the world's structure. Solar bones are defined as the admixture of time and light—that is, as the very building blocks of the space-time continuum. These structures stand against a space-time compression that would obscure social function and suspend temporal progression. Marcus connects meaning to structure via repetition, framing a worldview in which humans use measurement and pattern to bring themselves into being. The novel's plural title—like the water, like the concrete—counters the quantifications of financialization through a number/agreement ungrammaticality evocative of the novel's persistent interest in parts and wholes.

The governing synecdochic logic of the novel comes to an ambivalent culmination in the "that vast unbroken commonage of space and time" (2016, 223), to which Marcus turns multiple times in the novel. It's not an idealized space; like Honig, McCormack sees limits to the positive valence of the commons. Yet, in contradistinction to a world of microniches and divided expertise, McCormack proffers a view of unity, ultimately connecting all the world's shards and fragments. Alongside infrastructure and ritual, grammar and narrative are devices that provide structure even as we move forward into a fearful unknown where "bread is poured and water is cut" (194), and there are "no markings to steer by nor any sounds to sing me home" (223). As Marcus's ghost leaves a world he critiques as becalmed and stagnant and moves forward into an unknown and empty space, McCormack chooses to elevate the bleaker dimensions of Marcus's vision above the more hopeful parts, the only solace coming from movement itself.

While Barry's vision is bleak throughout and ends on an optimistic note, McCormack does something of the opposite in his novel, gesturing toward beauty, connection, and promise only to end with a dark, soundless nothingness. In this move, McCormack acknowledges the limits both of the individual and of humanity. The insights Mitchum Huehls offers about the "abyss of politics" in Chris Abani's fiction can be illuminating here. Abani's context is a far more immanent landscape of "war, poverty, racism, and sexual violence" (2017, 158), the sorts of issues that a comfortable middle-class life in Mayo can obscure or project outward. But Abani's work shows the distance that separates hope and intervention from justice and genuine equality:

Ultimately, Abani seems to suggest that the massive discrepancies between the human and the global, the personal and the structural, that define contemporary existence for twenty-first century postcolonial subjects require us to abandon a model of politics in which political judgments, actions and interventions are justified by human experiences past and present. *The human is neither the predicate, nor the horizon, of politics.* . . . [Abani's] texts' emphases on the relationship between individual experience and the vastness of geological time and the natural landscape offer an illuminating inquiry into what politics might look like . . . under and expansive and rapacious globalism. (158–59, emphasis mine)

Huehls's attention to grammar and landscape reads each as a human invention that exceeds humanity.

Such focus to scales beyond the human perception of time leads Huehls to "a notion of history distinct from temporality" (2017, 164), downplaying the personal or phenomenological as a means of contestation in favor of attention to "a confrontation with the geological abyss" (173), a notion he sees as congruent to Mark McGurl's "new cultural geology" and its "asymmetrical" relation of human and nonhuman (McGurl 387, 389, quoted in Huehls 2017, 174). In a vision in which "our shadows have grown tired of us and got to their feet . . . to leave this world altogether and head off towards some other jurisdiction beyond the horizon" (McCormack 2016, 194), Marcus similarly extends his grasp to a nonhuman dimension; the shadows foreswear the humans on whom their existence would have been thought to depend, freeing themselves from the "predicate," as Huehls might have it, and moving past human ideas of limits. Through the choice to extend his novel—and its sentence—beyond the scope of human time and geography, McCormack acknowledges the need for a far broader scale in confronting the ambivalences and contradictions that have created the non-linear individual, readily admitting to terror.

4

Catachresis and Crisis

New Builds on Old

In January 1980, the newly elected Taoiseach Charlie Haughey made what was only the third ever live televised speech by a sitting Irish prime minister. Haughey spoke solemnly of the moment's economic straits, intoning that, regarding "the state of the nation's affairs . . . the picture I have to paint is not, unfortunately, a very cheerful one. . . . As a community, we are living away beyond our means" (quoted in Kerrigan and Brennan 1999, 143). Haughey sought consent for reductions in public spending, but his main goal was to avert strikes by day laborers, farmers, and others, unifying the nation in advance of the release of a tighter budget. Yet Haughey was throwing stones while living in a very expensive glass house: Abbeville, a storied Big House in the form of a Georgian mansion in north Co. Dublin. Karl Whitney has suggested that Haughey's attraction to the 250-acre estate sprang from contradictory impulses toward "aping and modifying the model of its eighteenth-century owner. He wanted to play the king and the rebel simultaneously" (2014, n.p.). Haughey also owned a private island, Inishvickillane, one of the Blasket Islands off the coast of Kerry, where he had just built a home, and, at the time that he gave his speech, he owed Allied Irish Bank over £1.1 million. Gene Kerrigan and Pat Brennan write that "AIB agreed to take £750,000 in settlement. Haughey was getting a £390,000 gift. The bank left a notional debt of £110,000 on the books, to which interest would not apply, which Haughey was to clear as 'a matter of honour'. This, of course, was never paid off. . . .

160

The £390,000 could be written off as a bad debt and claimed against tax liabilities. As ever, the taxpayer would pick up the tab" (1999, 143). While Haughey's corruption and financial self-dealings were criminal, at the moment he gave his speech the public was impressed by his somber mien and willingness to tighten the state belt. His eventual fall from grace coincided with the nation's rise to heady economic regions; he was forced to sell Abbeville in 2003, though he lived in the house until his death in 2006.

As Haughey's story suggests, the way that the Irish government explained the 2008 economic crisis as a logical outgrowth of the personal financial choices of its citizens is not without precedent in Ireland. In 2008, the six largest private banks in Ireland were liable for some €400 billion in loans. At this moment, as Colin Coulter and Angela Nagle remind us, "two thirds of the workforce in Ireland were drawing salaries of €38,000 or less. . . . Most ordinary Irish people simply did not have the resources to have 'lost the run of themselves'" (2015, 11). Despite this, Brian Lenihan spoke on RTE to the charge that the crisis was caused by banks and should be borne by them, calling it "absolutely wrong" and countering that "we all partied" (2010). This transfer of blame to citizens embeds risk and responsibility at a personal level quite at odds with the factual conditions of the crash, which arose primarily due to structural problems, including a regulatory climate that favored large investors and multinational corporations, a property market overheated by speculative lending, and a general financialization of the economy. In Bryan Fanning's framing, this sort of "unholy combination" was to blame, in particular the way that "investment in commercial and residential real estate became detached from economic demand for such property. A new 'rationality' prevailed where it appeared reasonable for banks to borrow from other banks to invest in the property bubble" (2014, 160).

In the previous chapters, we have seen the ways in which risk, precarity, and hazard shape the neoliberal individual and the bleak prospects for a collectivist future under such conditions. In this chapter, I turn to the ways that the construction of a society of individuals is an index of precarity that we can trace through shifts in fiction about housing and real estate. Historically in Ireland, one mode of tracking class disparities was through novels about Big Houses like Abbeville, narratives which frequently affirmed a social hierarchy of wealthy landowners and dependent tenants. To borrow Vera Kreilkamp's apt account, this stratification opened out to other modes of distinction: "Ascendancy houses signalled . . . not just the typical disparities of class and wealth between landlords and tenants, but also difference of political allegiance, ethnicity, religion and language" (2006, 60). In the twenty-first century, with the English language firmly entrenched, religion sidelined, and differences in ethnicity and political allegiance no longer breaking along the same lines, new wealth disparities have arisen, and a sense of economic and social insecurity pervades for a growing swath of the population. I have been arguing that, within this context, the discourse of class is submerged, alongside other collective discourses. Community organized around extended families, and such social institutions as the church has been succeeded by a society of atomized individuals, a shift taking place at the same time as so-called natural risks like famine have been overshadowed by the daily gamble of international markets.[1] Ulrich Beck's formulation of "risk society" is apt here (1986), tracing how our current social formations have obviated industrial-era discourses of social class; instead, "reflexive modernity" locates risk at the level of the non-linear individual.

Literary texts about houses and other buildings offer a way to think about the real estate dimension of Ireland's economic crisis. Buildings are an ideal site to examine the way that economic

---

1. This is not to say that natural risks are no longer important—we need only think of the ecological catastrophes stemming from climate change that follow one after another. My point is, rather, that responses to these disasters, like the distribution of losses and gains in the markets, do not hold an upper class to account. Instead, they demonstrate a conflation of brute luck (situations we do not choose) with option luck (deliberate gambles) in the lives of the poor. This distinction is Dworkin's (2000).

forces interact with narrative, each with attention to structure. Both commercial and domestic property markets exist as simultaneously concrete and abstract. The term "housing," a fusion of home and property, gets at the paradoxical position of domestic space as both shelter and capital in a neoliberal economy, while real estate as a term carries within it the assertion of substantiality and the sense of a profession. Moreover, the relationship of an individual to macroeconomic forces presents problems of analogy and scale that fiction is well positioned to consider. The novel is a form that by design focuses on individuals, as Annie McClanahan notes when she unearths the tensions that arise in the assumption "that the difference between individuals and the market is merely a matter of scale . . . that aggregate economic behavior follows the same laws as individual economic choices" (2018, 32). Picking up the formulation of an Americanized Irish individual from chapter 2 and the discussion of environment, scale, and infrastructure in chapter 3, I consider how physical spaces and the stylistic and rhetorical techniques used to depict them in Irish fiction can help us track the conversion of subjects to consumers and the naturalization of the neoliberal belief in the futility of public or collective action.

In 2015 Abbeville was sold by the firm that had held it in receivership, to the Nishida family, Japanese hoteliers with plans to develop it. That same year, amid a mixed economic recovery that some optimistic commentators were hailing as a "Celtic Phoenix," Wetherspoons, a British-based chain of affordable superpubs, began plans on a Dublin City Centre location. Wetherspoons is known for its practice of renovating existing properties and often inflects its properties with regional markers, somewhat obscuring the familiar neoliberal business model in which a multinational corporation expands into new markets, undercuts local competitors, and levels cultural differences. During the years surrounding the Brexit vote, Wetherspoons' CEO, Tim Martin, toured his locations in England and Scotland to campaign for "no deal," going so far as to print up "#StopBrexit Manifesto" beer mats for use in Wetherspoons and other pubs.[2] Martin's support of an isolationist Britain is more ideological than practical or even actual, given that all paths will complicate not only Martin's expansion plans outside Britain but also his supply chain and development plans, including the expansion to Dublin.[3] Nevertheless, Wetherspoons acquired a pair of buildings in the City Centre, on Lower Abbey Street, both dating to the 1830s, one a former bank branch and the other an old Baptist temple. Paul Murray's 2015 novel *The Mark and the Void* appears to allude to this transaction (and perhaps as well to the Nishida acquisition) when it describes the "fevered boomtown climate" during the years of economic expansion in Ireland: "In the beginning, the boom was fuelled by IT and pharmaceuticals. Now it was construction. Dublin was undergoing its very own Haussmannization. Cranes cluttered the skyline, new builds were everywhere; the old architecture, meanwhile, was being transformed, hospitals becoming shopping malls, churches becoming superpubs, Ascendancy manors becoming five-star golf resorts" (150).

Murray's narrator, Claude, a French investment analyst working for the fictional Dublin-based Bank of Torabundo, sees the redevelopment of Dublin through that of another city with medieval bones: Paris. The reference to Haussmann also rests on capitalist parallels between the two cities and eras. As David Harvey explains,

> Haussmann clearly understood that his mission was to help solve the surplus-capital and unemployment problem through urbanization. Rebuilding Paris absorbed huge quantities of labour and

2. https://www.crowdfunder.co.uk/stopbrexit-beermats (accessed 2 June 2022). In November 2019, some of Wetherspoon's shareholders suggested that the beermats and other lobbying constitute the sort of political expenditure that requires strict reporting in order not to violate the United Kingdom's Companies Act.

3. Most news stories focus on Martin's efforts to replace French and German wines and beers with Australian, American, and British alternatives, including use of an English herbal liqueur, Strika, in place of Jägermeister, but the workforce populated by EU labor will also change shape.

capital by the standards of the time and, coupled with suppressing
the aspirations of the Parisian workforce, was a primary vehicle
of social stabilization. . . . Haussmann needed new financial institutions and debt instruments. . . . In effect, he helped resolve the
capital-surplus disposal problem by setting up a proto-Keynesian
system of debt-financed infrastructural urban improvements.

Harvey goes on to point out that modern cities also rely on dispossession as a feature of "urban restructuring through 'creative
destruction'" (2008, n.p.), as we can see in the repurposing of formerly communal buildings as commercial ones and specifically in
the move by Wetherspoons to reconfigure the Baptist Chapel. That
project stalled for several years after the 2015 purchase, finally opening in May 2019 under a name that paid tribute to the bank, the
Silver Penny.[4] The name and the reconception of history that it enacts
downplay the chapel, instead emphasizing the bank as a supposed
link to more than one thousand years of currency as a measure of
value in Ireland; an explanatory plaque that Wetherspoons itself created fabricates a lineage back to Sigtrygg Silkbeard, a little-known
Norse Irish king of Dublin who is credited with establishing Ireland's
first mint. In providing this genealogy for currency, one highlight-
ing a king of mixed ancestry over his much more famous rival, the
high king Brian Boru, Wetherspoons rewrites the historical narrative, ignoring the violence of settler colonization and valorizing the
principle of capitalist exchange.

Another Wetherspoons Dublin City Centre acquisition has even
more stark ideological implications. Slated for completion in summer 2019 (though it missed that deadline), Camden Hall is a former

---

4. https://www.jdwetherspoon.com/pub-histories/republic-of-ireland/county
-dublin/the-silver-penny-dublin (accessed 2 June 2022). It's worth noting for the
sake of completion that the former St. Mary's Church of Ireland, marriage site
of Arthur Guinness (1761) and venue for the first public performance of Handel's
Messiah (1724), was bought in 1997 and converted over the next seven years into
a superpub now known as the Church.

backpacker's hostel that was brought into commission as emergency homeless accommodation in mid-2011, "in response to a sudden rise in rough sleeping in the city," and, uncoincidentally, at the height of Ireland's austerity measures (Kelly 2015). Alongside the growing chorus of concerns about wages for Wetherspoons workers, we can see the congealing of an economy of precarity that ironically retraces a centuries-old colonial pattern of eviction of the Irish poor from their homes and extraction of wealth from their labor.

Murray's narrator refers to "Boomtown Ireland": this term is American in its origin, used recurrently to connect Dublin's prosperity to both US capital and an ethos of rugged individualism and free enterprise.[5] Claude's description refers not just to creative destruction but to "new builds." Here we see the lean argot of development in the use of a verb as a noun. Since this nominalization doesn't take place via a morphological change, it's called a "conversion" or "zero derivation"; the very same word is used as a different part of speech (classical rhetoric uses the term *anthimeria*). Such nominalizations abound in the twenty-first century, from reality TV's climactic moment of "the reveal," to a request in corporate-speak, "the ask."[6] Along with the series of "becomings" at the end of Murray's passage, the "new builds" encourage us, as Franco Moretti and Dominique Pestre discuss in their analysis of World Bank reports, to see "actions and processes" as "abstraction[s], where temporality is abolished," contractions of time in which development "seems to come into being all at once. It's magic" (2015, 90). Magic: partly because the processes operate independently of humans and partly

5. I am grateful to Peter Hitchcock for pointing out the connection as well to the Boomtown Rats, whose name is an early indication of the Irish westward gaze; they drew inspiration from the name of a childhood gang in Woody Guthrie's fictionalized autobiography of 1943, *Bound for Glory* (Metzer 2015, 40).

6. Hitchings (2013) notes that all these nominalizations have longer histories than we might imagine, though his argument is a bit disingenuous, given that, for instance, "ask" as a noun is pretty rare outside card playing, according to the *OED*. "Build" has long been a noun, but not in the context here.

because of the compression of time, both factors that speak to an absence of responsibility and causation. Murray's churches, pubs, and manors do their own becoming, with no developer or lender to blame when a global financial crisis hits. The happy fascination of our contemporary lingo with nominalizations would seem to suggest part of how we got to crisis, austerity, and disparity.

In concert with other economic discourses of the Global North, during the economic boom times of the 1990s and 2000s, Ireland provided scant sustained cultural counternarrative to what Eamonn Maher and Eugene O'Brien identify as the "close identification between cultural and economic forces" (2015, 6); rather, the interpretive landscape privileged—and continues to privilege—a financial viewpoint, "as if economics had now become the new master discipline" (5), with growth, development, and progress as unquestioned virtues. The era's persistent interest in real estate instantiated an outgrowth of neoliberalism's monetization of the domestic, an acquiescence to the reframing of the home as capital. In the wake of this triumphalist economic mindset, Ireland experienced a massive implosion of housing prices; at the same time, nonresidential properties also stood unfinished and unfunded. Thematically, many post-boom novels register the instrumentalization of space, the conversion of family homes to investments, and the replacement of public things with private ownership; their irrealist and ungrammatical formal choices inflect this attention.

While not all novels of the austerity periods can be read as merely or primarily allegories of their historical moment, we can note the correlation of irrealist plots and techniques with a moment in which global economic wisdom has hewed to unproven and questionable remedies, a homeopathic placebo in which the victim (the public) is blamed for the disease while the virus that caused it remains un(der) regulated, its role as vector only visible via traces like gothic and magic in texts that otherwise function on a realist plane. Following a short discussion of updates to the Big House genre, this chapter explains the particular usefulness of the trope of catachresis (the misuse of language at the level of metaphor and elsewhere) in examining novels about real estate, reading the catachreses that inflect Elizabeth Bowen's Big House fiction with the tensions and contradictions that remain hallmarks of crisis-era reworkings of the genre. What follows unpacks another dimension of crisis-era catachresis: grafted, monstrous intertexts born of a global popular culture, focusing on Irish thrillers in the tradition of American crime fiction. Finally, I consider the ways that the rhetorical discourses about banking and debt in what we can call a neoliberal economic intertext leave imprints, a catachresis of unreconciled traces, even in novels working to resist or offer counternarratives, using the structures of feeling that originate in the Big House tradition to shift blame from its historical locus, a dissolute upper-class, onto, in our present era, a precarious polity whose alleged overconsumption and riskiness is faulted for the economic crash.

Accumulation by Dispossession, Then and Now

Ireland's particular iteration of the home-as-exchange value dynamic is overlaid on a national history of recurrent accumulations by dispossession at the hands of outside invaders, a pattern that has redirected attention and blame away from the current homegrown rentier class, thereby enabling it to shield itself from culpability. No matter the attention Wetherspoons directs toward Sigtrygg Silkbeard, his family were not the earliest invaders, and they were followed by successive waves from England. Some colonizers in the late seventeenth century received seized lands from King William III, known as William of Orange; it is this group in particular who comprises the Anglo-Irish Protestant Ascendancy. Throughout the heyday of Ascendancy control, ownership of land by Catholics was largely banned, and the settlements of land roughly resembled feudal arrangements, with much land cultivated through tenant farming. In 1870, shortly before the founding of the Land League, an astonishing 97 percent of Ireland was in the hands of landlords; an aristocratic 1.5 percent owned about one-third of the nation.

In peripheral regions, economic organization reflects uneven development in contradictory ways. Friedrich Engels visited Ireland in 1856 and wrote to Karl Marx of what he perceived as a feudal economy. Historian Aidan Beatty (2019) points out that that while nineteenth century Ireland's economy retained precapitalist features, this was less through a delayed "development" of the sort external observers like Marx and Engels sought to detect and more through an enforced primitivism: "The Irish 'misery' and pre-capitalist ontology [Marx and Engels] identified were, in large extent, post-Famine phenomena" (832). Largely through the efforts of the Land League and other reformers, as the nineteenth century drew to a close, the economic control of the Protestant landowner class became diluted by Catholic landowners and smaller farms. The Ascendancy remained socially dominant through the Celtic Revival and into the period of revolution and civil war, 1916–25, which led to further economic and political reforms and redistribution, particularly in rural communities, where rates of home ownership climbed to 69 percent by 1946, reaching 88 percent by 2004.[7] Ironically, the rural growth somewhat masked a more troubling phenomenon as economic prosperity took hold in the Republic: Michelle Norris offers evidence of a decreasingly progressive distribution of capital assets during the Celtic Tiger years, resulting in an anomalous *decline* in home ownership. "At the start of the Celtic Tiger boom in 1991," Norris writes, "80 per cent of Irish households were owner occupiers, but by the end of the boom in 2006 homeownership rates had declined to 77.2 per cent, and they have declined even further to 70.1 per cent by 2011. A contraction of this scale in homeownership is almost without precedent in modern developed economies. . . . This development had obviously resulted in the increased concentration of housing wealth in the hands of the landlords" (2016, 253). The rates in 1946 and 2011

----

7. The rate of urban home ownership had a belated growth, only 23 percent in 1946, reaching 73 percent in 1991 (Fahey, Nolan, and Maitre 2004, 1–3).

are nearly identical. These numbers support the idea of a brief departure from a larger pattern of subordination and dispossession, followed by a resurgence of inequality, aligning with Thomas Piketty's argument that the twentieth century was an anomaly in terms of its redistributive economies. Rory Hearne (2021) argues the post-crash market has shored up the domestic and international rentier class: "For the last decade, Government has done everything possible to inflate house prices and rents, in order to attract in the global property investment funds and to recover the profitability and balance sheets of the banks [and has] prioritised the interests of property, finance, developer, investor, landlords over those who are looking to get an affordable home" (n.p.)

Certainly the dozen years following the economic crash saw a renewed housing "crisis" in Ireland. The scare quotes come from novelist Niamh Campbell, who explained in the summer of 2020 that, "speaking from Dublin now, the biggest threat to artists' survival is rack-renting. A housing 'crisis' created through a combination of opportunism and indifference means the post-crash atmosphere of reinvention and community is less and less viable" (n.p.) As with the global financial crisis and the environmental crises discussed in the previous chapters, both the actual precarity and the discourse surrounding it are products of a capitalist regime rather than natural, inevitable economic ebbs and flows. Campbell's analysis recognizes the role of a rentier class in the manufacture of scarcity and the production of a biopolitical subject whose ongoing precarity is an outcome of the uneven distribution of austerity and a necessary factor in the ongoing transfer of capital to the wealthy. If Campbell begins here with a nod to a Big House–inflected rhetorical register of colonizing absentee landlords and local Irish tenantry, she ends by parodying the cant of neoliberal platitude, underscoring the cruel optimism of a self-capitalizing "reinvention" or the creation of meaningful community under conditions of scarcity.

Irish fiction has long used narratives focused on property and housing to trace the effects of various instantiations of economic inequality, notably in the Big House genre, beginning with early

novels that are an outgrowth of texts concerned with "the fundamental question of legitimacy" and the interactions of "competing
power groups" in Ireland (Hand 2011, 27).[8] I expand here upon what
affordances arise if we examine some post-boom fiction with an eye
to the persistence of the structures and themes of Big House novels.
The anxieties in Maria Edgeworth's and Sydney Owenson's early
nineteenth-century texts come to be hallmarks of the Big House
genre: absentee landlords, the decay of Anglo-Irish family lines, and
the usurping of control by an emergent bourgeois class of Catholic interlopers. Another major symbolic attribute was the burning of
the Big House; this feature becomes historically important during
the Irish Revolution and Civil War. These thematic emphases provide continuity more than constancy; likewise, the formal features
of the genre have evolved over the centuries, inflected by and reshap-
ing generic contact zones such as epistolary novels, gothic novels,
realism, and modernism. Each of these forms is put under pressure
by the Irish context in ways that reflect the imperial context and
how a semi-peripheral state might register unevenness. Relatedly,
Joe Cleary suggests that "there has been a distinct tendency . . . to
identify realism with Englishness, and to identify the Irish novelistic
tradition . . . as inherently 'fantastic' or 'anti-realist'" (2007, 49).[9]

8. Hand begins his *History of the Irish Novel* (2011) in 1665, and Connolly importantly underscores that there is "far greater evidence of generic and
sub-generic diversity at work" than most narratives of early Irish "national tales"
acknowledge (2011, 4). My précis here traces a through line while attentive to the
wealth of texts and their wealth of thematic interests.

9. This conversation, entertainingly framed through Eagleton's question of
why Ireland never produced a *Middlemarch*, remains well beyond the scope of the
present project. Nevertheless debates about the obligation to represent, the limits
of representation, and the ideological valences attached to realism and its alternatives inform my argument, from Lloyd's discussion of the "crisis of representation"
(1993, 6) to Cleary's call to recognize that "intrinsic properties" can matter less
than "reference to other dominant modes" (2021, 211) in defining what is realist;
he notes that modernism's innovations are now "familiar everywhere" (223, where
he also helpfully distinguishes between realism and verisimilitude).

The ways that Big House novels struggle—or refuse—to conform to continental and imperial forms speaks to the imposition of conventions. If the normative expectation for a novel is that it will have an internally coherent form, then the Big House tradition recurrently troubles expectations, from the incursions of national myth in Sydney Owenson, the hybrid linguistic interpolations of Maria Edgeworth, the gothic strains in Sheridan Le Fanu. Edith Somerville and Martin Ross's 1894 novel *The Real Charlotte* simultaneously operates as a comedy of manners and something else entirely—Terry Eagleton calls it "an allegory of the collapse of the gentry" (1995, 215), paralleling its grasping protagonist with Heathcliff, each embodying the "typically uncouth minor Ascendancy figure" (20). To attempt to account for the apparent uncontainability of the Big House novel, it might help to turn to WReC (2015) and reject metropolitan norms so we view it instead in the context of other novels from peripheral and semiperipheral locales where "the pressures of combined and uneven development find their most pronounced or profound registration" (62), articulated in what WReC calls "peripheral realism":

> Not every work of from the peripheries will consciously encode disjunction and amalgamation as literary innovations . . . but there is very characteristically a propensity to reactivate archaic and residual forms, to use these to challenge, disrupt, compound, supplement and supersede the dominant (often imposed) forms, in order to convey the palimpsestic, combinatory and contradictory "order of the peripheral experience. Even the narratives of (semi-) peripheral authors who hew quite closely to the line of the dominant realist traditions display irrealist or catachrestic features when registering the temporal and spatial dislocations and the abrupt juxtapositions of different modes of life engendered by imperial conquest, or the violent reorganisation of social relations engendered by cyclical crisis. (2015, 72)

The account here of textual unevenness as a companion to social, political, and economic dislocations and incongruities speaks to the colonial context of the Big House's origin, to the genre's persistence in the face of newer disruptions, and to the perceived heterogeneity of form.

In a similar vein, Stephen Shapiro parallels the resurgence of gothic tropes with periods of convulsive economic transformation, a narrative of uneven development that aligns with the passage between "two phases of long-wave capitalist accumulation. Gothic representational devices become recalled and revitalized in the synapses that both link and distinguish the dendrites of two time-spaces of capitalist development and its reformation of inter-regional trade relations" (2008, 31). Shapiro offers as an example *Dracula*, an Irish novel that uses its title character as a stand-in for absentee landlords during the Irish cholera epidemic and decade of famines.[10] Taken alongside WReC's ideas of hybrid or amalgam forms, this suggestion that a specific cultural mode might respond to a particular crisis with enumerable generic features offers a chance to talk about the period of crisis and austerity as interacting with its context of global capitalist reorganization. Shapiro's model is useful for seeing the correspondence of mid-nineteenth-century Paris to late twentieth- and early twenty-first-century Dublin that Murray gestures toward, which is in turn analogous to the way the gothic devices of the Big House correspond to a post-boom uncanny irrealism. Echoes of the Big House genre in the twenty-first century arise in the descriptions of new construction going up without actors and in the discourse attending to the unfinished housing developments known as "ghost estates." Crucially, gothic tropes once commonplace for the Big House now are deployed for the middle-class home, a redistribution of agency and responsibility that disperses blame for the crisis onto individual

10. Nota bene: real estate is not a focus of Shapiro's argument. Interestingly, Le Fanu's 1864 *Uncle Silas* precedes the 1880s shift that Shapiro notes, in much the same way that Luke Gibbons has argued Irish modernity in general had a jump on the rest of Europe: "Irish society did not have to await the twentieth century to undergo the shock of modernity: disintegrations and fragmentation were already part of its history so that, in a crucial but not unwelcome sense, Irish culture experienced modernity before its time" (1996, 6).

actors and downplays attention to the role of institutional players like regulators, the EU, and banks.

This is not to cast the Big House genre as a progressive form. The dominance of Big House novels as a means to register the shape of Irish social and economic interactions throughout the era of Ascendancy and decline was problematic; not only could it help to reinforce the idea of a land becalmed outside of time but it also obscured and thereby excluded some populations (Travellers, urban dwellers, immigrants). Relatedly, Malcolm Sen has pertinently cautioned that "what might have been fit categories to read the history and literature of the Irish Big House fall short as critical trajectories that explain the ecology of contemporary Irish literature" (2019, 25). Sen urges attention to environmental and imperial scopes, rejecting the adequacy of an interpretive model that attends only to "gothic excesses of capitalist accumulation" because "the register of spectrality cannot be fully processed or critiqued if these un-inhabited spaces are rendered" (25) in this mode. Sen's call for a reconfigured perspective attune to environmental as well as economic crises is a useful corrective, so long as we do still pay attention to those accumulated capitalist excesses that irrupt in twenty-first-century Irish texts. For just as the old buildings do not disappear, neither does an old genre; rather, both sit available to be repurposed by a neoliberal capitalist regime. Big House tropes do not vanish as the Ascendancy itself recedes. Instead, the Celtic Tiger culture replaced old structures with new binaries, modeled closely on those of other prosperous neoliberal economies, including have/have-not, urban/rural, mobile/static, native/foreign, and emigrant/immigrant. In renovations of the Big House genre, archetypes persist: the decaying house, the degenerating family line and repressed family secrets, the deracinated landlord, the usurpation of control. I argue that we even see the persistence of the trope of the destruction of the Big House, with some variations. Throughout the repurposing we see authors logging the reorganization of the conditions of capital accumulation in the post-boom era, a shoring-up of regimes of accumulation by the powerful under fresh guises as well as under the cover of well-established narrative grooves.

Shifts in capitalist phases appear in novels featuring supernatural, uncanny, and irrational cultural markers of a society's interactions with an increasingly inequitable economic system, one that again concentrates wealth and inheritance in the hands of the few and naturalizes this configuration. The neoliberal conversion of home into capital creates disjunctions that are expressed through a number of ungrammatical modes, including the sorts of syntactic reorganizations and broken tensual and morphological formations explored in my previous chapters, as well as an added layer of "misused" language, or catachresis. Catachresis mirrors and responds to an economic condition that locates responsibility and powerlessness not as ends of a spectrum, but, paradoxically, as the same. This sense of not being able to escape or fix the economic crisis but of being held responsible and needing to take blame: alongside the formal and thematic continuities, it is this structure of feeling, this climate of feeling, that creates a particularly Irish effort to attain the good life.

Catachresis

"Catachresis" is the Greek word for "abuse"; in its original Greek rhetorical context, it refers to the use of inexact language in place of precise language.[11] The narrow definition of catachresis is a wildly unlikely or mixed metaphor—a verbal chimera with the head of one image and the tail of another, but, in a wider conception, catachresis is a vast rhetorical umbrella covering not just mixed metaphors, but such rhetorical tropes as metalepsis, prosopopoeia, and anacoluthon. Umberto Eco recalls the Venerable Bede's view of metaphor as a genus in which all other metaphors are species (1983, 217); he also contends that "the metaphor or catachresis invents a new term using at least two already known (and expressed) and presupposing at least another one that is unexpressed" (239). Eco's semiotic attention is

11. The Latin term is *abusio*, though some sources specify that this is a combination of two metaphors while catachresis is a larger, more general category of trope.

to the tension between catachreses that remain strange, requiring "interpretive labor" (234), and those that become codified and understood: dead metaphors (to use a term that itself is metaphoric). Some catachreses are clumsy outgrowths of such dead metaphors, evidence of sloppy or clichéd thinking: "'As I look at it with a broad brush, there are a lot of things going south at the same time,' said Morris Goldstein, a former IMF official. . . . 'Where's the good news coming from? There's no silver bullet out there.'" ("Block" 1998, 98).[12] Here we see a conflation of visual, tactile, geographic, and magical figures of speech as practiced by a titan of finance. Catachresis can be semantic: an *Essay on Irish Bulls* cowritten by Richard Lovell Edgeworth and Maria Edgeworth (1803) includes as one example the catachrestic: "The best way of boiling potatoes [is] in cold water."[13] Not all catachreses are so inadvertent: as Eco notes, catachresis finds novelty in unexpected juxtapositions, working like other literary devices of estrangement. In William Shakespeare's *Timon of Athens*, a servant of Lucius quips "Tis deepest winter in Lord Timon's purse; that is, one may reach deep enough, and find little" (2020, 87, 3.4).

Deconstructionists emphasized the aggression of catachresis. Jacques Derrida reads it as the incommensurability of signifier and signified, "the use of the sign by violence, force, or abuse, with the imposition of a sign on a sense not yet having a proper sign in the language" (1974, 57). For Paul DeMan, catachresis inspires terror: "[Mixed modes] can dismember the texture of reality and reassemble it in the most capricious of ways, pairing man with woman or human being with beast in the most unnatural shapes. Something monstrous lurks in the most innocent of catachreses" (1978, 21).

---

12. This example is drawn from an occasional feature in the *New Yorker*, "Block That Metaphor!" (12 October 1998, 98). The headline of the original *New York Times* article from which the quote was extracted raises its own metaphoric questions: "A Frenzy of Global Anxiety Kicks Up Dust That Had Been Settling" (26 May 1998, D1).

13. The *OED* defines Irish bulls as "usually humorous, manifestly self-contradictory or inconsistent statements."

Tilottama Rajan explains this "disfiguration" as a system in which "logic, rhetoric, and grammar mutually disrupt each other" (2002, 48), calling attention to the "mixed status" of catachresis as a "prosthesis that grafts a body back onto the nonhuman" (48). As Marcel Cornis-Pope helps to clarify, this ready movement between the linguistic and the material lays bare the mystification of language that tends to conceal its reliance upon the replacement of the "phenomenological object with a rhetorical figure that does not share any of the sensory determinations of its referent" (1991, 96). The heterogeneous, irreal, and uncanny images conjured up by catachresis unsettle both representational language itself and the boundaries that it would erect.

De Man sees catachresis deriving its authority "by dint of the positional power inherent in language" (1978, 21), a phrasing that correlates to Gayatri Spivak's attention to the grafting of Western ideas onto colonial territories (1993, 67). In particular she notes the application of ill-suited terminologies as an ideological manifestation of the arbitrariness of language. This final key dimension of catachresis is on evidence for Spivak in terms like "proletariat," which require grafting, since they never fully fit local particulars.[14] Spivak's analysis reads catachresis as having the potential to open spaces of resistance. Catachresis flourishes as well in less liberatory contexts, like the euphemistic designation of "redundancy" for "unemployment" and even in the sorts of linguistic contortions of Republican political consultant Frank Luntz, who popularized "death tax" and "energy exploration" and called healthcare reform a "government takeover." Positional power determines not only perception but also policy. In the wake of the financial crisis in Ireland, citizens became conversant with the terminology of a "haircut" for the disparity between the stated value of an asset and the amount a bank is willing to value it as collateral. The term can be read as a catachresis in

---

14. Eco's idea of "interpretive labor" (1983) can be deployed here to speak to the way that work is displaced onto marginal communities; people are made to conform to imposed categories.

its ungainly metaphor, with money as its tenor and hair its vehicle. While the metaphor might collapse if we consider that hair is atop or outside, not intrinsic, a more generous scan of the analogy would note that hair does grow, making it a suitable comparison for value, so long as the basic assumption of endless compounding growth in capital is to be believed. Beyond this ideological assumption built into the metaphor, it functions as a grafted monstrous entity in De Man's sense, with the human hair growing out of something not human, even intangible—a sensory confusion. The unsuitability of the term's implications of a painless cosmetic process rounds out its catachrestic valences; haircuts frequently end with emphatically non-metaphorical cuts to public services.[15]

Catachresis in its ideological form is pervasive in the charged political environment of the post-crash era, coincident with its use to indicate moments of emotional overwhelm, when logic fails. Chapter 2 argued in part that other ungrammaticalities are used to convey feeling so powerful that logic recedes; the relationships between ideas get lost and they exist, suspended, alongside each other to be observed or experienced but not altered.[16] As linguist Gretchen McCullough has written, we can detect a "general principle of internet language these days that the more overwhelmed with emotions

---

15. The chatty explanation from the European Central Bank (2016) of haircuts uses a million-euro home, apparently an old Big House, as its relatable example: "It may be worth €1 million now, but there is no guarantee that, when the time comes to sell it, it will actually be possible to get €1 million for it. Maybe the house has been damaged in a storm or the area it is in has become less desirable. . . . Coming back to our example, an old manor house (for which there is little demand) in an area known for its thunderstorms (putting it at risk of damage) would receive a larger haircut than a brand new two-bedroom flat in a city centre" (n.p.).

16. The nominalizations mentioned earlier offer an instructive connection: the Stanford Literary Lab found that in World Bank annual reports, the word "and" has roughly doubled in frequency since 1946, a phenomenon credited to "long lists of nouns that create the illusion of activity, sometimes despite a 'total absence of all logic'" (Schussler 2017, C6). See Mieszkowski (2009), which treats "linguistic affectivity" as a deeper challenge to the interaction of language and emotion.

you are, the less sensical your sentence structure gets" (2014, n.p.).[17] Retaining McCullough's notion of a "lack of the sensical," the key here is that writers seeking to evoke moments of heightened emotion draw on catachresis as one way to communicate the supplanting of rationality by feeling, a crucial dynamic in an economic system where consumer and investor confidence are as important as 'the fundamentals of the economy' in helping to buoy the market via Paul Krugman's "confidence fairy."[18]

Catachresis, like the larger category of ungrammaticality, subtends a structure of feeling in which citizens do not feel they are actively empowered or responsible. The implications extend from questions of individual efficacy and autonomy up to evaluations of who is accountable for the economic crisis. For this reason, moments when texts venture into irrealism and catachrestic ungrammaticality serve as irruptions of impossibility, recognitions of the gap between what is promised or expected and what is likely. Novels press up against the limits of rational explanation, requiring irreal elements to round out their narratives or resolve contradictions, themselves a

17. Anne Helen Peterson's 2020 book *Can't Even*, about the burnout generated in millennials by a capitalist system designed to ensure their precarity, evokes this sort of affective overload in its (ungrammatical) title.

18. See Clarke and Newmann (2012) for an elaboration of the idea of the alchemy of austerity. They cite Krugman in support of their characterization of this "intensive ideological work—work that we identify here through the image of the (political and financial) wizards attempting to find the alchemy that might turn disaster into triumph—the triumph being a new neo-liberal settlement" (300). Consider also the aesthetic linkage that Joe Cleary makes between emotional restraint and a minimalism I would argue is congruent with neoliberalism: "For Mark McGurl, '[American] Minimalism was in any case founded on a scepticism of the idea that fiction is emotionally rich when it is emotionally 'articulate.' . . . Minimalism had very little to say about emotion. That's because it was engineered as a way, not of explaining, but of beautifying shame'. . . . [Colm Tóibín's 2009 novel] *Brooklyn* more particularly bears out McGurl's contention that the style is connected to a lower middle-class sense of shame and self-discipline: its plot and style both confirm McGurl's claim that 'minimalism is an aesthetic of risk management, a way of being beautifully careful'" (2015, n.p.).

catachrestic mimesis of an economy that rises and falls via financial alchemy, without clear rational motive. In concert with Eco, Michel Riffaterre (1978) has characterized ungrammaticality as the point at which one's effort to understand a text left the mimetic level and moved to the semiotic; I build on his sense of mimesis and contend it corresponds to the invisibility of grammar—it is at the perception of an ungrammaticality that we perceive as well the political. If grammar is in effect how we naturalize laws, then analysis of literary ungrammaticality can likewise function as an disclosure or excavation of naturalized norms. Certainly this is how Gloria Wekker means it when she speaks of Edward Said and "a racial grammar, a deep structure of inequality in thoughts and affect based on race" (2016, 2) in the construction and maintenance of white innocence. The utter ungrammaticality of catachresis can lay bare the architecture by which power supports itself.

Ghosts and Stalled Time

The Last September (1929) and *A World of Love* (1954) are famously the only novels Elizabeth Bowen set completely in Ireland. Both take place largely in the farm country of north Cork, on fictionalized estates—Danielstown and Montefort—that evoke the environs of her own ancestral home, Bowen's Court. The parallels between the two novels have been detailed frequently. Each features an estate owner who has failed to reproduce and has a niece on the brink of sexual maturity, each of whom is deprived of a lover (in some way inappropriate for her, in any case) by death. The myriad romances in each are star crossed, with impossible affections attempting to span generations, bright women directing affection toward less honest, uninspiring men, and love triangles that allow queer erotic energy to percolate. Each explores the ill fit of British sensibility and Irish landscape, made vivid in part through the gothic irruptions of the ghostly past, unruly bodies, and the lives of objects.

In examining the traits that link these novels to the sorts of ungrammaticalities I see in fiction of the recent recession era, I resist

tendencies toward claims of an extraordinary present while also filling in a genealogy of the Big House genre to see what happens to its
features as social, political, and economic conditions change. Published in 1929, *Last September* ends with the genre's signature con-
flagration but *A World of Love*, postwar, can be read as what would
have happened to Danielstown had it not burned down, as well as
what happens to the Big House novel once its Ascendancy scions
cede power to British new money and the Catholic bourgeoisie. The
Ascendancy itself remains embalmed in the past; for Bowen, such a
situation requires a novel that self-consciously references earlier Big
House novels as well as her own fiction, folding back in on itself. *A
World of Love*'s fires are metaphoric rather than literal, in overt,
even heavy-handed ways, including a summer heat wave, love letters consigned to flames, and a final path that is blazed via the love-
at-first-sight romance between an Irish girl and an American man,
setting forth the means by which an increasing swath of Ireland's
population can indebt itself. The past looms as a crumbling ruin,
more likely brought under the control of American capital and torn
down than dramatically destroyed.[19]

Formally, *A World of Love* reveals residues of the generic pressure upon it in its inverted syntax, its heavy use of nominalization, its
occasional ungrammaticalities, and, most notably, its use of double
negatives (also called "negative concord"). These negative constructions permeate a passage in which Antonia, Montfort's owner, has
a flashback that recalls the energy of a love affair: "No part of the
night was not breathless breathing, no part of the quickened stillness
not running feet" (Bowen 1954, 77). This sentence evokes the rush

19. Keown is correct when she writes that that Bowen's generic shifts and her
"self-parodic references to her earlier work and other big house novelists (Sheridan
Le Fanu, Bram Stoker, Sommerville and Ross, Molly Keane) turn *AWoL* into a
modernist, self-questioning reinvention of the big house novel and of her own oeu-
vre. She wryly plays on literary conventions whilst also developing the big house
and Irish novels into something new—in the way she plays on literary history as
much as actual history" (2010, 225).

Antonia feels when remembering her deceased cousin, Guy. Bowen evokes momentum here via negation; elsewhere in the paragraph she relies on layers of gerunds that similarly describe the atmosphere and slow the impetus. The phrases themselves are difficult to resolve logically: "breathless breathing" both is and isn't a contradiction, a catachrestic construction that opens up space between a word and its absence in the same way that "quickened stillness" suggests time becalmed and racing. The overall effect here is of the creation of a mood rather than the advancement of the narrative; we are in a lyrical moment without progress or trajectory, an echo of the stultifying weather and stagnant relationships.

The house and its inhabitants—like its genre—seem suspended in an earlier era: Lilia in a hat long out of fashion, her daughter Jane donning a vintage gown from Montefort's attic, Antonia long past her prime. But, in the present of the text, Antonia feels time to be in motion again, seeking to banish the past: "Ghosts could have no place in this active darkness—more, tonight was a night which had changed hands, going back again to its lordly owners: time again was into the clutch of herself and Guy. Stamped was the hour, as were the others" (Bowen 1954, 77). Again, Bowen presents contradictory momentum, as time moves, but "back," a trajectory reflected by the inverted syntax in which "stamped was the hour," a reversal that also holds temporality in place via the time stamp. The passage further raises questions in the sense within the free indirect discourse that time reverts to its lordly owners, a phrase that evokes an aristocratic class and landlordism. It also makes time a spatial, ownable property. The end of the passage, with its climactic statement that Antonia and Guy "conceived of no death, least of all death-in-life— an endless rushing, or rushing endlessness, was their domain . . . ceaseless energy . . . waiting for the signal to go on again . . . for not come it could not and never did" (78) reveals again the proprietary grasp upon time alongside nominalizations and negative concords that accrue to undercut the movement in the passage.

Here as elsewhere in the Big House tradition, genre provides a set of tools for talking about time at the hinge between different iterations of capitalist society. [20] The formal techniques Bowen uses to suspend time anticipate those of Claire Kilroy in *The Devil I Know* (2012) and Anne Enright in *The Green Road* (2015), novels whose housing plots enact WReC's prediction that residual forms are reactivated in peripheral zones. As mentioned above, "irrealist or catachrestic features [register] the temporal and spatial dislocations and the abrupt juxtapositions of different modes of life engendered by imperial conquest, or the violent reorganisation of social relations engendered by cyclical crisis" (WReC 2015, 72). Bowen's two Big House novels come at moments of social reorganization: the end of the Irish Civil War and the end of the Irish Free State, and their jarring temporalities and uncanny objects speak to these moments of transition. In the thirty years between *The Last September* and *A World of Love*, the relative economic security of the focal family declines. Money remains a persistent concern in and of *The Devil I Know* and *The Green Road*, each of which reaches back temporally to the Bowen era and echoes Bowen's formal expression. Kilroy's novel retains an Ascendancy family at its center, following the end of the line to Tristram St. Lawrence, while Enright traces the story of the middle-class Madigan family and their land from the mid-century up to the very height of the boom. Both Kilroy and Enright revive residual, catachrestic themes and tropes, encoding disjunction through temporal shifts, recursive narrative sections, and traces of ghosts that defy space-time.

The Devil I Know tells its allegorical story by way of its reliance on such Big House tropes as baroque setting, dissipated aristocracy, and supernatural forces: the last in a line of Ascendancy scions, Tristram St. Lawrence returns in 2006 to the crumbling castle where he grew up, entering into real estate deals of increasingly high stakes with his old schoolmate Hickey, members of Dublin's political-economic elite, and a mysterious figure known as M. Deauville. Set in

20. In its effort to refute the linear measurement of time, the novel allies itself with the sorts of timelessness described by Moishe Postone and Jacques Le Goff; we are not yet in the sort of neoliberal present I trace in more recent fiction.

2016, four years after its publication, the novel, like *City of Bohane* and *The Green Road*, reflects back through multiple embedded time frames upon the period prior to the economic crash. In Kilroy's case, the final frame is a speculative one, as her novel is set in the future, timed to coincide with the centenary of the Easter Rising that Ireland celebrated in April 2016. Structured as what at first appears to be a trial but turns out to be merely a fact-finding hearing, the book reflects and implicates Ireland's own incomplete, ineffectual efforts to come to terms with its spectacular boom and subsequent crash. The shadowy M. Deauville, never seen by anyone except Tristram, reveals himself to be the devil, if he even exists. Deauville initially appears to be Tristram's Alcoholics Anonymous sponsor, with the suggestion that substance abuse is akin to the type of rash investment addiction seen in Tristram and other characters, who giddily pursue property acquisitions in days-long benders. The implication is that Ireland is tempted into extravagant, imprudent investments by the very forces that ought to stabilize it.

Well beyond the spectral Deauville, the novel is laced with references to the supernatural. A faithful old servant, Larney, converses with Tristram throughout the novel but is actually already dead. Tristram himself is assumed by many of the characters to have died. There's even some hint that he may be already/still dead during the course of the narrative—he is repeatedly referred to as "uncanny." This term appears alongside characterizations of Tristram's status as conduit. By profession he is a translator, a job he explains as requiring him to be "hollow . . . a perfect conduit" (Kilroy 2012, 6), a comparison that gains force when he notes its parallel to the way capital moves through the shell company Deauville creates, (73) such that, later in the novel, "money moved through me as freely as languages" (231). The catachrestic interchangeability of the two systems of signs—money and language—indicates the imaginative, alchemical dimension of finance. Tristram repeats several times that uncanny is a term used by others, an unnamed "they," about him: "That was the word [they] used" (6, 73, 231). The indefinite pronoun itself acts as both a conduit and empty signifier, opening space for Tristram to be constructed by others.

In this way, the uncanny becomes the intertextual; Tristram exists as a combination of acts of imagination by others, as evidenced by his full name, Tristram Amory St. Lawrence, which blends historical and fictional antecedents including Joyce, Sterne, and Fitzgerald. Kilroy invests Tristram with his pedigree as thirteenth Earl of Howth (historically, the title is extinct). In using a defunct earldom, Kilroy creates an occult genealogy for her tale of greed and excess. Goethe's *Faust* offers another clear intertext for Kilroy, given the novel's ongoing references to property speculation as alchemy; *The Devil I Know* projects a vision of the contemporary economy as magically generating wealth. The accumulated intertexts work to resist the relentless pressure of the present, providing history and grounding in opposition to neoliberalism's present of nonplaces and empty conduits.

Devil's domestic topography functions as a history of the plutocracy in Ireland, spanning an ancient castle with titled aristocrats, a Big House now devoid of its Anglo-Irish gentry, and a sprawling modern suburban ranch home. Such varied domestic spaces seem for much of the novel to be peripheral to the plot, which focuses on investment properties: tracts to be developed into more homes, hotels, flats, skyscrapers. The new construction featured in *Devil* is sleek, modern, and anodyne, part of the push to reconceive Dublin within global metropolitan supermodernity. When Tristram and Hickey go to secure financing for a hotel they seek to build, they travel to a district peppered with skyscrapers all "built of the same jade glass," entering a boardroom that "occupied the penthouse suite of one of the glass towers. A panorama of cranes spanning the horizon was engaged in a courtly dance" (Kilroy 2012, 138). An architectural model of the proposed hotel project is set out for display. "The skyscraper hotel closely resembled the building we had assembled in, which in turn resembled the building next to it, and the building next to it again, and so on throughout the docklands and across to the opposite bank of the Liffey. Those dollar-green towers were a contagion that had ripped through Dublin" (139). The initial description of the skyscrapers makes reference to jade, cranes, and courtly dancing, a decidedly Orientalist undertone evoking the Asian Tiger antecedents of the Celtic Tiger, an image supplanted by the sequential accumulation of buildings now compared to spreading disease and to dollars, the elegant dance replaced by a violent gash. This latter image of the skyscraper as defacement, associated with Americanness and a blotting out of local culture, brings the image in line with the nonplace of the boardroom, where, later on, Tristram, Hickey, and their investors will go on a multiday, multicontinental acquisition binge, buying—in a conflation of space and time—properties they will never see, places that are money, not locations.

Throughout the novel, past, present, and future dissolve into one another, not only in Tristram's indeterminate vitality but also in Kilroy's shifts of verb tense: "I don't know why I'm talking about all of this in past tense. Nothing is past. Everything is tense" (Kilroy 2012, 33).[21] Tristram's pun highlights the fundamental unease that accompanies a sense of unfixed time, but it also suggests the paradoxes that underlie the act of narration itself. As another mode of invention, like alchemy or real estate speculation, fiction is laced through with its own illogicality. Later, in his testimony offered on the ominously titled "Final day of evidence 24 MARCH 2016" (337), Tristram notes that "nothing can conclude matters for me" (353). On the one hand, the word "final" incontrovertibly implies an end, while Tristram's remark invokes the endless, inescapable recurrence hinted at by his name.

The novel ends without resolution on the legal and financial front; its closure comes from the enforced suicide of the protagonist at the requisition of the devil. Although foretold, this suicide is not within the novel—the future events themselves have speculative outcomes in the even further future. In this flattening of temporal difference, Kilroy moves gradually into present tense through a series

---

21. Another intertextual echo here, of Faulkner's oft-quoted "The past is never dead. It's not even the past."

of declarative sentences that seem to pressure the narrative to leave past tense narration aside: "Deauville had come to collect. A debt must be settled. That is the nature of a debt. The Devil linked my arm and we began the descent. I closed my eyes but my eyes would not close. They would not close. I tried and tried. I'll keep trying. I must keep trying. I can only keep trying. I am afraid of what I will see" (Kilroy 2012, 361). The doxa here about how debts function—itself a neoliberal analysis of macroeconomics that stands in contrast to the Keynesian model that prevailed throughout much of the twentieth century—is conveyed in brief, syntactically straightforward sentences as though to emphasize its austere truth. Such an oversimplification stands in contrast to the recognitions earlier in the novel, via intertextual references, of the intersectional complications of global finance and national history; it contrasts as well with the contradictory closed eyes that would not close, which echo Bowen's catachrestic constructions. The unworkability of the narrative of an easy exit from debt by way of austerity is revealed in the text's separation of meaning from syntax, grammatically simple sentences that turn Beckettian and link Tristram's journey to the persistence and repetitions of the past. The novel oscillates in its close between a critique of neoliberalism through a strategic intertextuality and a capitulation to the pressures exerted by the endless present.

Devil falls somewhat short of its target in its adoption of the Alcoholics Anonymous movement's rhetoric of powerlessness to characterize the addictive properties of speculation, which gives the events leading up to the crash a feeling of inevitability. Also troubling is Tristram's belated realization that he has been blind to his beloved Edel's treachery. Edel, Hickey's wife and Tristram's lover, is revealed to have been the grasping mastermind who stripped Tristram's family home of its artifacts. While Edel's acquisitive eye—she steals a valuable chandelier from Tristram's Big House ruin—breaks the association of women with an uncommodified domesticity, her clichéd role as temptress, like the very role of the devil, absolves Tristram of some responsibility for his downfall. Both choices suggest a neoliberal narrative of inescapability.

Nevertheless, the novel's overt critique of property speculators, corrupt ministers, and feckless bankers, as well as of the toothless fact-finding enquiry that structures the narrative, is mirrored by a critique of the Irish public itself. Recurrent efforts to expose truth or indict wrongdoing meet with no change, progress, or even outrage; Tristram's efforts to shed light have no effect on the Easter Rising Centenary getting underway at the novel's close. The Irish public is implicated in its absence, a ghostly populace who appears only to engage in frantic bidding wars to inhabit the nonplace flats Hickey constructs. *Devil* reveals the futility of insight without meaningful breakthrough or change. The judge overseeing the hearing is never heard to speak, and the format in which Tristram merely offers testimony acts as a recording of history as though it is unchangeable. The postdated setting in particular underscores the way in which the critique of neoliberalism stands in tension with the novel's narrative mode: we are left to think there is no alternative, even about time that has not yet passed.

The Green Road also grapples with temporality, arranged into two sections that in themselves suggest a catachrestic asymmetry. The first half of the novel is titled merely "LEAVING," a spatial gerund that embodies a temporal paradox of ongoing departure. Each chapter within this section is titled with the name of a member of the Madigan nuclear family, as well as a place and a date; the dates advance chronologically, but, despite the section title, these chapters don't actually tell stories about leaving Ardeevin, the family home. "LEAVING" concludes with a chapter about Rosaleen, the matriarch, who feels suddenly and entirely like she is in the "wrong" home, a "woman chased into a corner by her own house" (Enright 2015, 168), in an uncanny perversion of a long-standing association of women with domesticity. The solution to a feeling of wrongness is enacted in the financial realm: Rosaleen decides to sell her home, and the "leaving" of the title comes at last to apply to the temporal and spatial matrix of home, which we can infer, from the steady reflections on globalization and modernization throughout "LEAVING," is representative of residual constructions of the Irish family and mode of living that ill suit the "cosmopolitan mobilities" (Negra 2013, 55) of the new millennium.

Part 2, "COMING HOME 2005," covers a few days in late December 2005, with a brief coda some months later. Enright begins with chapters whose titles are just place names—Toronto, Shannon Airport, Co. Dublin—shifting to more evocative, elusive titles, some of which share the nominalized gerund format of the titles of the two parts of the novel, which both provides a sense of ongoing activity and creates a further lack of symmetry. This jarring organizational choice makes no meaningful distinction between place and time, a structural catachresis that immerses Ireland fully in a global world while problematizing notions of linear progression.

The text from its outset undermines the processes by which humans seek to impose order: in its opening chapter, "Hanna, Ardeevin, Co. Clare 1980," Enright decouples space and time, beginning the novel with the word "Later" (2015, 3). Already looking forward, the novel recounts Rosaleen's reaction to an unwelcome announcement from her elder son, Dan, that he intends to study for the priesthood. Taking what Dan calls "the horizontal solution" (13), Rosaleen stays in bed for two weeks. Enright narrates this period—endless for twelve-year-old Hanna—recursively, repeating the first paragraph of the novel in its entirety at the chapter's conclusion. This circularity sits in tension with the linearity of the horizontal solution and the tight geometry of the chapter, which is organized in two trips to the pharmacy and two trips to Galway, lovely structural parallels that still do not reconcile time into an easy progression. The narrative both relies upon and bridles against structure, as when Hanna feels "her uncle's eyes resting on her, and in them something like pity. Or joy" (6), a nonparallel comparison similar to Hanna's realization later that her mother's ideas were "either true or beside the point" (34). Such grammatically correct constructions remain semantically unresolved, catachreses that hint that the narrator's efforts at knowledge and explanation are inadequate, as are the characters', not to mention those of the reader, who must also work circularly in trying to assemble a narrative logic.

For instance, we eventually discern that Rosaleen's withdrawal from the family arises as a consequence of her conviction that Dan is becoming a priest because he's gay; her reemergence comes because she deduces (falsely, we learn later) that the existence of a girlfriend means he isn't gay. But there isn't a clear answer, a theme underscored when, amid Rosaleen's weeping, her husband, Pat, leaves the dinner table, and dessert's apple tart has to be cut differently. Dan immediately cuts it in fifths, rather than sixths with one left for Pat for later: "Five was a whole new angle, as he moved the cake slice through the ghost of a cross and then swung it eighteen degrees to the side. It was a prising open of the relations between them. It was a different story, altogether. As though these might be any number of Madigans and, out in the wide world, any number of apple tarts" (Enright 2015, 12). The infinite narratives and infinite possible selves multiply outward and forward throughout the novel, specters of potential stories untold.

"LEAVING" thus combines temporal advance with lack of progress in ways redolent of Bowen's negative concords, emblematized by a clock in Rosaleen's chapter. She keeps thinking it is ten o'clock, only to recall, recurrently, that the "clock had been stopped for years, maybe five years" (Enright 2015, 153). The uncertainty about time intersects with the novel's persistent uncertainty about space. Staring at a wall painted a dusty rose (a color evocative of 1980s decor), Rosaleen recalls that "under that was the 1970s terracotta, Tuscan Earth it was called, up on a chair herself, coat after coat of it, to cover the wallpaper beneath, fierce yellow repeats of geometric flowers that kept breaking through" (145–46). This sentence, conversational in its rhythm, shifts ungrammatically from the temporal excavation of paint to Rosaleen's memory of painting the wall; the way that the syntactic anacoluthon breaks the sentence from its original direction is paralleled by the flowers that break through the coats of paint. The irrepressible wallpaper—à la Charlotte Perkins Gilman—casts an uncanniness over the scene, which assumes an increasingly menacing aspect as the evening drags: "Something wrong with the house. . . . Rosaleen was living in the wrong house, with the wrong colours on the walls. . . . And where could you put yourself: if you could not feel at home in your own home? If the world turned into a series of lines and shapes, with nothing in the pattern to remind you what it was for" (165).[22] The final sentence fragment sets forth a condition but no main clause, a grammatical incompleteness that indicates the emptiness of form and pattern without a goal. The irruption of the gothic elements disrupts the seamless identification of woman with home, the references to decorating trends in particular serving to underscore how commodified such spaces are.

Enright structures the novel's climax around Rosaleen and her home as well. A chapter entitled "The Hungry Grass" begins with a massive shopping expedition by Constance in preparation for a lavish Christmas dinner, during which Rosaleen, having already announced her plan to sell the family home, further declares her intention to move in with Constance. Soon after Constance resists the latter pronouncement, Rosaleen flees to the Green Road for a walk, during which she senses the presence of her long-dead hus-band, Pat. Pat had spoken expansively in courting her, telling stories steeped in folklore that blurred distinctions between living and dead, culminating with his promise to "worship her with his body, with his entire soul, until the day he died. . . . And that is the way he saw the land, with no difference between the different kinds of yesterday. No difference between a man and his ghost, between a real heifer and a cow that was waiting for the end of the world. It was all just a way of talking. It was the rise and fall in the telling, a rounding out before the finish" (Enright 2015, 263).

The non sequitur on which this passage hinges is the vow of life-long devotion juxtaposed with a series of denials of difference. The

22. It is possible, of course, that the fragment merely restates the question in the previous sentence, though its lack of question mark suggests Enright seeks to do more. The fragment resonates intertextually with Bloom's musing in the "Hades" episode of Joyce's *Ulysses*: "If we were suddenly all somebody else" (1990, 110), a reflection that acknowledges the relativity of individual subjectivity, suggesting, as does Enright, the illusion of individuality by paralleling the subject to a sentence fragment that has only a subject.

implosion of temporal distinctions calls to mind Claire Bracken and Susan Cahill's insight that Enright "enacts a disruption of linear and chronological time, with past times interrupting and breaking 'open' the narratives" (2011, 7). Pat's stories of Ireland's mythic past, told in 1956, shape Rosaleen's interaction with the landscape in 2005, in a novel published in 2015. At least four moments embed within one another here and parallel Enright's complex temporal shifts throughout the novel, in which each episode is set within multiple past moments, forming a novel of past progressives, of events that are temporally complete and yet psychologically ongoing: there is no difference between the different kinds of yesterday. Enright thereby testifies to the power of history to speak within present events; setting the story of Rosaleen's serendipitously canny real estate deal in 2005 reminds readers that the economic highs of 2005 contained multiple yesterdays—of the previous decade's growth as well as the stagnation of the decades prior, not to mention the deep yesterdays before that. By 2015, 2005 is itself another yesterday, one that cannot be ignored or minimized by those emerging from the recession. Ireland cannot absolve itself from the materialism of the boom, nor treat the dismal aftermath as disconnected from what came before. At the same time, the variety of yesterdays here contests neoliberal notions of teleology, a cautionary warning for a nation eager to move past its recent recession: if there is no difference among the different kinds of yesterday, then no narrative of progress can downplay or obscure those moments that challenge fantasies of an upward trajectory.

As the frantic search for Rosaleen escalates, she crawls into a "little famine house" (Enright 2015, 278), a space suffused with ghostly domesticity and heavy with history. To enter, she realizes that she must cross hungry grass. Stuart McLean explains that hungry grass is said to exist on sites where someone has died, "in spots where a corpse had fallen mouth downwards" (1999, 65)—the idea is not restricted to famine deaths but has strong associations with that time. Those who touch or cross hungry grass are cursed with hunger themselves, no matter how long ago the original contact. Rosaleen connects immediately to the Great Hunger and graves left unblessed because "the priest was too busy, or the priest was fled. Sometimes the grass was on the threshold of a house where all the people died, with no one left to bury them" (Enright 2015, 278). McLean reads Hungry Grass as expressive of a magical "logic of contagion and contact-transmissibility" (1999, 64) that spans "temporal distances. . . . Its temporality appears resolutely non-linear, implying a disturbance of the diachronic ordering of pasts and presents. Both Derrida (1994) and Zizek (1994) [argue] such a slippage is a prerequisite for the appearance of the spectre or revenant, as a figure testifying not to the chronological separation of past and present, but to their continuing and inescapable inter-implication" (65). Pat's stories and his reanimation in the novel conform to this interpenetration of temporalities, as does the diachronic disturbance that begets the hungry grass. And the term itself blurs cause and effect, actant and object, place and sensation in a discomfiting, discordant catachresis.

Enright's interest in asymmetry and catachresis does not rest with a simple allusion to this resonant terminology. While Rosaleen's sense of eviction from Constance's home chimes with the likely history of the ruined cottage, the chapter in which she enters it is an unnamed subchapter of "The Green Road"; it is not part of "The Hungry Grass," that title having gone to the Christmas dinner at Ardeevin, an imbalance that itself destabilizes linearity and underscores the relevance of the dinner table events. Each character conforms to type throughout the episode (most hilariously in Emmet's multiple etymological Sanskrit lessons), the contagion of the past meaning that they all remain hungry forever, for connections they cannot provide one another. In disallowing mystical reifications of the land and the past, the novel asserts that neither can be a solution to the alcoholism, materialism, self-centeredness, and emotional coldness that complicate the Madigans' relationships with their mother.

In keeping with earlier Big House novels, *The Green Road*'s house is a metonym for the nation's fortunes. At the same time as she deploys irreal and ungrammatical elements in ways reminiscent of their intersection in Big House fiction, Enright shifts the form's conventions to focus on a middle-class family, complete with upstart

Catholic usurpers in the form of Constance's in-laws, the McGraths, real estate people who know before the Madigans that Rosaleen plans to sell the house. (In the pub on Christmas Eve, Emmet receives a donation to his charity, "a wedge of apricot-coloured fifties" from Michael McGrath, who is engaged in the financialization of property through his work conveyancing; he is the "son of the real estate McGrath who was minting it these days" [2015, 221].) The McGraths are figured as emblems of excessive consumerism through their consumption of champagne and of real coffee (rather than the more lowbrow or Irish alternatives of, respectively, instant coffee or tea). And their sanguine expectations for Rosaleen's timing prevail: the bidding war and swift sale of the Ardeevin house are completed just as the Irish housing market approaches its apogee—in the case of a used house in Ireland (outside Dublin), the average value increased from 1991 to 2007 by 489 percent (O'Callaghan et al. 2014, 125).[23] While the sale is lucrative, and Rosaleen shares the proceeds with her children, all the novel's interpersonal relationships remain fraught and unresolved; like land and history, money cannot heal. Just as the nation learned it could not borrow its way out of economic crisis, the Madigans discover they cannot spend their way out of family crisis, revealing the fundamental catachresis that propels affective economics. In setting the novel at the moment when Ardeevin can yield the greatest profits, Enright proclaims how little difference such a windfall makes, emphasizing the false promise of personal gratification through upward mobility.

While the novel makes some pointed critiques of the frictionless materialism of some of the Madigans, particularly Constance and Dan, its indictment of Celtic Tiger excess maintains a distinction between the uncalculating and ultimately failed effort to spend one's way into emotional comfort and the profit-seeking of the rentier class. "The house sold in three weeks, closed in eight. . . . Whoever bought

23. As a point of comparison, the change in US home prices in the same period was about 116 percent.

it did not move in—a developer, by all accounts—so the place stayed empty while Rosaleen's bank account filled up with money" (Enright 2015, 302). Throughout, Enright's attention to the emotional forces surrounding the transaction makes clear that the family has not operated out of a desire to capitalize on the moment, much less out of greed, undermining the suggestion that a grasping and risk-taking middle class is responsible for the crisis, or that there is a workable analogy to be made between the behavior of citizens and banks.

The Development Thriller

A developer buys Ardeevin, "development" being an ideal occupation for the neoliberal era, a nominalization that manages to be vague yet convey activity and productivity at the same time. The business and busyness of this sector are evidence that while 2008 is a crisis, it is not in any way a rupture with what has come before. Rather, and specifically via the related Irish embraces of financialization and Americanization, the boom era lays groundwork for the crash and austerity as an extension of the regime of development. Because of the overlapping issues of a complex system of derivatives, packaged American mortgages, and domestic real estate bubble, features of the crash that combine with domestic ambivalence about consumerist substitutions for an earlier nationalist and religious context, the real causes of the economic crisis are obscured, in some cases willfully, and sometimes more inadvertently.

The thematic and symbolic attentions of Dublin crime novels offer a morality play on the cultural logic of development in Ireland. As Jason Buchanan has convincingly demonstrated, attention to and concerns about overdevelopment in Irish literary fiction predate the crash, at least regarding domestic property (2013). The mass-market crime novel registers widespread anxieties about commercial real estate as the boom reaches its peak. Declan Hughes writes a series of books that frets about Dublin during prosperity, advancing his sequential narratives into the recession era in later installments; Alan Glynn's trilogy begins just after the bust. Both sets of novels struggle to resolve critique with the limitations of a genre that privileges American-style individualism. Through attention to the narration of temporality and to representations of construction projects, I argue that efforts to challenge or subvert dominant social and economic relations are themselves subverted by, in the words of Diane Negra and Anthony McIntyre, the installation of "corporatism in the heart of everyday life" (2019, 2).

The regnant image of commercial development novels is the crane, which figures as the establishing shot in many a scene of City Centre construction. I reprise briefly moments from Murray's *Mark* and Kilroy's *Devil*: "Cranes cluttered the skyline, new builds were everywhere" (Murray 2015, 150) and "A panorama of cranes spanning the horizon was engaged in a courtly dance" (Kilroy 2012, 138). And, from *Winterland*, the first installment in Glynn's trilogy, in 2009: "Down in the docklands, Richmond Plaza dominates the horizon. Next to it there are two enormous cranes, which look like mechanical high priests, supplicants kneeling before some holy monolith" (59). In all three instances, emphasis falls on the scale of the cranes, always in plural, in relation to the cityscape. Ireland remains agog at its own modernization. As with Kilroy's aestheticized, aristocratic cranes, Glynn's span multiple eras and registers; he anthropomorphizes them as sacerdotal celebrants of a prehistoric epoch. The combination of personification with the evocation of an earlier era renders the cranes as uncanny: they both are and are not alive; they exist in both past and future, of and yet not integrated into the skyline. The temporal overlay thereby naturalizes their presence as having already been there at the same time as it strains to integrate them into the landscape.

A similar spatial confusion accompanies the rhetorical positioning of commercial development, depicting it as both Irish and alien. The overt Orientalism of Kilroy's cranes and skyscrapers falls in line with the language of the Celtic Tiger and texts complicit with or agreeable to its terminology, such that *Winterland*'s investors in Richmond Plaza foresee "'all of this being developed. I see it becoming a sort of new Hong Kong on Europe's Atlantic rim'" (Glynn 2009, 125). With the echo of the far more common term "Pacific rim," Glynn parallels Dublin to Hong Kong, another English-speaking island long held by the United Kingdom. Elsewhere a politician forecasts a Europe with Dublin at the forefront, in which "cities like Frankfurt and Brussels, The Hague and Berlin, these would all be just like American and Asian cities, just like Houston or Kuala Lumpur" (78). The choice of cities here is telling of a mindset keen to displace capital cities with capitalist cities and a nationalist Irish perspective with a federalist European perspective; the pair of mid-European cities signals the leadership of the EU by bureaucrats, and the American and Asian representatives, while major cities, are known more for their chaotic landscapes of skyscrapers than their economic importance.

In both spatial and temporal modes, then, Glynn—and, to gesture forward, Hughes—underscores Ireland's ambivalence about and inability to reconcile itself to its own modernity. This uncertainty is reflected in the generic trajectories of each series of novels. Sarah Townsend reads middlebrow genre conventions in the post-Tiger era as "enfeebled would-be guarantors of middle-class futurity" (2020, 252), holdovers from an earlier "emergence of a corporatised consumer culture" (250). Her analysis of the romance novel and the police procedural sees their conventions as straining to contain the contradictions of late capitalist society. While Glynn and Hughes forswear the stable professional environment of a bureaucratized police force, their outsider detectives work in service of the same "production of . . . social consensus" (251), a consensus working to manufacture the image of a trajectory of progress alongside a growing understanding of the limits and costs of that consensus.

Winterland showcases the Irish economy and the property and financial markets just past their intoxicating peak. The complex, conspiratorial plot centers on developers of an enormous skyscraper, who are frustrated by bureaucracy and keen to override safety regulations. In a plotline that could act as a case study of Beck's risk society, the support structures required to prevent the building's destruction in high winds are not installed, since the cost is high and the chance of wind shear remote. Those urging greater caution are silenced by bribes, threats, or murder. Glynn thus presents developer malfeasance as not merely criminal but also evil, offering an analogy between such rash negligence and the risky financial gambles made by banks and developers: the odds of a market downturn seemed small enough that fiscal caution was cast to the wind. While the literal wind hazard is exposed and ameliorated in *Winterland*, Ireland's burgeoning property development proceeds, unchecked even by recession, evidence that the crisis is not so much a rupture with the boom as an intensification of its redistribution of wealth upward.

The cost of this redistribution and endless growth for the bourgeoisie and working class is high. The novel's clever hook is that two men of the same name are killed on one night. Set early during what the novel refers to as the "downturn" (Glynn 2009, 35), the plot is set in motion by a mistaken-identity murder, a gangland thug named Noel Rafferty shot in a professional hit. The actual mark, however, was his uncle, a structural engineer, targeted for standing up on principle to Paddy Norton, whose thirty years in commercial development were threatened by the elder Noel's insistence on safety protocols. Long ignored as potential major characters in novels, engineers seem in the era of big development to come into their own. In parallel to the subplot in *Solar Bones* concrete pour, Noel is holding up the relentless, voracious need to build. (The development's name, Richmond Plaza, etymologically "rich world," gestures toward the United States.) The death of Noel's nephew is collateral damage to the powerful men who arrange it, even more than the death of this Noel, which shortly follows. But the slip is indicative of a convenient assumption, one that most everyone in the novel falls prey to, thinking that the criminality of a smalltime drug dealer, DVD pirate, and cigarette bootlegger is the threat to Irish society, when, the novel suggests, the real menace is far bigger and resides within the state and economic structures themselves. The attention directed to so-called street crime forms a tidy analogy to the misattribution of blame for the financial crisis: just as the traffic in DVDs is not a substantial factor in the financial misdeeds in Dublin, domestic consumption and personal mortgages are not the primary cause of the recession.[24] But the economic contexts that are mapped onto individual lives emphasize personal accountability. As Anne Mulhall explains, "With the individual interpellated as fully responsible for their own condition, the forces of capital and their institutional and political collaborators are exonerated of any responsibility" (2016, 30).

Glynn's novel expresses outrage at the transfer of blame, yet it also works within its neoliberal and thriller milieus, characterizing the government as irrelevant: all agency and power reside in the private sector. The politician who advances the will of capital on behalf of his shadowy associates is depicted as a vain tool. Efforts to seek redress are nonofficial, with the implication that normal channels of due process are no longer operative and are even irreparably corrupt. Rather, the novel's heroes engage in vigilantism, appearing as risky in their actions and as dismissive of the legal system as the developers they hunt. Not by coincidence, the American power broker whose capital enables the construction manages to avoid tarnish.[25] The outcome of the plot is invisible to anyone except the reader; one message of the book is that power will go to great extents to conceal its workings, with the implication that conspiracy is everywhere and routinely hidden from the public. Meanwhile, at the novel's end, the skyscraper grows, of its own volition: "It's as though the building, like a wounded organism, is busy renewing itself, carrying out its own repairs, determined to survive" (2009, 467). Glynn's Darwinian language animates the construction project and absolves the system of any accountability, his choice of present tense enhancing the sensation of continuous movement. Once a few corrupt elements have been removed from the equation, progress is organic and regenerative, laced with an eerie inexorability. *Winterland* accedes to the primacy of the economic, angry at bad actors but reflecting

24. Mercille (2014a) has been particularly clear on this point.

25. Glynn's two sequels more fully critique neoliberal power, focusing on the American capitalist and his global reach; it could be argued that this shift of focus to the United States further obscures the culpability of the Irish plutocracy.

the status quo as inevitable. The consensus that is assembled is one of curtailed agency.

Hughes's novels bespeak a similar belief in the frequency of conspiracy and the unstoppable advance of development. All feature detective Ed Loy, a private eye returned to Dublin after decades in Los Angeles, his path paralleling that of other emigrants coming home at the height of the Tiger, the booming property market of which acts as a backdrop and plot engine in the novels. Loy's absence gives him an outsider's perspective as he misses all but the final years of the Celtic Tiger, arriving amid the consumerist mania that he disdains in novel after novel. The story lines tend toward the gothic, with intricate, baroque elements: incestuous families, long-kept secrets, institutionalized abuse, and femmes fatale with mixed motives feature in each volume. In keeping with the norms of the genre but also negotiating the sort of space-time compression that bespeaks a Dublin in step with global modernity, Loy recurrently solves his cases in highly condensed time frames, usually exactly a week, involving at least one very long day/night.

Returning to Dublin reluctantly, an unapologetic and unreconstructed American immigrant, Loy focalizes with an American perspective, critical of Ireland and inclined to romanticize the United States. The America of the novels is midcentury modern in its mise-en-scène, gender roles, and uncritically meritocratic ideology. Hughes consciously evokes the American tradition of hardboiled fiction (a "loy" is a spade, equating protagonist Ed Loy with Sam Spade), a temporal allusion that parallels the Tiger years with the prosperity of the United States in the 1950s. The novels comment on Ireland's belated entry into car culture, tying Loy's love affair with the antique Volvo he drives to a midcentury American dream of freeways and seamless individual transportation. Hughes's fidelity to the well-worn rhetoric of the hardboiled novels, as well as its weary tropes, anchors his series to this earlier era. His settings and cadences pay tribute to Dashiell Hammett and Raymond Chandler. For instance, when Loy is hired in the first novel, *The Wrong Kind of*

Blood (2006), by a woman named Linda Dawson, the first of many tragic, doomed women in the series, he reflects in an early scene:

> I didn't want her to know I was coming. I was tired of hearing her tell me lies. This time, I wanted to catch her off guard so that at least she didn't have time to make up a second set of lies to explain the first. . . . Linda was standing by the white sofa in her living room, smoking a cigarette and staring out to sea. She was wearing a short black cardigan over a low-cut purple silk top, a tight black skirt that fell just above the knee, black stockings and black high heels. Her golden hair was piled high on her head, and her lips were the same bloodred shade as her fingernails. She looked like a quiet night was the last thing on her mind. (94–95)

Fittingly for a narrator who speaks like this, Loy is wary of the present in all sorts of ways, bemoaning the tacky fake tans of the women he sees, dismayed by the wimpy pastel cocktails consumed in tasteful, well-lit bars, scornful and nostalgic in the face of Dublin's changes. Construction cranes help to create the ambience that makes him uneasy: "Cranes bearing the Dawson name seemed to be trampling at will all over Bayview and Seafield; I could see three from where we sat. My first view coming in on the plane wasn't of the coast or the green fields of North Dublin; it was of four great Dawson cranes suspended above a vast oval construction site. It looked like they had just dug up the Parthenon, and were laying the foundations for another shopping mall" (11).[26] Hughes easily deploys the familiar trope of the obliteration of nature alongside modernity's desecration of an earlier, superior, sacred culture. The trampling cranes are violent and malevolent, while the subsequent "great" ones are magical, suspended; in both cases, they seem to operate without human

---

26. Hughes uses the invented placenames of Bayview and Seafield as apparent stand-ins for Dun Laoghaire and Sandycove, substantially Americanizing Co. Dublin's southern region.

hands, a characterization of cranes that echoes those of Glynn and Kilroy. Later in the novel, more cranes:

> As the sun burned off the last of the gray, the great cranes stood black against the sky: one here, three there, half a dozen above the largest sites, as far as the eye could see and farther, the cranes swooped and swung and loomed, hovered and turned and rose, until the ground beneath their feet seemed provisional, subject to their imperious whim. It was as if Dublin had become a city of cranes; like great steel titans of the property boom, they delved on the horizon, churning up the city's past and concreting it over so some unknown but inevitable future could be built, some enticing, elusive dream of the new. (2006, 154)

Not only does Hughes make an anthimeria in using concrete as a verb, he also includes a few extraneous "ands," a polysyndeton that here seems to gesture toward excess and a breathless unstoppability, a denial of logical sequencing that depicts the present as timeless. And, again, the cranes have their own automatonic energy, a reference in part to the seemingly inescapable teleology of big development.

The overdetermination of factors here—cranes without human operators, an economy striving for personal wealth, a distrust of the structures of civic society—underwrites a social configuration focused on the individual autonomy and accountability and places the onus of risk upon the individual. What becomes invisible is how personal risks have social roots and individual problems have institutional causes. It is worth revisiting Conor McCabe's argument about the eagerness of the Irish government to see the risky choices of individuals as precipitating Ireland's crisis: "Despite the fact that *commercial property was the crucial element in the collapse of these banks* [AIB, Bank of Ireland, and Irish Life and Permanent], mortgage-holders were routinely listed as the root cause of the problem" (2015, 59, emphasis mine). Julien Mercille has importantly noted that this narrative of a nation of spendthrifts is an "often repeated story" but argues that Europe's economic crises were not due to "fiscal irresponsibility or profligacy" (2014a, 14). Nevertheless, the cultural imaginary focuses on the individual for the assumptions of risk but speaks in terms of society in the dispersal of costs. The banks receive payouts from a strapped public in the name of austerity, a sleight of hand(out) that is a signature move in the neoliberal handbook. Philip Mirowski reads a core principle of the original neoliberals (the Mont Pèlerin Society and its outgrowth of a "Neoliberal Thought Collective") to be that "'free' markets do not occur naturally. They must be actively constructed through political organizing. . . . The political goal of neoliberals is not to destroy the state, but to take control of it, and to redefine its structure and function, in order to create and maintain the market-friendly culture" (2018, n.p.). Hughes's novels aptly lay out parallels between the free market entrepreneurs in Dublin and the criminal underworld that operates alongside and in conjunction with it, a connection sustained by its alignment to the emergence of a nomadic, "second-modernity individual" who "has neither the time nor the space to reflect" (Lash 2001, ix), a "combinard" driven to build personal capital.

Hughes's protagonist can be read via this lens. Even the term "private eye" invokes a distance from a public collective. The detective can be read as a proto–gig economy worker, often on a flexible schedule and self employed.[27] Loy collapses the distinction between work and leisure, in the mode identified by Boltanski and Chiapello (2005) of managerialist rhetoric that would have a self-motivated, nimble workforce willing to innovate and disrupt in ways that generally just equal working more and more. John Patrick Leary unpacks the much-venerated idea of "flexibility," a bodily metaphor alongside and akin to lean and nimble, all nonfat words: "Austerity culture seems to demand a sort of embodied moral discipline, like that of the ascetic . . . devoted to a single task, scornful of leisure that might

---

27. The Pinkerton agency notwithstanding. See Townsend's apt description of the romantic individualism of detectives prior to the police procedural and the bureaucratic stability of a professional investigative unit (2020).

detract from it" (2018, 94–95). In a like manner, Ed Loy cannot disentangle personal from professional—he is an independent contractor who keeps working even when he does not have an employer: "It didn't matter anymore if I didn't have a client. I had a stake in this that went beyond the job" (2006, 196). Loy's work ethic derives from the interpellation of diligence as a principle, and from Philip Marlowe, Sam Spade, and Walter Neff, investigators who mix business and pleasure in the service of the job. For Loy, this individuated worker is one aspect of his romanticization of America and its expansive anonymity and atomization: "I'd had it with Dublin . . . where my da knew your da and yours knew mine, where the past was always waiting around the next corner to ambush you. . . . I was going to the place you went to when you'd had enough past, enough family, enough history, the place where they let you start again, make yourself up, be whoever you wanted to be. A happy orphan, in a land where no one knew my name" (125). Loy's Ireland is inbred, stuck in the past, even atavistic; he refers later to "real old Irish tribal bullshit" (262) and goes on to equate a drug kingpin with a "tribal chieftain" (282), the language of primitivism resonating with the ambush imagery above. The United States, by contrast, is the site of an overtly metafictive parthenogenesis where people are self generating and future facing.

It is worth considering what affordances Hughes derives from the generalization that America represents the future, with Ireland figured as a regressive, atavistic past—particularly in novels that at the same time log what would seem to be a contradictory sentiment: an ongoing, horrified fascination with development, materialism, and income inequality. The thriller has roots in a midcentury version of velocity and acceleration; its pacing is congruent with the pacing of a newly forming car culture, as the investigator zips from crime scene to police station to witness and so on.[28] Such motorization was long

---

28. Tony Shalhoub's title character in the television series *Monk* (2002–9) was famously afraid to drive, a phobia that underscores how much this mode of transport is associated with private detectives.

delayed for Ireland, which had a lower rate of auto ownership than the rest of the EU as late as 1999 (McDonald 1999). While Hughes writes his series, car ownership in Ireland reaches a peak: a car for every two Irish residents over age fifteen in 2006 (Kelly 2007). Hughes's Tiger-era Dublin has much in common with a healthy mid-century US economy, a place where (supposedly) everyone is finally working and able to afford durable consumer goods. The thriller genre of the older era thus maps easily onto the increasingly atomized urban landscape of the latter, a place where car ownership at last allows people to be alone as they travel from place to place, such physical enclosure a synecdochic encapsulation of the move away from collectivist identities bound by nation, religion, or labor union.

Indeed, the plot of a Hughes novel hinges on access to a working motor; the absence of a car provides a backdrop to the opening scenes of the first volume. A great deal of attention is lavished on Loy's vehicle of choice, a 1965 Volvo Amazon 122S, which is treated as a possession of greater social distinction than the boom-era Mercedes and Range Rovers that clog Dublin's roads as Loy tries to investigate. Such overt status symbols are derided alongside other forms of conspicuous consumption in the novels. By contrast, the Volvo's understated retro-modern chic emanates from its midcentury Scandinavian design, of a piece with an era of optimistic futurism. For Hughes, ironically, a vintage car stands in for the future, not the past. The futurity the Volvo conjures is of the midcentury moment during which the Mont Pèlerin Society is working to dismantle a Keynesian postwar economic consensus and allow again for massive wealth accumulation. The car enables Loy to move across Dublin with impressive agility and scope, covering, in one twenty-four-hour period in the second novel, *The Color of Blood* (2007), some fifty-one miles.[29] The meticulously itemized and compressed time frame is dependent almost entirely on a personal vehicle, not transit, to move Loy around Dublin and environs, and, astonishingly, he usually

---

29. My thanks to Alyx Raz for their work on charting this journey.

manages to find parking and avoid traffic. Loy's journeys offer an analogy between the use of public roads for private ends in fiction and policy worlds, both treating the infrastructure as invisible, scarcely worth mention. Loy crisscrosses in a time warp, zipping seamlessly up and down Ireland's eastern coastline, in and out of the city center, even, in *The Color of Blood*, finding parking just off Stephen's Green in time to have dinner at the Shelbourne, in 2007, when boom times would make this particularly improbable.[30] This sort of fantastic parking karma sets forth geographic miracles to stand in for economic magical thinking: anything is possible in Boomtown Dublin, in a way that reflects a larger neoliberal sense of freedom from the past, and from time more generally. While on a thematic level Hughes hectors a materialist citizenry for its excesses, the mechanics of the plot participate in the boom's boominess.

The fact that Loy operates in space-time, doing his sleuthing in the flesh rather than conducting Internet research, hacking computers, or using drones, gives the novels an old school feel—he performs the role of detective as journeyman artisan. In keeping with this analog mode, the characters in the novels have and use mobile phones, but with a technological clumsiness that serves as a trace of the anachronistic genre. The first novel is set in the heyday of the Blackberry, mere months away from the release of the first iPhone, yet Loy seems unable to receive calls on his mobile, instead getting a beep when a voicemail has arrived. Like the Volvo, this technological backwardness is a remnant of the contradictions within Hughes's critique of the hyperspeed era, a tension between the midcentury genre's optimistic futurity and anxiety about predatory, frenetic development. The forced conversion of the older genre into development-era iteration extends the neoliberal imperative to configure the individual as a brand and a product. For this job, the correspondence of the emergent development thriller to its moment is near perfect.

---

30. An American equivalent might be a parking space on Central Park South, just across from the Plaza or Essex House.

The values and meanings validated by the plot and the detective's activities align the novel with a culture in which self-sufficiency, an appetite for risk, and a valuation of the individual over the (always dysfunctional) family speak to a nation earnestly replacing its faith in the church with a faith in the markets and embracing privatization as the realization of a rational market.

And, indeed, Hughes sees a new religion rising where the Parthenon has been:

> The garage had been replaced by something called the "House Beautiful Retail Park." . . . There was a DIY superstore, a carpet showroom, a garden center, a bathroom and tiling store, an electrical goods warehouse and outlets that sold furniture and lighting. The forecourt was thronged with determined shoppers loading their cars with crates and cartons. Rapt faces huddled in the stores, studying carpets and gazing at tiles and worshipping fridges and washing machines. The atmosphere was hushed, reverent, devotional. The kingdom of the house beautiful was at hand. I knew my father's body lay beneath all of this striplit splendor. For years I had dreamed of finding him, alive or dead, imagined the moment I'd uncover the truth. Now it was here, and I felt nothing; worse, I felt what the bustling congregation around me felt: an overwhelming desire to buy something. (2007, 267–78)

Loy's condemnation of himself and the shoppers he sees uses the language of religion to emphasize how empty he finds this sort of faith. Hughes does not reflect on the replacement of a collectivist religion with a personal one, instead using excess "ands" to convey hyperabundance. Hughes's unsubtle condemnation of consumerism in 2006 feeds very easily into the displacement of guilt from banks to the Irish public two years later. In fact, as the Irish economy ended its 1990s export-based expansion, "financialization and a credit-fueled housing boom sustained high rates of economic growth" (Mercille 2014a, 18), a neoliberal mode that required the very consumption soon to be condemned. Attention to the ways that the standard of living felt affluent in the waning years of the boom obscures the larger structural underpinnings of an economic system that requires consumption to survive. While Hughes's critique of materialism makes sense in the context of a cultural narrative in which religion has been replaced by individualistic practices grounded in commodified self-care and creature comforts, it papers over the fact that the crash stems far more from the development of the individualized mindset Loy embodies.

In contradistinction to the burning estate at the end of the Big House novel, Dublin development thrillers end with construction. Other novelists also use construction as a means of comment on the earlier form. The collapse of the ice house in Colum McCann's *Transatlantic* (2013) is one such inversion; that novel also begins and ends in a crumbling house on the brink of repossession by the bank.[31] Many other novels feature inversions of the burning big house as well: Donal Ryan's novels about a Tipperary community's journey through the boom and crash begins chronologically with *The Thing about December* (2013). At the novel's climax, Johnsey holes up with a rifle, only to die in an encounter with a SWAT team. His incredibly valuable house—on land of inflated value—isn't burned. Rather, the man himself goes down in a hail of fire, a symbolic inversion that genuflects to the value of the land and the lack of importance of Johnsey. Bobby Mahon, who narrates the first section of the next installment, *The Spinning Heart*, swears that, once his father dies, "I'll burn the cottage down and piss on the embers and I'll sell the two acres for as much as I can get" (2012, 10). To begin with the image of a burning house inverts the traditional Big House narrative (the father-son tensions here evoke Yeats's 1938 drama *Purgatory*). Jason Buchannan (2017) has read such burning as the collapse not to the past but of a future that will not come to pass.[32] Tana French's fiction recurrently dances around Big House tropes, from the burning of an old Ascendancy home in the final pages of *The Likeness*

---

31. This insight is Matt Eatough's.

32. Buchannan reads the Mahon cottage not as a Big House update but a famine cottage update, arguing gentrification is as destructive as famine.

(2008) to the choice of the killer in *The Trespasser* (2016) to turn off the stove so as to avoid burning the house down. Where once the burning of the Big House was a sign of an unsustainable social system, we see in French and in Ryan an effort to preserve capital/ evidence, because the asset is too valuable for such symbolism.

This idea of capital *as* evidence foregrounds questions of blame. Stripped of their historic colonial anxieties, the Big House tropes worry unstable class distinctions through a transfer of the negative qualities of earlier Ascendancy characters and ideals onto the middle class.[33] Historically the Catholic bourgeoisie were cast as upstarts, fumbling in the greasy till. Now their grasping, materialism, and social climbing are gendered as feminine and blamed for the economic crisis. Claire Bracken has discussed feminizing terms like "'yummy mummy' and the 'Celtic kitten,' [used to] characterise a nation perceived to be trivial and overly consumptive" (2013, 170). Rosemary Meade (2012) argues that "narratives of blame . . . ultimately fall back onto that most pervasive of ideological devices, the fetishisation of individual choice"; in this way, discourses about the crisis that look to affix personal responsibility disguise "the contradictions of late capitalism as a global system" (33). This disguise is the result of what John Clarke and Janet Newman call the "intensive ideological work" (2012, 300) by "wizards" who redirect attention away from risky financial speculation towards the costs of a social safety net, tidily effecting an "alchemy that might turn disaster into triumph" (300). For the Irish plutocracy, triumph looks like the retention of economic power and wealth in the hands of an elite who escape blame for the crash.

This brings us back to Claude, Paul Murray's banker, who is asked by a struggling novelist named Paul to serve as an Everyman for his own recession novel. As to be expected from a novel with this

---

33. Of course the class politics are not as straightforward as thumbnail history would have it: Seamus Deane has argued that "the Protestant Ascendancy was historically a predominantly bourgeois rather than aristocratic social formation" (Kreilkamp 2006, 19).

sort of premise and a love interest named Ariadne (a refugee from the 2010 collapse in Greece, all of whose paintings bear the name *Simulacrum*), Murray plays with the metafictive qualities of money itself, as in this passage, where Claude has been asked to offer analysis on Royal Irish Bank, already bailed out for €7 billion once and seeking recapitalization:

> The report is going slowly, very slowly. Financial institutions are chimerical creatures at the best of times, but Royal's books are like nothing I've ever seen. Every figure is a door into a world of illusion—of shapeshifting, duplication, disappearing acts. Deals are buried or recorded more than once; borrowers are split into two or lumped together; mysterious sums arrive and depart without explanation, like ships full of toxic waste that pull into a harbour in the middle of the night and the next day are gone again.
>
> Royal Irish: the name sounds like a bad poker hand, one that looks unbeatable until it capsizes and you lose your shirt. (Murray 2015, 150)

The passage implies *unheimlich* and alchemical dimensions to contemporary finance, which we can see articulated by Clarke and Newman's reading of austerity as "magical thinking" (2012). Crucially, they note "a remarkable display of 'shape changing'" that shifts attention from private to public sector, "from a crisis located in the banking and financial centres of the USA and UK to a global crisis . . . ideologically reworked . . . from an economic problem (how to 'rescue' the banks and restore market stability) to a political problem (how to allocate blame and responsibility for the crisis): a reworking that has focused on the unwieldy and expensive welfare state and public sector, rather than high risk strategies of banks, as the root cause of the crisis" (300).

The magical thinking that underpins the neoliberal global economy is metonymically reproduced in Claude's description of Royal Irish's books, a word that itself reminds us of the parallel of credit and fiction. (It's worth noting that the plural, "books," is the default means of expression for even a single ledger, with the implication that "every figure" contains multitudes.) Here, numbers are the passageways into magical thinking, variations of which are listed paratactically, without conjunctions to specify their relation. The data in Royal Irish's bookkeeping is similarly paratactic—Claude seeks to trace a coherent narrative from a text that gives figures "without explanation." The passage has an occult valence with its references to burial, borrowers split in two, and mysteries, becoming even more ominous with the introduction of the toxic waste, a metaphor which carries echoes of "toxic assets" and introduces a seemingly superfluous nautical code. Of course, actual ships do move toxic waste around but here, to dissect the metaphor, the books and sums are the tenor, with the harbour and ships the corresponding vehicles.[34] It's a bit confusing since we can't assign ship or waste specifically to the sum, which has to act as repository for both parts of the image, an asymmetry that reflects the ungainly image of debtors divided and "lumped together again," financial Frankenstein monsters.

The paragraph overlays imagery of unholy couplings and decouplings, of the joining of things that ought not be joined, calling to mind a chimera, an animal embodying the very notion of catachresis in its assemblage. This corpse imagery connects the passage to a protest-cum-performance art installation of zombies in the Financial Service Centre's plaza, picking up on the parlance of "zombie banks," which conduct business while insolvent.[35] To introduce the ship code, as Michael Riffaterre (1978) would call it, into this relatively coherent metaphor is to make the passage itself a catachresis as well, a turn only amplified at the beginning of the subsequent paragraph,

34. A Greenpeace report (2010) notes that "profits derived by illicit waste management operations were recycled into perfectly legal activities by Swiss and British financial companies and trusts, through a number of offshore havens such as Panama, Guernsey, British Virgin Islands (BVI), Liechtenstein, and Ireland" (18).

35. The term has its origin in the savings and loan crisis of the 1980s, coined by Kane (1987); it revived in the bailout years of the global financial crisis.

with its weak joke about Royal Irish as a bad poker hand. In making explicit the gambling dimension of contemporary global finance, Murray also alludes to the actual gambling term Claude evokes, the Royal Flush, the highest possible poker hand, which would mean this is the one hand when betting is not a gamble but rather a sure thing.

Sure enough, this "bad poker hand" looks "unbeatable" until—and now the ship code resurges and the liquid flow connotations of flush pay off as well—it "capsizes." If the ship of toxic waste capsizes, the chemicals spill *beyond* the harbor, creating a natural disaster and public health crisis, an analogy that links Murray's novel to *Solar Bones*. The convergence of imagery across the novels suggests a shared anxiety about environmental pollution that dovetails with shared anxieties about the global economic system, both read as inescapable hazards to which the public is exposed without its consent. Public exposure: the blaming of the public instead of the banks is an ethopolitical catachresis—the real responsibility ought to rest with the financial sector, but in an asymmetrical, ungrammatical patch, public spending is reduced instead.

As was the case with the novels considered in previous chapters, the texts examined here provide evidence of a correlation of irrealist plots and techniques with a moment in which global economic conditions have been misrepresented to blame individual consumers. Chimerical, gothic, and magical catachreses indicate the ragged seams of a logic assembled to naturalize the economic inequalities of the post-crash era.

5

Outcasts and Animals

In his 2014 play *Breaking Dad*, part of the Ross O'Carroll Kelly satirical series, Paul Howard used the term "Celtic Phoenix" for an imagined recovery taking place in the comedy's 2022 setting.[1] The play premiered in April, and by summer the Celtic Phoenix had migrated, without irony, into the business sections of the European newspapers, where upward-turning leading economic indicators were heralded as signs of austerity's success and a return to Tiger-era growth.[2] While *Breaking Bad*, the TV series Howard alludes to, was itself an economic parable of a middle class unable to pay medical expenses, the humor in *Breaking Dad*'s reference to the Celtic Phoenix relies on the hubris of the wealthy character who speaks. Howard cleverly manages to convey and critique the relentless buoyancy of the plutocratic class, whose rosy optimism was protected throughout the crisis by bailouts and austerity measures borne by a public sector with which they scarcely engage. Underneath this sanguine egotism sits the biting message: the attribution of growth to the supernatural overlooks the real pain of most citizens in an economic recovery in which both house prices and homelessness are on the rise, in which unemployment may go down but wages don't go up. Part of the value of the satire is its recognition of the fact that there was a burning and that the ashes are with us still.

1. A scan of Nexis Uni suggests that the term had made two unironic appearances prior to April 2014.

2. Krugman and others read austerity as prolonging the recession: "Harsh austerity in depressed economies isn't necessary, and does major damage when it is imposed" (2015, n.p.)

2014 was also the year that the GDP's growth rate in Ireland turned positive again, thanks in part to some clever bookkeeping that allowed large global corporations to engage in wealth accumulation via a tax avoidance technique known as "the Double Irish," a scheme that sounds like something out of *The Mark and the Void* but is real. The Double Irish had the side effect of making the economy look more robust than it actually was, since profit actually made elsewhere, on money actually not in circulation in Ireland, was calculated as part of the Irish GDP. Migration numbers provided some context that the official data obscured. Una Mullally noted at the time that "29,000 people who emigrated last year were students prior to leaving. The previous year, that was 20,200. That's a whopping increase in just-graduated students leaving within a tiny 12-month period" (2014, 14), further suggesting that reported increases in available jobs were more about quantity than quality. And even those jobs were still hard to come by: the unemployment rate for the year was nearly 12 percent. Meanwhile, what Conor McCabe has called the comprador class of Ireland began a new cycle of accumulation: "The opening months of 2014 saw a return of property exuberance to the national media, as a bubble took hold in certain parts of Dublin. At the same time it was reported that a number of speculators who had been bailed out by NAMA were in the process of buying back their loan book at marked-down prices" (2015, 62). The disconnect between the excitement about a Celtic Phoenix cyclically regenerating itself and the hard reality of ongoing privation for most of Ireland parallels the disconnect between the magical thinking that fueled the speculative bubble and the real bodies that could not find work and/or emigrated.

2014 was also the year that Marie Kondo's *The Life-Changing Magic of Tidying* (*The Life-Changing Magic of Tidying Up* in the United States) was released in English.[3] Promising a transcendent

---

3. Kondo's book is by no means the first of its kind, though its reach exceeded that of others before it. First published in Japan in 2011, it has been translated into thirty languages and has sold over ten million copies worldwide. But its antecedents laid the groundwork for its success, creating a neoliberal landscape in which the

spiritual experience through extreme decluttering, the book famously asks readers to hold an object in order to establish whether it "sparks joy"; if not, it is thanked and discarded. Objects that do not pass this test are called "clutter," while objects that inspire "bliss" and "speak to [the] heart" cease to be objects at all and become part of a "life-style" (2014, 31), moving, like the Velveteen Rabbit, out of the object realm entirely and into an intangible, numinous state. The basis for this method lies in a series of overlapping assumptions, including a commitment to take good care of possessions and a belief that accumulation is in itself problematic. While reducing overall consumption can be an important part of combatting climate change, Kondo's focus is the individual and the psyche, with the suggestion that we can be overwhelmed by too many things and are oppressed and even damaged by the control that objects assert over us. Only through a mystical interaction with them can we wrest back our authority, recognizing that the objects are so powerful that we must severely limit their numbers to retain our dominance. When Kondo refers to objects as "vibrant," she latches onto the zeitgeist, echoing Jane Bennet's influential *Vibrant Matter* (2010), which examines the agency of nonhuman things and forces. Bennet's attention to materiality recognizes that agency exists outside of humans or as humans operate in conjunction with things; included in this are uncanny dimensions, as in her cover image featuring floating bricks that look like magical loaves of bread but are actually remnants of houses lost to coastal erosion. Leaving aside the ontological questions, the Kondo empire embraces the conjunction of human and other, in marketing as well as method, noting on one of its websites that her name is now used as

---

KonMari method embodies its era's "postfeminist domestic perfectionism" (Negra 2009, 152), and its resultant orderly home signifies taste and opulence. Negra persuasively analyzes what she calls "hyperdomesticity" as a feature of the economic prosperity that took hold in the mid-1990s: "Postfeminist culture places a premium on showplace domesticity, with the achievement of a comfortable domestic life also a marker of personal virtue. In this realm also, status correlates with the achievement of/entitlement to comfort, composure, and serenity" (128).

a verb, an anthimeria that operates as an ungrammatical, chimerical assemblage.

As in the United Kingdom and the United States, Kondo-ing has been popular in Ireland, revealing curious tensions within a country that had been excoriated less than a decade before for its excesses and later deemed the "poster child for austerity" due to its willingness to slice public expenditures to the bone.[4] Ireland's relationship with affluence had been brief, as a country that counts a Great Hunger in its collective memory and was long considered a "state of the semi-periphery" (Arrighi quoted in Coakley 2016, 178), complete with "economic backwardness" and high rates of emigration, even as "increasingly liberal economic policies" weakened what little "indigenous industrial base" was present while "dependence on external capital" expanded (178–83, passim). During the years that the boom took hold, as Sharae Deckard lays forth, "financial success seemed to repudiate all the horrors of domination and dependency, to elevate the semi-peripheries to core players in the world-economy; this triumphal present was imagined as eternal, with no future crisis in sight. Futurity was something to be denied, rather than face the historical evidence of cyclical boom-bust; memory was something to be renounced as a bad dream" (n.d., 3). This conception of a timeless time marked by simultaneity (Castells's formulation, 1996) "erased the nightmare of colonial modernity, repressing national traumas and the ongoing asymmetries and economic polarities of neoliberalization" (Deckard, n.d., 3). The poverty and precarity that structured so much of Irish life was blotted out by a fantasy of the good life achieved; even for the "two thirds of the workforce in Ireland . . .

4. The term "poster child for austerity" appears in too many places to list all of them; most scholars engage with the term critically: see O'Flynn et al. (2014); O Rian, McCabe, and Mercille (2014a); and Coulter and Nagle (2015), just for starters. The popular press use of the term seems to originate with an article by Larry Elliott in the *Guardian* in November 2011 that quotes David Begg, the general secretary of the Irish Confederation of Trade Unions, as saying, "We were the poster child for globalisation. Now we are the poster child for austerity" (Elliott 2011, n.p.).

drawing salaries of €38,000 or less" in 2008 (Coulter and Nagle 2015, 11), the standard of living *felt* higher, with loans available, new cars within reach, a mobile phone for every hand. In the context of what seemed at the time like a miraculous windfall, the accumulation of objects signified departure from precarity. When the bust led to recriminations for citizens and the introduction of austerity cuts, the boom times and their physical corollaries functioned as a site of collective shame and scapegoating.

Scapegoating is an interesting concept in this context, as it involves the transfer of guilt or blame to animals, inanimate objects, and marginalized people. Micheal O'Flynn, Lee F. Monaghan, and Martin J. Power explore this dynamic and conclude that, "as financial, economic and fiscal crises unfold, scapegoating becomes a convenient and pervasive process in response to the ills of a polarizing world-system. With the exception of a few 'rotten' bankers, it is the unemployed, single mothers, public sector workers and immigrants in Ireland who are the 'logical' targets for routine pillorying" (2014, 933). O'Flynn et al. analyze a strategy that they call "democratizing blame" (925) wherein politicians, bankers, developers, and major media outlets collaborate "to spread the blame as widely as possible" (926) through remarks such as Brian Lenihan's oft-repeated "We all partied" as well as Enda Kenny's assertion that Irish people "all went a bit mad with the borrowing" (quoted in O'Flynn et al. 926). Distributing culpability so that supposed welfare cheats and hypothetical lazy public sector workers are read as significant causes of the crisis deceitfully conceals the massive role of the ruling class; affixing responsibility upon a populace for its heavy consumption of Jumbo Breakfast Rolls, designer clothes, or even sunroom extensions cultivates a feeling of shame relatively large compared to the role of consumer spending as a proportion of the total problem. As Julian Mercille has demonstrated, "Europe's problems have not been caused by fiscal irresponsibility or profligacy" (2014a, 14).

Nevertheless, in the wake of 2008's crash, Ireland moved swiftly to rein in public spending via drastic austerity measures, more swiftly than any other nation. The need to reject the earlier material excess chimed with consumers who internalized the narratives that their personal spending was integral to the crisis, that their shopping weekends in New York had caused banks to fail. This ambivalent relationship to objects was fertile ground for Kondo's aesthetic and moral imperative, which offers an apparent freedom from materialism and what Kondo refers to as the "burden of excess." She encourages acolytes to discard, donate, and recycle what they do not need. This process of course assumes that there are needier people for whom one's excess is of use, who are not themselves burdened by enough. Kondo turns doing without into a game: "My clients tell me that now life is more fun because when they run out of something they enjoy seeing how long they can last without it" (2014, 123), one with grotesque analogues to the cuts made by the elites to public services in Ireland, where hospital bed shortages and emptied out pension funds persisted even as the rhetoric of a Celtic Phoenix took hold.

One of the hardest parts of the KonMari method is getting rid of objects with sentimental value. Kondo reassures readers that their memories do not need physical embodiments. Moreover, she argues, "no matter how wonderful things used to be, we cannot live in the past. The joy and excitement we feel in the here and now are most important" (2014, 114). While, again, the emphasis here is on the experience of pleasure, it presumes an unchanging economic backdrop that recalls Deckard's characterization of a "triumphal present . . . imagined as eternal" (n.d., 3). As I have argued, this view of a timeless time or neoliberal present can create feelings of becalmed immobility and a sense that things cannot change. It further shifts blame for this state of affairs onto the materialistic subject unwilling to part with belongings that do not spark joy within her. The magical dimensions of both the Kondo and financialized discourses further firm up the paradoxical sensation that the materialistic subject is not in control, and yet it is her fault. The Irish mode of scapegoating thus seems to be one that turns inward. As Larry Elliott explains, "Ireland's response has been almost Pavlovian, reacting to the demands to inflict pain on itself with a consensual approach that has bordered on passivity" (2011, n.p.).

The link between things, responsibility, and the irreal speaks to a pervasive cultural feeling during the period of crisis, a feeling about inanimate objects and our relationship to them. The juxtaposition of excess and scarcity that marks contemporary precarity draws on the anxieties that have accompanied centuries of technological advances. Humans can worry that somehow, machines, be they Victorian gizmos or contemporary AI robots, are robbing us as people of our ability to control our own destinies, something we see reflected in concerns as diverse as the discussion of algorithms and twitter bots, our relationship with objects like self-trackers and phones, and the rise of self-driving vehicles.[5] Concern about these technologies beyond human control stems partly from their complexity and the idea that we cannot actually understand instruments "we" have ostensibly invented. The popularity of a steampunk aesthetic is a symptom of our fascinated anxiety, expressing itself via attraction to Rube Goldberg–style contraptions. Adorable in their analog intricacy, they represent a way of dialing back the technological advances of the digital era and making how things function a mechanical, visible process.

The complex digital technology hiding inside a smooth iPhone, a device we are not allowed to open or tinker with, offers an analogy to the neoliberal assertion that a market economy is too complex for human control. Friedrich Hayek has asserted that such complexity is beyond human comprehension; in Henry Staten's words it "necessitates that human subjects submit themselves to its higher rationality rather than try to control it with their own" (2017, n.p.), a tenet that generates neoliberal subjects and creates the uneasy dynamic recognizable in media coverage of credit default swaps and collateralized debt obligations, financial instruments so complicated as to be beyond the understanding of laypeople, and even, if the bankers in Paul Murray's novel *The Mark and the Void* (2015) are representative,

---

5. I thank Stephanie Hershinow (2018) and her connection of self-tracking and big data to *Clarissa* for helping me to think about these interactions.

by those who packaged and sold them. Tying this unimaginably complex economy to what John Clarke and Janet Newman have called "the alchemy of austerity," in which political and financial wizards undertake the ideological work of "shape changing" that shifts attention from private to public sector, we can trace a series of transfers: "From a crisis located in the banking and financial centres of the USA and UK to a global crisis . . . from an economic problem (how to 'rescue' the banks and restore market stability) to a political problem (how to allocate blame and responsibility for the crisis): a reworking that has focused on the unwieldy and expensive welfare state and public sector, rather than high risk strategies of banks, as the root cause of the crisis" (2012, 300). Let us also include the magical transfer of blame from a financial sector onto individual consumers and the invisibility of the marginalized as further alchemical tricks. Through these sleights of hand, incomprehensibility merges into magic itself in ways that evoke for us all sorts of uncanny objects used to talk about the economy, from Adam Smith's invisible hand to Marx's dancing table, with its grotesque wooden brain.

In "The Fetishism of the Commodity and Its Secret," from *Capital* (1867), Marx begins by noting how very obvious the use value of a commodity is. Taking the transformation of wood into a table, he states that there is "nothing mysterious about it" (1990, 163).[6] But something weird happens to the table when it moves beyond use value: "As soon as it emerges as a commodity, it changes into a thing which transcends sensuousness. It not only stands with its feet on the ground, but, in relation to all other commodities, it stands on its head, and evolves out of its wooden brain grotesque ideas, far more wonderful than if it were to be dancing of its own free will" (163–64). Key here is that the use value of the table is separate from its value, which is beyond the sensuous, and it is in this extrasensory

6. While Marx doesn't reference them, his discussion calls to mind Aristotelean material, formal, and efficient causes, as he uses the transformation of wood into a table as his example of how a human "changes the materials of nature in such a way as to make them useful" (163).

realm of the marketplace that we have the animatronic table, capable of standard posture at the same time as it is inverted.

But what are these grotesque ideas of the wooden table? They speak to the way that social relations between people manifest as "social relation[s] between the products of labor . . . the commodity reflects the social characteristics of men's own labour as objective characteristics of the products of labour themselves, as the socio-natural properties of these things" (164–65), a process of substitution that Marx calls "fetishism." Unfortunately, the table vanishes from Marx's discussion, which underscores the social dimensions of labor and value, taking pains to remind readers that value does not inhere naturally in objects but accrues via social interactions. Crucially, a few pages later, we see another vitalized dimension of Marx's argument, when he observes that value "transforms every product into a social hieroglyphic," wherein the principles of exchange seem to be natural and beyond human control, as when "magnitudes vary continually, independently of the will, foreknowledge and actions of the exchangers" (167). Indeed, the movements of exchangers—people engaged in the market transfers of commodities—are themselves subject to a "form of a movement made by things, and these things, far from being under their control, in fact control them" (167–68). For Marx, unlike Hayek, market freedom is not a genuine freedom. As David Harvey explains it, "Market forces, which none of us individually control, regulate us" (2010, 42). Marx ends his subsection on commodity fetishism with another animation of objects: "If commodities could speak, they would say this: our use-value may interest men, but it does not belong to us as objects. What does belong to us as objects, however, is our value" (1990, 176). The irruption in this part of *Capital* of animated objects that very nearly dance and speak coincides with the question of agency or control.

Nonhuman objects and assemblages are a noticeable, persistent feature of contemporary texts. My interest is in what feels like an upsurge of depictions of objects operating as part of a body or network with humans, functioning outside of human control, or even acting to limit human possibilities. These animated objects work to create or underscore a feeling of powerlessness in the humans in the novels I discuss in a way congruent with earlier gothic fictions while also inflected by a neoliberal moment in which the feeling of powerlessness stems from genuine redistribution of agency, a precarity of control akin to economic precarity. The uncanny elements act as a trace of the concealed distribution of blame and agency in the boom, bust, and recession, a means of unmasking the power of capital, the state, and plutocracy in contemporary Irish lives. In the preceding chapters, I have argued that cultural and economic conditions in Ireland (the boom, bust, and aftermath as part of a neoliberal antipolitics) have been generative of, and also shaped by, a set of narrative and linguistic tendencies—namely, irrealist elements like discontinuous plotlines and gothic tropes alongside formal choices like experiments with verb tense, syntax, and voice, as well as a growth in catachrestic and otherwise ungrammatical constructions. Throughout this book I have connected irrealism to crisis, austerity, and imbalanced recovery, underscoring formal dimensions including genre, imagery, narrative choices, and syntactic structure. I have linked this formal investigation to efforts to account for murky, seemingly unforeseeable or inexplicable economic outcomes through recourse to the irrational, the magical, and the uncanny.

To conclude the series of embedded views of increasingly more localized scales of investigation, the remainder of this chapter looks at examples of the lives of objects and animals in Irish novels of crisis, austerity, and recession. I also consider cases of marginalized, invisible, or objectified humans, be they people who fail to master the rules of self-actualization in a neoliberal economy, people who are not neurotypical, or people who are marked as racial others and asylum seekers.[7] In ways that have Irish antecedents in Big House fiction

---

7. Gessen notes that, as of 2019, "migrant advocates prefer to say 'person in need of international protection' rather than 'asylum seeker.' This usage, which has yet to migrate to the United States, emphasizes that people are claiming what is theirs by international law, as opposed to asking a national government for a handout. It also foregrounds personhood" (2019, n.p.).

yet are reflective of their particular economic and temporal setting, contemporary novels feature a number of nonhuman and human/ animal/object assemblages that operate outside human control, from galvanized machines and ghostly forces to the power grids and other infrastructural elements examined earlier. In each case human agency is curtailed by external forces that neoliberal subjects feel they cannot control, evoking the pressures of a global economy seen as too complex, magical, and disembodied to understand, much less direct. Recalling Mel Chen's (2012) attention to a hierarchy of animacy which distributes agency inequitably, my analysis highlights the incongruity of objects acting on subjects to underscore the regular and continual displacement of some humans from positions where they have self-determination. Depictions of objects with animacy unsettle this hierarchy; they can have the effect of affording power to objects at just the moment that, as Bonnie Honig writes in characterizing Wendy Brown's critique of thing theory, "humans are lamentably and increasingly deprived of it" (Honig 2017, 29), or it can be a redemptive project, like Chen's or Honig's, "different from (although indebted to) the varieties of vitalism and thing theory that attribute agency to things and decenter the human" (28). Honig's important insight that things can have "magical and malicious powers" (3) points to the multiple possible valences, congruent with Chen's revolutionary perspective: "Matter that is considered insensate, immobile, deathly, or otherwise "wrong" animates cultural life in important ways . . . animacy has the capacity to rewrite conditions of intimacy, engendering different communalisms and revising biopolitical spheres, or, at least, how we might theorize them" (2012, 2, 3). Bearing in mind the affordances and costs of such reconfigurations, I examine how the formal choices that shape each narrative's lack of control simultaneously reveal each novel's ideological relationship to the body, responsibility, and power. I tie the appearance of objects, whether magical or mundane, to the deployment of the passive voice, the use of second person, and other grammatical constructions that diffuse subject power and read conjunctions of the animate and inanimate alongside paratactic grammatical conjunctions that resist logical sequencing.

Ovines Sensitive

In *The Lives of Women*, Christine Dwyer Hickey's haunting 2015 novel, galvanized objects indicate an Americanized mindset that lays groundwork for the selfish actions of the adults in the novel. Early on, the suburban neighborhood in an unnamed Irish locale features identical home maintenance chores transpiring in unison: "Bins are left out on Tuesday mornings. On Saturdays, cars are given their sponge baths. . . . On Sundays, lawnmowers rumble" (40). The regularity suggests an enforced schedule; impetus does not arise from an individual desire but from an all-containing structure. The grammatical absence of actors leaving out the bins or giving the cars sponge baths suggests ghostly forces, invisible hands. But most ominous and telling are the self-propelled anthropomorphic lawnmowers, which give the scene an agentless mechanical momentum, merging technology and ghosts, as described by Elaine, a girl confined to her bedroom—a gothic touch that underscores the uncanny dynamism of the trappings of suburbia.

Dwyer Hickey's plot centers on a botched abortion resulting from a secret relationship between an adult man and a blind teen, the effects of which we see play out on our narrator, Elaine, over many decades. Her narrative ends with a ghostly image: "There will still be those nights of waking suddenly to the sound of something scuttling: inside the wall, under the bed, on the far side of the ceiling. Bleats of shadow will inhabit my days. There but not there, caught but not caught, always one scurry beyond my line of vision" (2015, 278). The imagery here is of conflations: sound is light, a haunted space is also time, and nights are the same as days, which will themselves, in a final space-time compression, be inhabited not by shadows themselves but by their sheep-like noises. Further, the passage merges present into future tense, ending with an ungrammatical sentence devoid of verbs, and therefore of time or movement. Curiously, the fragment is also devoid of an agent.

Dwyer Hickey's choice to set the narrative in the 1970s represents a starting point in an agentless social model that will reach its apogee with the height of the real estate frenzy. Her choice of decade aligns neatly with the onset of the sort of financialization that rose to dominance in the early seventies. At this moment, which coincides with Ireland's entry into Europe, derivatives, hedging, and leveraging reconfigure the market so that, in Richard Godden's formulation, "what is being traded is risk" (2011, 415). This shift in which the "production of commodities" is definitively supplanted by "circulation and capital" (415) decisively redirected the financial markets toward astronomic growth and loss, setting in motion the exponential increases in inequality that have underwritten decades of strong economic figures: the supposed health of the economy features unimaginable wealth for the few alongside a stagnation and decline in security for the masses. The disconnection of the market from the concrete is structurally akin to the severing of actors and actions; we see timeless time and agentless action that suggest, in the words of Hamilton Carroll and Annie McClanahan, "a world whose most important activity remains persistently unseen, a world that shifts behind our backs in ways that exceed our capacity for knowledge, a world in which what we thought we controlled turns out to have its own hostile intentions" (2015, 659).

The rumbling lawnmowers in *The Lives of Women* have analogues in *The Green Road*, where, following the climactic Christmas dinner pronouncement discussed in the previous chapter, the assembled Madigans "heard Rosaleen's little car coughing into life outside and the wheels chewing the gravel" (2015, 255).[8] When the next chapter shifts to Rosaleen as focalizer, "the car drove itself," until they came to "the edge of things. Then the car stopped. . . .

8. This is by no means the only place in the novel where Rosaleen's possessions are animated, nor Enright's only novel with such imagery; Claire Bracken (2016) notes that cars also function as organisms in both *What Are You Like?* and *The Gathering*. Certainly Enright's fascination with the uncanny precedes the economic crisis, repeatedly signaling a discomfort with objects less about the supernatural than the material and suggesting an early and ongoing understanding of the problematic relationship of Ireland to its own prosperity.

The fields were indifferent. . . . But she [Rosaleen] got a slightly sarcastic feel off the ditches, there was no other word for it—sprinkles of derision—like the countryside was laughing at her" (261). The judgmental landscape activates and inverts the long-standing Irish poetic tradition of the *dinnseanchas*, the lore of place or the idea of an enchanted land—here instead that land controls the narrative. Indeed, when Rosaleen shouts out, "The mountain took her on . . . it sent her voice back her way, and there was mist, she saw, coming down for her too" (260). Rosaleen's voice is rebuffed by the land, which at best ignores her but seems to be overtly scornful and even menacing. Enright vests the earth with agency at this moment, in a way that underscores a feeling of human powerlessness.

Returning to Rosaleen's car: Enright characterizes the sound of its locking mechanism as a "bleat," a resonance with Dwyer Hickey's bleats of shadow and a way here of turning the car into a herd animal—the end of this scene features Rosaleen's conflation of a cow and a plane as she sleeps, an admixture of vehicle and animal recalling the catachrestic chimeras of the last chapter. Enright gives the car a mouth, chewing and coughing; if the landscape is a sort of mind, extrasensuous, the vehicle is a body, specifically the part that communicates. Its personification differs from that of the land; it acts with and for Rosaleen, more part of an assemblage with her, both striving to articulate some sense of the wrongness of their environment. Driving away from her home affords Rosaleen a sense of control, however illusory, since, in ascribing the menace and scorn to the immediate objects, the character fails to see the actual forces of capital operating on her.

Sara Baume's 2013 novel *spill simmer falter wither*, which I will discuss in detail in the next section, also contains animate cars. Its narrative mode features a speaker, Ray, addressing his dog, One Eye. Ray observes several times that cars seem animate, as when "the bulb of the left headlamp is out, and so it must seem to oncoming traffic as though our car face is winking. See how all the cars have car faces, headlamp eyes and a shiny-toothed number plate smirk" (150–51). Like Rosaleen, Ray senses judgmental affects from the object world, attributing to them the same disregard and contempt as he has received from the human world.

Indeed, a unifying element among these novels featuring vitalized objects is their marginalized subjects. Certainly Eileen and Ray exist on society's edges; even Rosaleen feels powerless. All are subject to the whims of the social forces acting upon them. Likewise, Lisa McInerney's *The Glorious Heresies* (2015) looks explicitly at the extent to which our choices interact with our environment, how much control we really have, particularly in her portrait of her charismatic, frustrating protagonist, Ryan Cusack, who recognizes the disconnect between agency and inevitability:

> So it was during a class on Newton's Laws of Motion that Ryan had an epiphany. Third Law, as it happened, and probably his third epiphany that month. Maybe even that day, if he was to scale the epiphanies down to their basest elements. Small truths. Snatches of caught breath as playback skipped just enough for him to grab onto something new . . . but shit happens right up to the point where it's happening in the face of someone who doesn't want to see it. That was the truth and the truth had fuck all respect for Sir Isaac Newton and his axioms. So here, Ryan realized, was a case of the pig-headedness of people versus the Laws of Physics, and while flesh and bones have to obey the push and pull of the universe the real meat of men, their thoughts and actions and utter arrogance, ignores the processes the universe has run on for aeons. (55)

Newton's third law states that every force or action has an equal and opposite. Ryan recognizes that this physical reality is undercut by the unwillingness of responsible adults in his life to see or put a stop to the physical beatings he experiences at the hands of his father. While part of what Umberto Eco calls our "codified lexeme" (1983, 233) the well-known figure of speech "pig-headed people" nevertheless remains chimerical; here, it helps to create a contradictory definition of "the real meat" in which the physical world is less real than an intangible realm. Ryan distinguishes flesh and bones from meat, the latter a source for consumption that remains somehow disembodied. The conversational parataxis that opens the passage reflects the equality posited by Newton's law, but this is supplanted by a hypotactic logic in which cause and effect mirror the nonphysical inequalities that shape Ryan's abuse. The passage speaks beautifully to the deeper emotional damage wrought by physical violence, laying the groundwork for Ryan's ongoing injury even once he is physically large enough to counter his father's attacks. The invisibility of his cuts and bruises to those who could intervene pushes Ryan to act out in class; he is scolded for vandalizing his desk with black marks at a moment when "there were marks on Ryan's face" (57). In a sequence that weaves together three separate narratives, Ryan makes clear his need to be seen and his invisibility in a system that worries more about the wooden desk than the boy.

That Ryan's desk is more visible and matters more than he does speaks to the logics of its use value and social relations, both contexts in which a boy like Ryan does not register. Elsewhere in the novel McInerney uses wooden imagery to show people equated to objects, depicting the hapless couple Georgie and Robbie in a way that recalls Marx's table even more explicitly. The bad fortunes of these characters, even more ne'er do well than Ryan, propel the plot: "Georgie and Robbie had little to hold them together, and there were more photogenic couples. He looked jointed enough to be folded away when not in use, and it wasn't often anyone had use for him. She was short and freckled, prone to weight where it wasn't wanted. The size of her breasts had made her barrel-like in her school jumper; ould fellas had breathed rough suggestions when they passed her on the street" (2015, 29). McInerney's language suggests from the outset that these members of Cork's precariat are assemblages of a sort, "held together" by external forces and only barely. Repeatedly throughout the novel, McInerney uses syllepsis to jar the reader's sense of comfort by disrupting expectation in its divergent applications. Here her syllepsis hinges on the word "use," so that Robbie is compared to a foldaway table in the same sentence that underscores his social marginality. Georgie is also wooden, a barrel; something else the two share is the way that no one wants to look for them—Georgie when she runs away from home, and Robbie when he is murdered. They are socially invisible, with little personal agency; Ryan says he is "fucking invisible" (66) to people who ignore the marks on his face, clear indicators of multiple beatings at the hands of his father in the preceding days. Robbie's silent presence on a barstool and Georgie's treatment by the guards underscore their lack of full, embodied existence in the eyes of those around them. Like Ryan, they are buffeted by a social context that is designed for others, to enrich others. Like her animal and object imagery, McInerney's stylistic choices restrict her subjects on the page in ways akin to those that control their lifestyle and economic options via outside forces.

In a surprising convergence with Enright and Dwyer Hickey, McInerney also opts to include uncanny ovine imagery in her novel, in reference to Georgie: "The ghost of who she was an hour ago bleated its dissent" (2015, 102). Sheep serve as sacrificial animals in our collective imaginary, known for their compliance and supposed stupidity, for their collective nature; even the word itself does not distinguish between singular and plural. While the sacrificial dimension of the bleating shadow, car, and ghost arises from the sense of a creature subordinated and overpowered, at the same time these objects are chimerical, both sheep and thing. This convergence recalls the anastrophe of Paul Lynch's "bovines insensitive" in *Red Sky in Morning* (2013, 181), a figuration that personified the role of the working class and whose form of expression gave rise to a feeling of inescapability and limited agency in the novel. Those plodding, numb animals to which Lynch's exhausted railroad workers were compared resemble the sheep of the novels here, signaling a collective of circumscribed power and understanding. What distinguishes these novels is the choice to bring this sheep image to the surface via its sound, the bleat. Its status as nonverbal utterance offers a sort of chimerical form of articulation that is verbal but not language. In contrast to Lynch's bovines, who did not feel, the disembodied bleats here are pure affect, to use Jean-François Lyotard's formulation: "The sentiment is a phrase. I call it affect-phrase. It distinguishes itself in that it is *unarticulated*" (quoted in Nouvet et al.

2016, 3, emphasis in original). The lack of content to the expression is key here: as explained by Claire Nouvet, Julie Gaillard, and Mark Stoholski, the affect-phrase "has no addressor, no addressee, no referent, and no meaning" (2016, 3). That the utterance is in essence nonlinguistic, free floating, outside of time, emphasizes its marginalization, but "the inarticulate affect nevertheless 'occupies' articulated discourse in some fashion" (4). The unintelligible bleat thus functions as an ungrammaticality, a trace of the novels' moment of austerity: an inarticulate plaint, a protest in form without explanation, bleating is an indictment as well of a passive populace.

You

The animal inarticulacy of the bleat raises questions of what utterances can be read as communicative, issues addressed by the distinctive mode of narration in Sara Baume's *spill simmer falter wither*. A tale of an isolated man and a rescue dog who is his companion for a year, *spill*'s spare story is an austerity parable, from its reduced scope to its gothic excess, both narrated via a sparse minimalism, a signature of a moment of reduced expectations and horrific consequences. The story of Ray and One Eye features two short sections of third-person narration as a prologue and epilogue, but the vast bulk of the novel is a second-person address to the dog by Ray, a diegetic mode that downplays Ray's first-person statements in favor of what Margarita Estévez Saá sees as a sort of communication "between humans and animals without necessarily trying to impose our views and our voices, and silencing those of the non-human animal" (2020, 123). The novel's narrative choices and its characterizations of Ray and One Eye extend voice to the marginalized at the same time as they reveal the limited agency available to those marked as outsiders; as in McInerney, Enright, and Dwyer Hickey, irreal and ungrammatical techniques gesture to crisis-era inequality and precarity. This moment finds expression as well in Melatu Uche Okorie's collection of short stories *This Hostel Life* (2018), which also takes the lives of the marginalized as its subject and uses a variety of textual innovations, including a blended mode of second-person narration in "Under the Awning," to undercut neoliberal claims to individualism and personal agency. The story plays with perspective in both its frame and embedded narrative, decentering the white voices surrounding both protagonists while registering the limits on Black bodies and stories in contemporary Ireland. Okorie's attention to objects also reframes discussions of agency and self-determination. The fact that both writers deploy heterogeneous second-person narration suggests that this uncommon mode may be particularly well suited in this moment to the narration of marginalized subjects.

Extended second-person narration is historically rare, a complex mode that is itself chimerical and hard to sustain. In line with Monika Fludernik's observation that the second-person mode "seems to contradict expectations of customary patterns of verisimilitude" (quoted in Herman 2004, 339), we can see second person as a mode that finds conventional narration inadequate to its purposes. I would argue that, in the texts I consider here, second person avoids the objectification of third person and the affective burden of first person, extending voice to a perspective generally excluded. Such an affordance may explain why, though it remains infrequent, second-person mode is used to voice experiences of overlooked, ignored, and discounted people, those historically considered incapable or undeserving of the subject position. Claudia Rankine's *Citizen* (2014) is a particularly powerful instance, one that Angela Hume argues "accounts for how certain bodies are attenuated or made sick under capitalism and the state, while simultaneously being regarded as surplus by these same structures" (2016, 79). This mode is clearly distinct from that of apostrophe in lyric poems, in which the second-person mode is momentary and, as Barbara Johnson so effectively demonstrates, can be more of a mere performance of address, a "form of ventriloquism through which the speaker throws voice, life, and human form into the addressee, turning its silence into mute responsiveness" (1986, 30). Given my interest in the uncanny, in animacy, and in assemblages, it's important to note that the use of apostrophe that Johnson delineates is one that, as in her example of Percy Bysshe

Shelly's "Ode to the West Wind," "gives animation, gives the capacity of responsiveness . . . not in order to make it speak but in order to make it listen to him—in order to make it listen to him doing nothing but address *it*" (31). This mode of apostrophe exploits its "you," denying it embodiment.

While apostrophe in this way denies the subjectivity of the second person, recuperative uses of it acknowledge the relationality of pronouns. To discuss it in the terminology used by Mieke Bal, who in turn cites the linguist Émile Benveniste, second personhood "indicates the reversible relationship of complementarity between first- and second-person pronouns whose use produces subjectivity and constitutes the essence of language precisely, Benveniste says, because pronouns do *not* refer" (1993, 307). In relying on second-person narration, a text can materially constitute a narratee—an important move for a speaker who is deemed marginal. Indeed, in *spill*, both Ray and One Eye are socially excluded and treated as irrelevant because they do not serve the economic and biopolitical ends of contemporary Ireland. Yet, beyond the general feeling of incongruity, *spill*'s specific mode of intradiegetic narration does not correspond to any of the traditional narratological classifications of second-person address. Even within this unusual, seldom-used form, Baume's technique is an outlier; it is not apostrophe, nor is it thinly disguised first person, or a deictic gesture to include the reader. Its novelty comes not from its addressee—anyone who has spent time with an animal companion is fluent in this mode—but from its duration, which extends for the full year of the novel. Baume is clear that status quo modes of address fail to encompass the experiences being related: in an interview appended to the novel, she explains that her efforts to write the story from the point of view of the dog and from Ray's perspective did not work (2013, 282). The narratological choice itself can be seen as a hybrid form, particularly given how well this aligns with the characterization of both man and dog as themselves chimerical creatures.

Ray notes that his name itself orients him toward chimeras: "My name is the same word as for sun beams, as for winged and boneless sharks. But I'm far too solemn and inelegant to be named for either" (Baume 2013, 8). The beams of light themselves, neither particles nor waves, are interstitial forms, just as a winged shark evokes something neither arial nor aquatic, its bonelessness suggestive of a creature not quite vertebrate.[9] Ray's brief lyricism is undercut by the catachrestic juxtaposition of solemnity and "inelegance," a word that itself points up that elegance has no easy opposite. His brutal self-characterizations emphasize his ungainly disconnection and discomfort: "When I move, my clodhopper feet and mismeasured legs make me pitch and clump. My callused kneecaps pop in and out of my shredded jeans and my hands flail gracelessly, stupidly" (7).[10] Baume creates the sense of awkwardness through a physical lack of parallelism and a permeability of boundaries. Ray's self-location in ill-fitting, in-between places comes early in the novel, foreshadowing the isolation and exclusion he experiences in the quasi-social interactions he has with shop clerks and people in his village. Most telling, however, may be his intermixing with One Eye, which opens the novel. Ray is drawn to One Eye's picture on a storefront notice from an animal shelter; he bends over to see better, such that "the shadows shift with my bending body and blank out the glass of the jumble shop window . . . I see my head sticking out of your back like a bizarre excrescence. I see my own mangled face peering dolefully from the black" (4). Here Ray and One Eye become a single composite creature, whose two heads create the formal possibility of the novel's simultaneous first- and second-person narration. The

9. Taxonomically, sharks are vertebrates, but their skeletons are entirely cartilage.

10. While, in her interview with Estévez-Saá, Baume declines to characterize Ray and her other protagonist to date, Frankie, as "as representations of disability in fiction" (2020, 124), the way that Ray elaborates on the flailing of his hands is one that, in conjunction with some of his other traits, might be read as autistic. Costello-Sullivan offers a nuanced consideration of a similar marginalized character in Catriona Lally's *Eggshells*, noting the challenge for Ireland "to integrate diverse neurological perspectives and citizens as it labors under the shadow of their shameful treatment in the past" (2021, n.p.).

man-dog chimera gives space for Ray to dream the dog's dreams, an irreal possibility that the book never undercuts.

Of course, the hybrid narrative voice accompanies recurrent attention to a single perspective, most prominently in the way that Ray talks about One Eye's "lonely peephole." Ray always couples these words to one another, emphasizing singularity as well as the sense of body as dwelling. His phrase makes the idea of seeing strange, calling attention to the separation of a mind that perceives and a body that is inhabited, part of the novel's larger attention to the body, whether Ray's or someone else's, as an object: "He's a triangular man . . . the silhouette of a root vegetable" (Baume 2013, 6). After One Eye almost bites a child, "I feel like I swallowed a free bird and it's lashing its wings against the bars of my bones" (191). Baume's flora and fauna metaphors are congruent with the novel's overarching attention to the blurriness between humans, animals, and objects. But, even more, the latter metaphor raises questions about the ways we choose vehicles and tenors. The complicated image relies on a pair of comparisons, a racing heart to a bird and ribs to a birdcage or jail. The body serves as both captor and captive, undermining the substitutions on which the metaphors rely in a way that can be read, through Umberto Eco's construction (1983), as catachrestic.

Eco's discussion of catachresis recognizes its fundamental interpenetration with the very idea of metaphor itself. Noting that this figure of speech "invents a new term using at least two already known (and expressed) and presupposing at least another one that is unexpressed" (1983, 239), Eco attends to the way that some metaphors become "institutionalized . . . transformed into a codified lexeme" (233); the idea of the ribcage is itself such a codification. Beyond such well-worn phrases, Eco posits "an institutive catachresis (language creates metaphors even outside of poetry, simply out of a need to find names for things). And if institutive catachreses require interpretive labor, it is because the latent proportion (which could be expressed in a simile) does not exist before the metaphor: it must be found" (233).

Interestingly, Eco's example of an institutive catechesis is "inflationary spiral/spirale inflazionistica," a term that in both English and

Italian the Google Ngram Viewer shows to be vanishingly rare prior to the early 1930s, after which its rate of frequency in each language's publications rises and falls in an accurate correspondence to the inflation rates as compiled by the US Bureau of Labor Statistics. As concern over inflation peaked during World War II and again in the 1970s, the number of times the term was used also rose. As Eco wrote in the late 1970s, Italy's inflation rate was even higher than that of the United States, about the same as Ireland's, wavering between 17 and 20 percent. In this context, the question of interpretive labor and the work of finding a metaphor becomes more tangible, underscoring the unfamiliar economic terrain for nations experiencing simultaneous increases in inflation and unemployment—a combination the midcentury Keynesian compact had said could not exist. The need to find a new metaphor arises within a new economic landscape.

Back to Baume's lashing free bird: this is the first time the phrase appears in the novel, and Ray here identifies its accompanying emotion as rage, reflecting on how he experienced anger earlier in his life: "I never broke anything and I always tidied up afterwards. My anger was a tea-candle, one more useless sensation amongst a snowslide of useless sensations I suffer but never act upon. Now it's a whole cathedral of tea-candles, an inferno" (2013, 191). Ray becomes the grammatical subject here only at the moment of naming his suffering and denying his agency, a feeling that elides the difference between past and present tense. The initial metaphor of the tea candle—a flame so small as to be powerless—strains alongside its elaboration in the present, when the traditional religious setting for such candles leads to the recognition of their combined power. Yet the sense that the feeling is useless persists as well, in part through the reference to a snowslide, the frozen counterpoint to the flames. If Ray's metaphoric vehicle here is an avalanche, the tenor expressed is that of the suffocation or smothering of affect, a diminution that creates another catachrestic strain, overriding the presumed power of the crashing snow as well as the inferno itself. Somehow fire and ice, extremes of temperature that gesture toward a global environmental crisis that is a backdrop elsewhere in the novel as well, are marshaled in support of powerlessness. The effect is not unlike that of humanity in the face of the planetary devastation we have wrought, emphasizing nature's force and our own smallness.

Baume's knotty metaphors recall the animacy hierarchy as explained by Mel Chen, here in ways that would seem to exonerate humans from culpability. Chen explains that they "read this hierarchy, treated by linguists as an avowedly *conceptual* organization of worldly and abstract things with grammatical consequence, as naturally also an ontology of *affect*: for animacy hierarchies are precisely about which things can or cannot affect—or be affected by—which other things within a specific scheme of possible action" with attention to the hierarchy's "leakages, its 'ambivalent grammaticalities'— to map the ways in which such a conceptual hierarchy cannot but fail . . . must continually interanimate in spite of its apparent fixedness" (2012, 30, emphasis in original). Ray's entire existence has been about dehumanization and ostracism, such that his experience repeatedly shows the leakages of grammatical animacy hierarchies like the one in the tea-candle metaphor, in which he is acted upon by natural forces and by his own emotions. His subject position in the sentence in which he explains deemphasizes him by locating his first-person pronoun in a restrictive clause within a prepositional phrase, subordinate to anger both grammatically and conceptually.

The second time the novel refers to the "free bird," it is a "free bird of fear inside my chest but beneath its wings my organs are putrefying, bit by bit" (Baume 2013, 271). Ray says this to One Eye moments before putting the dog out of the car and releasing its handbrake so that it will plunge off a cliff into the sea with himself still in it. Again we see a disordered temporality: Ray is not yet dead but speaks of his body's decay, a connection also to the toothache that troubles him throughout the novel, as well as to the way that his father's corpse decayed in the attic. The novel then bifurcates into two alternate endings, one in which the car "will roll us home to the salmon-pink house, grudgingly yet irresistibly" (271), whereupon Ray makes sausages for himself and One Eye, and the other ending, in an epilogue, that shows One Eye as a "tiny figure, right on the cliffslope's edge, like a sock puppet to the theatre of the open sea" (273), looking down where the car has just fallen before turning to run in seeming recognition that he is alone again. The second-person ending affirms animal community and domestic normalcy; its vitalized car, of a piece with others in the book, is part of a world that imagines life beyond animacy hierarchies and other exclusionary mechanisms. The second ending, the placement of which gives it primacy and truth-value, returns us to the third-person narration that opened the novel, a state of affairs that was abusive and dangerous for One Eye and for the provisional bond he and Ray develop. To return to Bal's explanation of Benveniste (1993), the third-person section relies on a pronoun that refers to someone absent or excluded. Narrative norms stand in for social norms, and the novel ends conceding to them.

Throughout *spill*, Ray's connection to One Eye is a recognition of their shared ostracism; each comes from a troubled past, insufficiently nurtured and socialized. Baume poignantly emphasizes that, in human and dog alike, this inability to interact normatively with others does not diminish the desire for connection. Being shunned creates an outcast; Ray comes to see that, for all his strangeness, it is the creation and sustenance of normalcy that is the problem. "See the bare branches of the cherry trees. The houses with people inside and the shops with goods inside and the church with all its chalky gods inside, and everything and everybody remaining inside, because it's Christmas, of course, and there nowhere to go. . . . See the takeaway, the chip shop. The pub, the other pub. The grocer's and the hairdressing salon, all shut. See the community we were insidiously hounded from. See how community is only a good thing when you're part of it" (Baume 2013, 266). The list of structures begins with the equation of people and goods, moving through a spatial map of any small village in Ireland, given shape by its businesses and its church; the image is of banal normalcy, and, indeed, the turn that Ray makes to point out the flip side of inclusion and normativity is rejection and atypicality. *spill* demonstrates the way that old Irish ideas of narrowness and exclusion, of conformity and judgment, have not vanished so much as been succeeded by another, even more powerful, version of othering.

The othering that drives Ray to suicide indicts an Irish society that has not so much left behind its stifling conformities as evolved them into modern form. Melatu Okorie's story "Under the Awning" (2018) makes clear that the systems of community that create in-group and out-group dynamics persist in a twenty-first-century Ireland often self-congratulatory about its efforts at inclusion. Using second-person address as a means to shed fresh light on the supposedly well-understood or now-diminished racist logics of belonging, Okorie exposes white fragility and the systems of rhetorical engagement that shore up the existing structures. Like Baume's, Okorie's narrative brackets its second-person narration with the third person. She begins with a scene of a writing workshop, making clear the protagonist's sense of alienation through her spatial position in the room: she is the last to enter and takes the first chair she comes to, without looking around or engaging with others. Her seat turns out to be "directly opposite" (25) the leader, a framing that emphasizes her feelings of anxiety. Asked to read the entirety of her story aloud, she does so, "stuttering" (26). The story she reads is related to us in italics, occupying well over half of the entire narrative; it is a second-person story that itself begins with a character feeling awkward about her spatial position: "*You stood under the awning outside the Spar shop, staring straight ahead, barely moving, a pink plastic folder tucked under your arm, waiting for the drizzle to stop*" (26, italics in original). The importance of physical placement is underscored by the prepositional phrase that comprises the frame story's title and opens the second-person interior story. This focus persists as an interest of the interior story, which notes that the seat beside the speaker on the bus is the last one to be taken and makes repeated use of inner/outer distinctions. Gazes are also a motif in both layers of the narrative; the protagonist is not questioned directly about her choice of second-person address but instead sees "expectant eyes raised in her direction" (38). Within her story, "you" speak to your mother without looking at her and make moves to avoid being seen.

While other characters I've discussed in this chapter like Ray, Ryan, and Georgie struggle with invisibility, both Okorie's protagonist and the subject of her story seek to be less visible physically. Ultimately, however, their struggles align with those of the other characters in that each seeks to be truly seen, though neither of Okorie's endings holds out much hope.

Just as Baume's Ray never tells us his name, instead giving us something of a riddle to solve, Okorie's pair of narrators in "Under the Awning" are not directly named, although the feedback from the writing group pushes the frame protagonist (whom I will call "the girl," as Okorie does) to insert a protagonist's name into the interior story, to which the girl responds in revision, naming "you" Didi. The choice not to name characters extends beyond these two; Okorie does not give proper names to anyone in the writing workshop, instead using single letters in alphabetical order, a stripping away of identifying details.[11] These choices work, like the second-person mode of address, to demonstrate the breadth or wide applicability of the experiences related. As the girl puts it in explaining her choice of second person, "I didn't want to personalise it by using a first person and giving the character a particular voice" (2018, 38). The refusal to render as individual a set of experiences that are common does not sit well with the writing group, whose critiques coalesce around two related issues: the formal decision to narrate in second person, and the failure of the episodes narrated to align with their own self-serving understanding of race in Ireland. The group's reaction to Didi's experiences of racism and exclusion exhibit recognizable signs of white fragility, most notably in their insistence on the limits of the story's reach. In suggesting that the events it relates are too "bleak and negative" (37), or that a white character is being "misread" (38) by Didi, the writing workshop members decline to reflect on their own perspective and instead seek reassurance. Their critiques of Didi

---

11. Flynn (2021) makes the connection to Beckett's tramp in *Waiting for Godot*, which underscores the existential concerns of the interior story's protagonist.

as "paranoid" (38) and full of "self-loathing and self-hatred" (39) further personalize her experiences, bracketing them as one person's story rather than representative of larger racial dynamics. As Claire Bracken explains it, this portion of the story "signals the egocentric nature of the classmates (respondents all begin with 'I'), as well as demonstrating the fundamental failure to listen to accounts of racism in the Irish context and a refusal to see and hear the regulatory operations of biopower at work" (2020, 152).

In this light, the choice of second-person narration is as much an ideological one as a formal one, rendering the comment from C particularly ironic: "There is something about writing in the second person that prevents me from caring about the character. I always know I'm reading a work of fiction" (Okorie 2018, 37). C resists occupying the position of the marginalized Didi, even retracting empathy, a move that underscores the imperative that a Black voice assimilate to white expectations. The girl's efforts to respond to the feedback she receives make up the final movement of the story. Okorie begins this section by making clear that the girl wants to keep her mode of address but makes changes anyway. Her own efforts to adapt are mirrored by the changes she forces upon Didi's thoughts within the story. In the original, Didi had felt comfortable telling Dermot, a white man interested in integration and charity work, about a number of the uncomfortable, hurtful experiences she has had. Dermot's responses had been to diminish the significance of specific events and to question Didi's analysis of the motives of the white people involved, leading her to list a number of even more disturbing experiences that she wants to tell him but doesn't. In the revised version, Didi does the work of placing herself in the position of another and trying to imagine his response: "*You tried to reason out his point of view in your head. Your classmates who asked their friends to mind their bags were actually not doing anything wrong; the bus driver who dropped you off two stops away from your bus stop could have done so due to road works; the man in the supermarkets who asked your mother for a BJ is just sick; and the children who called out 'Blackie' at you whenever they saw you passing could just be what they were, children*" (40). Didi here internalizes Dermot's perspective and diminishes her own; in the same way, the girl's choice to implement to suggested revisions, which she then emails to the rest of the group, signals her ability to see through their eyes.

Two aspects of these revisions are important here: first of all, as the girl minimizes the relentless impact of the continual prejudice to which Didi is exposed, she also shifts the grammar of her story in ways that are not in response to any of the critiques from the workshop. In the first draft we read, the unnamed protagonist's trajectory moves from finding in Dermot someone in whom she can confide, to telling him some of the aggression to which she's been exposed, after which he discounts her views and she lists what she doesn't tell him, beginning each of the next three long sentences with "*And you wanted to tell him about*" (Okorie 2018, 36), concluding with "*You wanted to tell him all these things but you didn't*" (36). Following this disclosure, she buys a diary, the implication being that writing will be a space where she can explore the things she doesn't say to Dermot. But I want to focus for the moment on the anaphora: Okorie's use of the same phrase multiple times emphasizes the monotony and inescapability of the racist attention the protagonist receives. Its polysyndeton works, like other moments of polysyndeton analyzed earlier, to level the distinction between the experiences; the combination of the two effects shows how the aggressions may seem of different sizes or intensities but their impacts all occur in an identical register. This section follows on the back-and-forth of the exchange with Dermot in which each sentence began with "You told him" or "He told you," a tennis match whose repetitions make clear the lack of progression, similarly showing the failure of conversation to advance or create understanding. The story features this pattern elsewhere—an early paragraph conveys homesickness with three successive sentences beginning "It meant" (27)—but it is in the final pages that it achieves a feeling of rhythm. Okorie's moments of anaphora forecast bleak prospects for understanding.

The girl's revisions for her writing group depart from the carefully patterned paragraph that concluded the first draft in other ways that suggest white control and foreclosure. Responding to their advice, she inserts an awkward sentence in which the mother in the story addresses her daughter as "Didi," a narrowing of focus that dilutes the story's representational force. Even more devastating to her precise sentence structures is the way all of the exchange with Dermot becomes a single sentence with multiple semicolons. The narrative moves all its dialogue from the spoken to the imagined, and displaces "You" from the agent in each sentence, instead giving subject position to the various aggressors. "You" is no longer the subject, just the object of the taunts and animosity. The conditional "could" in each segment of the sentence gives entry to the racial rationalizations that Dermot and the members of the writing group require of the girl. The new sentence lacks the grammatically tight structure that had been so meticulously crafted throughout the story, which begins the majority of its sentences with a pronoun or a conjunction plus a pronoun. The revisions address anxieties outside of the story that are presented in the guise of technical feedback, and the quality of the prose is correspondingly diminished.

Another salient feature of the revisions is the extent to which they satisfy the girl's readers—sadly, the answer is not much. The replies she gets are for the most part reiterations of the original criticisms. Her readers double down on the centrality of their own perspective and their need to believe that Ireland is not as racist as the girl's story suggests it to be: "I did think it could be useful to still temper the racism she experienced with examples of kind behavior to. In places there is so much bias, so much prejudice, that it almost swallows itself" (Okorie 2018, 40–41), says B, while D advises that she "work on the bleak picture. How you would do this, I don't know" (41). Both of these respondents also say they like the use of second person, suggesting a complicated resistance to the girl's insights; they want to tell her what to present to them while purporting to allow the voice to stand. Bracken astutely notes that the more overt support for the girl's narrative choice "come directly after she has sent through the story with changes, changes that (again with heavily loaded irony) supposedly resolve the story's characters' concerns about discrimination. Thus the email exchange ultimately compounds the lonely vulnerabilities of the narrator" (2020, 152). The fact that C, who claimed not be able to care about the second-person story, does not reply at all, "ruthlessly undercut[s] any affirmative vision of affective solidarity" (152). It is the report of this fact that ends the story, severing the lines of communication within the story and metafictively. The "continuity" between the live workshop and subsequent email exchanges had been, for Bracken, "a materialist plane that holds together actuality and virtuality in nondualist terms" (152), as the girl continues to offer emotional vulnerability in the face of critique. This reading recognizes the various relational networks constituted within the story that exceed conventional ideas of individual autonomy and agency, providing a connection to Baume's story. We see community as a space with the potential for exclusion as well as inclusion, for coercion as well as collaboration. While the writing group is largely painful for the girl, given all the misunderstandings and misreadings, the severing of sociality via that silence and apathy of C denies the girl agency in a far more aggressive way.

While Okorie concludes *her* story with this clear note of intentional disconnection on the part of a white reader, another moment within the girl's narrative suggests why. Dermot had staged an integration project that brought children from migrant and Irish families together to play football. The narration is clear that the program has at best a very limited success: the players divide into teams based on citizenship status, and parents stand in racially segregated groups on the sidelines, largely ignoring one another. Dermot later questions Didi as to whether she thought the event was successful, but *"you dodged the question. You are yet to feel comfortable telling someone something was grand when you didn't think it was"* (2018, 35). This latter sentence is the only one in either the frame or interior story that is in present tense; its use of the Irish catchall of "grand" positions Didi as fluent in the local dialect while its sentiment shows her as yet incapable of bland social insincerity. The tense shift elevates the message outside of its immediate context and extends it temporally, suspending the feeling of discomfort in an ongoing timelessness for Didi, for the girl, and perhaps even for Okorie herself.

Okorie has in interviews been emphatic as to the hardships of life for migrants to Ireland at the same time as she has resisted efforts to position her as writing therapeutically, to cope with her position as a person in need of international protection in direct provision or, mimetically, as a writer whose material is drawn mainly from personal experience. To invest her stories with such context would again be to make individual and personal what is structural. Despite repeatedly shrugging off of the burden of representation, Okorie does not downplay Irish racism and exclusion, acknowledging that "I have also felt the most isolated and a visible outsider here [in Ireland]" (Martín-Ruiz 2017, 180). The linking of isolation to visibility reconnects to the moments bookending the story of Didi. After Dermot silences her by failing to recognize the effects of ongoing systemic and personal racism on her, "*You cried for a long time on your bed after he left, confused at how alone you felt with so many people around you and the next day, you went into this same Spar shop and bought a diary*" (Okorie 2018, 36–37). The story's opening was at the Spar, where "*you were desperate not to stand out*" (27); the notion of being alone and too visible structures both moments, yet another place in which Okorie has granted the girl a lovely literary parallel—clearly we are meant to see that the story as first read aloud is well written. "This same Spar shop" suggests that the story here curls back on itself, the deictic indication acting almost as another signal of the present tense, locating Didi physically in front of the shop and perhaps placing her at the beginning of the story, a move that would render the racist environment enclosing and inescapable, much as the cold silence of C does.

"Under the Awning" is the second story in Okorie's collection *This Hostel Life*; the first is the title story, narrated in first person by Beverléé, a Congolese woman with limited French and even more limited English. Okorie has explained that she invented the language of the story: "I had to coin out what I'll call a mixture of Englishes" (Martín-Ruiz 2017, 181). In a couple of moments Beverlée slips into second person, as when explaining how direct provision works and why she is dissatisfied with it: "Dis direct provision business is all the same, you see, because even if you collect provision for every week or you collect for every month, it is still somebody dat is give you the provision. Nothing is better than when you decide something for yourself" (Okorie 2018, 3). In departing from the personal first person that comprises the rest of the story, Beverlée makes her statement more universal. And, indeed, the narrative tension in the story revolves around unequal treatment, when a man is given honey that other hostel residents are denied. Beverlée's friend Ngozi takes a stand against this, and the hostel manager closes the provision windows, punishing all for the behavior of one. The story ends as Beverlée must leave her friend and see to the laundry: "From the window outside, me I can still see her stand alone for the dining room, fighting for her honey" (23). Okorie frames Ngozi with the window, emphasizing her visibility and isolation and the futility of fighting alone.

The manager's response—a shutting down reminiscent of the way that C withdraws from conversation—pits members of the hostel community against one another. Some wonder angrily why sugar isn't an adequate substitute, failing to see the way that the absence of choice speaks to larger losses of agency. As Masha Gessen notes, "The thing about living in Direct Provision is that the management or staff of the hospitality company can enter your room anytime, whether to empty the trash or to check on the state of the room. You have forfeited not only agency but also privacy" (2019, n.p.). Gessen's move into second person for this part of the article alone echoes the rhetorical moves the girl makes in writing her story in "Under the Awning," with both recognizing the limited agency afforded by the second-person pronoun. Okorie's choice to use honey as Ngozi's flash point is read by Sara Martín-Ruiz as "literal and metaphorical" (2017, 175); the idea of asylum via migration to a land of milk and honey is ludicrously undercut by the biopolitical mechanics of Ireland's direct provision system. It is to this system that I now turn.

Loneliness and Community

At the moment that Kondo first offered a weary capitalist class freedom from the exhaustions of consumption, the world was in the midst of one of the largest mass movements of humans in history, a refugee crisis of unimaginable proportions, one that began in 2014 to give rise in Europe to far-right populist movements. The global horror at the discovery of a drowned toddler, Alan Kurdi, on a beach in Italy in 2015 raised sympathies and also anxieties at the perception of the EU "flooded" with migrants coming by sea. It was in the context of frequent reports of overcrowded ships in peril on the Mediterranean that the Brexit movement gained momentum. While fears of being overrun spurred "Leave" voters in the United Kingdom and hate speech in Ireland, neither Britain nor Ireland received many migrants, each taking in less than .5 percent of the total population of their respective nations.

Arriving refugees in 2014 could hardly have been further from Kondo's "burden of excess," often having had to leave behind nearly everything and losing what little they carried in transit. As Arielle Bernstein writes in a poignant reflection on Kondo's book in light of her own family's multiple displacements during the twentieth century, "Embracing a minimalist lifestyle is an act of trust. For a refugee, that trust has not yet been earned. The idea that going through items cheerfully evaluating whether or not objects inspire happiness is fraught for a family like mine, for whom cherished items have historically been taken away. For my grandparents, the question wasn't whether an item sparked joy, but whether it was necessary for their survival. In America, that obsession transformed into a love for all items, whether or not they were valuable in a financial or emotional sense" (2016, n.p.). The sorts of objects that are necessary for living don't enter into Kondo's equation, and she is blithe about the human ability to retain memories without physical corollaries or spurs. Those latter, "sentimental" objects that carry meaning for their owners are often the very things that refugees must leave behind.

The Asylum Archive was created by Vukašin Nedeljkovic in 2015, a photographic testimony to the period of direct provision for asylum seekers in Ireland. Nedeljkovic's intervention is designed as advocacy, so this "most appalling treatment of people" is not forgotten (2019). A collection of photographs from dozens of direct provision sites, the images are "devoid of people to emphasize the dual burdens of visibility and invisibility experienced by those seeking asylum in Ireland as a psychological, social and legislative process" (Nedeljkovic n.d., 1). Nedeljkovic's attention to the simultaneous visibility and invisibility of people seeking asylum chimes with the attention to the embodiment of the nonwhite characters in Okorie's story alongside the refusal of the writing group to acknowledge their reported lived experiences.

Just as Nedeljkovic's images are devoid of people, they are also devoid of personal possessions. As Charlotte McIvor notes, "The direct provision hostels and their residents don't seem to have a physicality," hence an archive of absence, traces, ghosts (n.d., 4). We cannot see enough in the photographs to construct imagined lives for the people who exist under the conditions Nedeljkovic documents, and this is one of the archive's complexly layered points: life itself is truncated by dehumanizing conditions. Claire Bracken has read the photographs as an assertion of the privations associated with Giorgio Agamben's notions of bare life: a mode of living reduced to mere existence, without humanity, dignity, or basic human rights, exiled to the peripheries of the political and legal system (2020).

Nedeljkovic organizes the archive's images into "Direct Provision Centres" and "Found Objects," among other categories. This latter group comprises both such carceral detritus as sign-in sheets and timetables, as well as abject toys—dirty dolls, a plastic "talking ball," a child's truck. The talking ball is one of those vile pedagogic objects that, in trying to make play educational or education playful, manages instead to make both play and education feel like chores. On the archive site, the ball is depicted in full and then in four close-ups (fig. 1). Nedeljkovic's framing and presentation emphasize the

1. "Talking Ball, found object in Railway Hostel grounds, displayed in a glass box, 37 cm L x 37 cm W x 37 cm H, 2011." Photograph by Vukašin Nedeljkovic. Courtesy of Vukašin Nedeljkovic, creator and curator of the Asylum Archive.

dirt and the eerie emptiness of the object representations on the surface of the ball. Its inverted label is a hodgepodge of catchwords that congeal into an ungrammatical and aspirational torrent: "VTECH Talking LITTLE SMART PRESS 'n play ball." Depicted in two colors and at least four fonts of varying sizes, this brand name-cum-instruction manual reads almost like a sentence fragment, one that butchers the conventions of capitalization, adjective ordering, and contraction formation. Particularly ironic is the way that "little" and "smart," each of which is presumably meant to refer to the tyke playing with this toy, instead apply grammatically to the ball itself, ordered such that the former seems to diminish the latter. The choice to position the ball so that this title is upside down indicates its ill fit with its context.

There's a poignancy to Nedeljkovic's title for the photographs, *Talking Ball*, which carries within it a contradiction: more than "speaking," "talking" implies some sort of process of interaction, a communicative exchange with an implied listener. It feels unlikely that the ball speaks or talks—conversation is not a feature of the asylum setup. The asylum seekers detained in the direct provision centres find their opportunities for such interaction severely circumscribed by their isolation from the cities and towns in which they've been placed. As T. J. Hughes argues, direct provision separates asylum seekers from resettled refugees and curtails humane support: "The capacity of a person to integrate into Irish society becomes undermined by these processing regimes and destabilizes the capacity for agency subsequently forcing asylum-seekers further to the margins of Irish society" (2020, 100). Analogously, the enclosure of the ball in a glass box removes its use value as an object of play and seals off the possibility that it could actually be heard. The framing of the ball and the photographs themselves remove the possibility of engagement, enacting precisely the estrangement enforced by the direct provision system and creating the profound loneliness that Okorie refers to as well as a feature of the institutional frameworks.

Another series of images in the archive are of an "Action Man" truck. The Action Man doll is the British market version of the American toy GI Joe, an action figurine in the shape of a soldier in production since the 1960s. Like the other toys in the archive's series, these photographs show objects devoid of context, on blank backgrounds. Deprived of relationality, they lack function and meaning. Nor do they include people, not even the humanoid action figure who would presumably ride in the truck. Nedeljkovic works with found objects, as his original caption indicates: "What Has Happened With the Child That Owned the Truck?—Found Object in Railway Hostel Grounds, Kiltimagh, 2011;" nevertheless, the absence of the man himself contributes to the loneliness that emanates from the photographs.[12] As in the talking ball images, these photographs emphasize

12. As of 2020, the caption has been updated to "Yellow Truck, found object in the railway hostel, Kiltimagh, 2011."

the dirtiness of their object. The Action Man label conflates man with machine and highlights the immobility of asylum seekers, as does the choice not to include any full images of the truck; our view of it is partial, and we cannot tell if it is functional enough to be useable as a toy. The caption's reference to a child uses the departed child to haunt the image, suggesting an untold story. The question format of the original caption creates narrative momentum that the archive makes clear is curtailed by the structural containment of direct provision, which thwarts movement in favor of endless suspension. As Gessen has explained in their aptly titled article "Ireland's Strange, Cruel System for Asylum Seekers," the condition of a refugee is one of waiting, of temporal abeyance. We see here the wages of a system that treats people as objects, that replaces them with objects. Those seeking to highlight feelings of immobility and powerlessness would do well to focus attention on those traces of humanity, looking past affective engagement. Nedeljkovic's strategic use of objects to tell human stories, like Okorie's and Baume's second-person narratives, resists any comforting rush of sympathy or sentiment. Their shared move to impersonality relies upon recognition of the limits of most conceptions of the human and the ways that ethical engagement requires an expanded understanding of networks, connections, and mutual obligations.

Postscript

One of the epigraphs that begins this book is Nietzsche's question "Is the philosopher not permitted to rise above a faith in grammar?" (1886, 34). Elsewhere, Nietzsche links cause and effect to subject and predicate: "It is only the snare of language . . . presenting all activity as conditioned by an agent—the 'subject'—that blinds us to this fact. . . . No such agent exists; there is no 'being' behind the doing, acting, becoming; the 'doer' has simply been added to the deed by the imagination—the doing is everything" (1887, 178–79). If there is no being behind the doing, then the lack of agency depicted in the novels and images in the last chapter uncovers a long-standing condition in which we do not have a self, essence, or unity.[1] Our neoliberal moment has in this case merely laid bare what was visible to Nietzsche long ago, and, with some variation, to Hannah Arendt more recently—that, as Bonnie Honig explains,

> even in the public realm, where we do have a coherent, identitied self, we do not have a self in charge of itself. The stories reveal an actor, but this actor is not "an author or producer." His story and identity are community property. . . . And this seems fitting to an account that views the self as multiplicity, privileges action over actor, insists that identity is not the condition but the product of action, refuses to identify freedom with autonomy, grants only to spectators a vantage point from which action can be witnessed

1. This is a condition variously identified by Lash (2001); Beck (1986); and those attentive to the nomadic individuals of secondary modernity as well.

fully, and assigns to them the task of immortalizing the event by turning it into a story. (1988, 88–89)

Honig here examines Arendt's interest in the public realm, where democratic action takes place, suggesting that it is through such action that the self is produced. Moreover, art is figured as action; the self and its narrative belong to the collective and only exist if they are "comprehensible" (88) to their audience, which is itself responsible for the story. The ungrammaticalities and irrealisms of the texts throughout these pages need us as their audience; their events become immortal through our witness—directly, in the case of the Asylum Archive, but also through our recognition of the messages of the broken narratives that urge us beyond our own multiple, fractured selves and our own becalmed time into motion and collective action.

References

Index

References

Allen, Kieran. 2015. "Interpretations of the Irish Economic Crash." *Ireland under Austerity: Neoliberal Crisis, Neoliberal Solutions*, edited by Colin Coulter and Angela Nagle, 66–85. Manchester: Manchester Univ. Press.

Althusser, Louis. 2001. *Lenin and Philosophy and Other Essays*. Translated by Ben Brewster. New York: Monthly Review.

Arrigihi, Giovanni. 1994. *The Long Twentieth Century*. London: Verso.

Bal, Mieke. 1993. "First Person, Second Person, Same Person: Narrative as Epistemology." *New Literary History* 24 (2): 293–320.

Banfield, Ann. 1982. *Unspeakable Sentences: Narration and Representation in the Language of Fiction*. New York: Routledge & Kegan Paul.

Barry, Kevin. [2011] 2013. *City of Bohane*. Minneapolis: Graywolf.

Barry, Sebastian. 2011. *On Canaan's Side*. New York: Penguin.

Baume, Sara. 2013. *spill simmer falter wither*. Boston: Mariner.

Beatty, Aidan. 2019. "Marx and Engels, Ireland, and the Racial History of Capitalism." *Journal of Modern History* 91 (4): 815–47.

Beck, Ulrich. [1986] 1992. *Risk Society: Towards a New Modernity*. Translated by Mark Ritter. London: Sage.

———. 2009. *World at Risk*. Translated by Ciaran Cronin. Malden, MA: Polity.

———. 2013. "Risk, Class, Crisis, Hazards and Cosmopolitan Solidarity/Risk Community—Conceptual and Methodological Clarifications." Working paper of the Fondation maison des sciences de l'homme, FMSH-WP-2013-31, April 2013. https://halshs.archives-ouvertes.fr/halshs-00820297/document (accessed 23 May 2022).

Beck, Ulrich, and Beck-Gernsheim, Elisabeth. 2001. *Individualization: Institutionalized Individualism and Its Social and Political Consequences*. London: Sage.

Bender, Abby. Forthcoming. "Nursing the Revival: Patrick Pearse, Breast-feeding, and Sacrifice." In *The Irish Revival: A Complex Vision*, edited by Joseph Valente and Marjorie Howes. Syracuse, NY: Syracuse Univ. Press.

Bennett, Jane. 2010. *Vibrant Matter: A Political Ecology of Things*. Durham, NC: Duke Univ. Press.

Berlant, Lauren. 2011. *Cruel Optimism*. Durham, NC: Duke Univ. Press.

Bernstein, Arielle. 2016. "Marie Kondo and the Privilege of Clutter." *Atlantic*, 25 March 2016. https://www.theatlantic.com/entertainment/archive/2016/03/marie-kondo-and-the-privilege-of-clutter/475266/?utm_source=share&utm_campaign=share.

Bhattacharyya, Gargi. 2015. *Crisis, Austerity, and Everyday Life: Living in a Time of Diminishing Expectations*. Houndmills: Palgrave Macmillan.

Bielenberg, Kim. 2014. "A Brick Too Far." *Irish Independent*, 22 December 2014. https://www.independent.ie/irish-news/politics/a-brick-too-far-the-day-it-all-turned-sour-30856122.html.

"Block That Metaphor!" 1998. *New Yorker*, 12 October 12 1998. https://www.newyorker.com/magazine/1998/10/19/block-that-metaphor-2.

Boast, Hannah. 2020. *Hydrofictions: Water, Power, and Politics in Israeli and Palestinian Literature*. Edinburgh: Edinburgh Univ. Press.

Boltanski, Luc, and Ève Chiapello. 2005. *The New Spirit of Capitalism*. New York: Verso.

Bowen, Elizabeth. [1929] 2000. *The Last September*. New York: Anchor.

———. [1954] 2003. *A World of Love*. New York: Penguin.

Bracken, Claire. 2013. "Postfeminism and the Celtic Tiger: Deirdre O'Kane's Television Roles." In *Viewpoints: Theoretical Perspectives on Irish Visual Texts*, edited by Claire Bracken and Emma Radley, 157–71. Cork: Cork Univ. Press.

———. 2016. *Irish Feminist Futures*. London: Routledge.

———. 2020. "The Feminist Contemporary: The Contradictions of Critique." In *The New Irish Studies: Twenty-First-Century Critical Revisions*, edited by Paige Reynolds, 144–60. Cambridge: Cambridge Univ. Press.

Bracken, Claire, and Susan Cahill, eds. 2011. *Anne Enright*. Dublin: Irish Academic Press.

Breaking Dad. 2014. Written by Paul Howard. Gaiety Theatre, Dublin, 30 April 2014.

Brennan, Michael. 2019. *In Deep Water: How People, Politics And Protests Sank Irish Water.* Cork: Mercier.

Bresnihan, Patrick. 2015. "The Bio-Financialization of Irish Water: New Advances in the Neoliberalization of Vital Services." Undisciplined Environments, 27 August 2015. https://undisciplinedenvironments.org/2015 /08/27/the-neoliberalization-of-vital-services-the-bio-financialization -of-irish-water/.

"Brian Lenihan 'We All Partied' on Prime Time 24/11/10." YouTube video, 1:37, 25 November 2010. https://www.youtube.com/watch?v=YK7w6f XoYxo.

Brody, Jennifer DeVere. 2008. *Punctuation: Art, Politics, and Play.* Durham, NC: Duke Univ. Press.

Brouillette, Sarah, and David Thomas. 2016. "First Responses." *Comparative Literature Studies* 53 (3): 505–34.

Brouillette, Sarah, Mathias Nilges, and Emilio Sauri. 2017. *Literature and the Global Contemporary.* Cham: Palgrave Macmillan.

Brown, Wendy. 2015. *Undoing the Demos: Neoliberalism's Stealth Revolution.* Brooklyn, NY: Zone.

Buchanan, Jason. 2013. "The Home of the Tiger: Economic Speculation and the Ethics of Habitation." *Studi Irlandesi: A Journal of Irish Studies*, no. 3: 137–56.

———. 2017. "Gentrification as Famine in Post-Celtic Tiger Irish Literature." Presentation to the Columbia University Seminar on Irish Studies, 5 May 2017.

———. 2019. "Like a Scattering from a Fixed Point: Austerity Fiction and the Inequalities of Elsewhere." *Studi Irlandesi: A Journal of Irish Studies* 9, no. 9: 179–201.

Cahill, Susan. 2011. *Irish Literature in the Celtic Tiger Years, 1990 to 2008: Gender, Bodies, Memory.* London: Bloomsbury.

Calvino, Italo. [1972] 1974. *Invisible Cities.* Translated by William Weaver. San Diego, CA: Harcourt Brace Jovanovich.

Campbell, Niamh. 2020. "How Does a Young Writer Pay the Rent?" *Guardian,* 21 July 2020. https://www.theguardian.com/books/2020/jul/21/how-does -a-young-writer-pay-the-rent-affordable-education-coronavirus-pandemic.

Cargill, Angus. 2011. "Sebastian Barry: On Canaan's Side." The Thought Fox: Books and Culture from Faber & Faber, 27 July 2011. http://thethoughtfox.co.uk/sebastian-barry-on-canaans-side/.

Carroll, Hamilton, and Annie McClanahan. 2015. "Fictions of Speculation: Introduction." *Journal of American Studies* 49, no. 4: 655–61.

Casey, Moira. 2014. "'Built on Nothing but Bullshit and Good PR': Crime, Class Mobility, and the Irish Economy in the Novels of Tana French." CLUES: *A Journal of Detection* 32, no. 1 (Spring): 92–102.

Castells, Manuel. 1996. *The Rise of the Network Society, The Information Age: Economy, Society and Culture, Vol. 1.* Oxford: Blackwell.

Chen, Mel Y. 2012. *Animacies: Biopolitics, Racial Mattering, and Queer Affect.* Durham, NC: Duke Univ. Press.

Clarke, John, and Janet Newman. 2012. "The Alchemy of Austerity." *Critical Social Policy* 32, no. 3: 299–319.

Cleary, Joe. 2007. *Outrageous Fortune: Capital and Culture in Modern Ireland.* Dublin: Field Day.

———. 2017. "Widening Gyres: Irish Expatriate Fiction between the American and Chinese Centuries." Unpublished manuscript.

———. 2018. "'Horseman, Pass By!': The Neoliberal World System and the Crisis in Irish Literature." *boundary 2* 45, no. 1(February): 135–69.

———. 2021. "The Irish Realist Novel." In *Irish Literature in Transition: 1980–2020*, edited by Eric Falci and Paige Reynolds, 211–27. Cambridge: Cambridge Univ. Press.

Coakley, Maurice. 2016. "Ireland, Europe, and the Global Crisis." *Journal of World-Systems Research* 22, no. 1: 177–201.

Coates, Ta-Nahesi. 2015. *Between the World and Me.* New York: Spiegel & Grau.

The Commitments. 1991. Directed by Alan Parker. Beacon Pictures, Twentieth Century Fox.

Conceição, Pedro. 2019. "Beyond Income, Beyond Averages, Beyond Today: Inequalities in Human Development in the 21st Century." https://digitallibrary.un.org/record/3846848?ln=en (accessed 6 July 2022).

Conger, Kate, Jack Healy and Lucy Tompkins. 2020. "Churches Were Eager to Reopen. Now They Are Confronting Coronavirus Cases." *New York Times*, 8 July 2020. https://www.nytimes.com/2020/07/08/us/coronavirus-churches-outbreaks.html.

Congressional Budget Office. 2011. "Estimated Impact of Automatic Budget Enforcement Procedures Specified in the Budget Control Act." 12 September 2011. https://www.cbo.gov/publication/42754.

Connolly, Claire. 2011. *A Cultural History of the Irish Novel, 1790–1829.* Cambridge: Cambridge Univ. Press.

Connor, Gregory, Thomas Flavin, and Brian Kelly. 2012. "The U.S. and Irish Credit Crises: Their Distinctive Differences and Common Features." *Journal of International Money and Finance* 31 (2012): 60–79.

Cooper, Melinda. 2017. *Family Values: Between Neoliberalism and the New Social Conservatism.* Brooklyn, NY: Zone.

Cooper, Melinda, and Angela Mitropoulos. 2009. "The Household Frontier." *ephemera: theory and politics in organization* 9, no. 4: 363–68.

Cornis-Pope, Marcel. 1991. *Hermeneutic Desire and Critical Rewriting: Narrative Interpretation in the Wake of Poststructuralism.* New York: Palgrave Macmillan.

Costello, Norma. 2014. "The Irish Are Protesting Because They Don't Want to Pay to Drink Crappy Water." *Vice,* 9 October 2014. https://www.vice.com/en_us/article/nnqk8g/irish-protest-groups-have-had-enough-of-paying-for-crappy-water-467 (accessed 27 July 2020).

Costello-Sullivan, Kathleen. 2021. "Disability, Embodiment, and Shame in Caitriona Lally's *Eggshells.*" In *Irish Shame,* ed. Joseph Valente and Seán Kennedy, forthcoming. Edinburgh: Edinburgh Univ. Press.

Coulter, Colin. 2015. "Ireland under Austerity: An Introduction to the Book." In *Ireland under Austerity: Neoliberal Crisis, Neoliberal Solutions,* edited by Colin Coulter and Angela Nagle, 1–43. Manchester: Manchester Univ. Press.

Coulter, Colin, and Angela Nagle, eds. 2015. *Ireland under Austerity: Neoliberal Crisis, Neoliberal Solutions.* Manchester: Manchester Univ. Press.

Cronin, Michael. 2002. "Speed Limits: Ireland, Globalisation, and the War against Time." In *Reinventing Ireland: Culture, Society and the Global Economy,* edited by Peadar Kirby, Luke Gibbons, and Michael Cronin, 54–66. London: Pluto.

Cullingford, Elizabeth Butler. *Ireland's Others: Ethnicity and Gender in Irish Literature and Popular Culture.* South Bend, IN: Univ. of Notre Dame Press, 2001.

————. 2014. "American Dreams: Emigration or Exile in Contemporary Irish Fiction?" *Éire-Ireland* 49, nos. 3–4 (Fall–Winter): 60–94.

Curran, Dean. 2013. "Risk Society and the Distribution of Bads: Theorizing Class in the Risk Society." *British Journal of Sociology* 64, no. 1: 44–62.

Davies, Dominic, and Elleke Boehmer. 2018. *Planned Violence: Post/Colonial Urban Infrastructure, Literature, and Culture.* Cham: Palgrave Macmillan.

Davies, William. 2018. *Nervous States: How Feeling Took Over the World.* London: Jonathan Cape.

Deckard, Sharae. 2016. "Review: Solar Bones Is That Extraordinary Thing." *Irish Times*, 21 October 2016. https://www.irishtimes.com/culture/books/solar-bones-is-that-extraordinary-thing-an-accessible-experiment-virtuosic-yet-humane-1.2838095.

————. 2017. "Capitalism's Long-Spiral: Periodicity, Temporality, and the Global Contemporary in World Literature," in *Literature and the Global Contemporary*, edited by Sarah Brouillette, Mathias Nilges, and Emilio Sauri, 83–102. New York: Palgrave Macmillan.

————. 2019. "Water Shocks: Neoliberal Hydrofiction and the Crisis of 'Cheap Water.'" *Atlantic Studies* 16, no. 1: 108–25.

————. n.d. "Neoliberal Memory and the Market: Financialization, Algorithmic Governmentality, and Boom Fiction in Iceland and Ireland." Preprint draft. https://www.academia.edu/36874836/Neoliberal_Memory_and_the_Market_Financialization_Algorithmic_Governmentality_and_Boom_Fiction_in_Iceland_and_Ireland (accessed 20 October 2020).

Deckard, Sharae, and Stephen Shapiro, eds. 2019. *World Literature, Neoliberalism, and the Culture of Discontent.* Cham: Palgrave Macmillan.

De Loughry, Treasa, and Mike McCormack. 2019. "'. . . A Tiny Part of That Greater Circum-Terrestrial Grid': A Conversation with Mike McCormack." *Irish University Review* 49, no. 1 (May): 105–16.

De Man, Paul. 1978. "The Epistemology of Metaphor." *Critical Inquiry* 5, no. 1: 13–30.

Derksen, Jeffrey. 2009. *Annihilated Time: Poetry and Other Politics.* Vancouver: Talonbooks.

Derrida, Jacques. 1974. "White Mythology: Metaphor in the Text of Philosophy." Translated by F. C. T. Moore. *New Literary History* 6, no. 1: 5–74.

Dolowitz, David P. 2000. *Learning from America: Policy Transfer and the Development of the British Workfare State*. Maidenhead: Open Univ. Press.

Dwivedi, Divya, Henrik Skov Nielsen, and Richard Walsh, eds. 2018. *Narratology and Ideology: Negotiating Context, Form, and Theory in Postcolonial Narratives*. Columbus: Ohio State Univ. Press.

Dworkin, Ronald. 2000. *Sovereign Virtue*. Cambridge, MA: Harvard Univ. Press.

Dwyer Hickey, Christine. 2015. *The Lives of Women*. London: Atlantic.

Eagleton, Terry. 1995. *Heathcliff and the Great Hunger*. London: Verso.

Eco, Umberto. 1983. "The Scandal of Metaphor: Metaphorology and Semiotics." Translated by Christopher Paci. *Poetics Today* 4, no. 2: 217–57.

Edgeworth, Maria, and Richard Lovell Edgeworth. 1803. *Essay on Irish Bulls*. New York: J. Swaine.

Edmond, Amanda M. Corey. 1872. *Religious and Other Poems*. Boston: Gould & Lincoln.

Elliott, Jane. 2018. *The Microeconomic Mode: Political Subjectivity in Contemporary Popular Aesthetics*. New York: Columbia Univ. Press.

Elliott, Larry. 2011. "Ireland Becomes Poster Child for Implementing Austerity Programmes." *Guardian*, 27 November 2011. https://www.the guardian.com/business/economics-blog/2011/nov/27/ireland-poster -child-for-austerity-programmes.

Enright, Anne. 2015. *The Green Road*. New York: W. W. Norton.

Estévez-Saá, Margarita. 2020. "'An artist, first and foremost': An Interview with Sara Baume." *Estudios Irlandeses* 15, no. 2: 117–28.

European Central Bank. 2016. "What Are Haircuts?" 3 November 2016. https://www.ecb.europa.eu/explainers/tell-me-more/html/haircuts.en .html.

European Parliament. 2020. "Waste Management in the EU: Infographic with Facts and Figures." https://www.europarl.europa.eu/news/en/head lines/society/20180328STO00751/eu-waste-management-infographic -with-facts-and-figures (accessed 8 August 2020).

Fahey, Tom, Brian Nolan, and Bertrand Maître. 2004. *Housing, Poverty and Wealth in Ireland*. Issue 34 of the Combat Poverty Research Series. Dublin: Institute of Public Administration.

Faiola, Anthony. 2010. "Irish Government, Seeking Bailout, Unveils $20 Billion in Spending Cuts, Taxes." *Washington Post*, 24 November 2010.

http://www.washingtonpost.com/wp-dyn/content/article/2010/11/24
/AR2010112401510.html.

Fanning, Bryan. 2014. "Review of Seán Ó Riain, *The Rise and Fall of Ireland's Celtic Tiger: Liberalism, Boom and Bust.*" *Irish Journal of Sociology* 22, no. 1 (June): 159–71.

Ferguson, James. [1990] 1994. *The Anti-Politics Machine: "Development", Depoliticization, and Bureaucratic Power in Lesotho.* Minneapolis: Univ. of Minnesota Press.

Finch, Laura. 2015. "The Un-Real Deal: Financial Fiction, Fictional Finance, and the Financial Crisis." *Journal of American Studies* 49, no. 4: 731–53.

Fisk, Gloria. 2017. "After the Debate Over World Literature." *Contemporary Literature* 58, no. 1 (Spring): 157–69.

Fitzpatrick, Brian. 2015. "From Detroit to Dublin, A Fight to the Right to Water." Foreign Policy in Focus, 23 January 2015. https://fpif.org /detroit-dublin-fight-right-water/.

Flannery, Eoin. 2014. "'Ship of Fools': The Celtic Tiger and Poetry as Social Critique." In *From Prosperity to Austerity: A Socio-Cultural Critique of the Celtic Tiger and Its Aftermath*, edited by Eugene O'Brien and Eamon Maher, 203–17. Manchester: Manchester Univ. Press.

Flew, Terry. 2014. "Six Theories of Neoliberalism." *Thesis Eleven* 122, no. 1 (June): 49–71.

Flynn, Deirdre. 2021. "'Where are you from originally': The Cruel Optimism of the Precarious Irish Public Sphere in Melatu Uche Okorie's 'Under the Awning.'" *Alluvium* 9, no. 1 (March), https://www.alluvium -journal.org/2021/03/08/cruel-optimism-precarious-irish-public-sphere -melatu-okorie/ (accessed 16 August 2021).

Foster, Roy. 2008. *Luck and the Irish: A Brief History of Change From 1970.* Oxford: Oxford Univ. Press.

French, Tana. 2008. *The Likeness.* New York: Penguin.

———. 2016. *The Trespasser.* New York: Penguin.

Galvin, Annie. 2018. "Post-Crash Fiction and the Aesthetics of Austerity in Kevin Barry's *City of Bohane.*" *Critique: Studies in Contemporary Fiction* 59, no. 5: 578–95.

Gessen, Masha. 2019. "Ireland's Strange, Cruel System for Asylum Seekers." *New Yorker*, 4 June 2019. https://www.newyorker.com/news /dispatch/irelands-strange-cruel-system-for-asylum-seekers.

Gibbons, Luke. 1996. *Transformations in Irish Culture*. Notre Dame, IN: Univ. of Notre Dame Press.

Glynn, Alan. 2009. *Winterland*. London: Faber & Faber.

Godden, Richard. 2011. "Labor, Language, and Finance Capital." *PMLA* 126, no. 2 (March): 412–21.

Goswami, Nina, and Andrew Alderson. 2006. "Revealed: the Reclusive Property Mogul Who Has Already Won the Olympics." *Telegraph*, 10 September 2009. https://www.telegraph.co.uk/news/1528481/Revealed-the-reclusive-property-mogul-who-has-already-won-the-Olympics.html.

Gray, Breda. 2019. "'Leaving Dublin': Photographic Portrayals of Post-Celtic Tiger Emigration—a Sociological Analysis." *Sociological Review* 67, no. 3 (May): 635–53.

Greenpeace Italy. 2010. "The Toxic Ships." Greenpeace, June 2010. https://www.greenpeace.org/archive-italy/Global/italy/report/2010/inquinamento/Report-The-toxic-ship.pdf (accessed 23 May 2022).

Gumbrecht, Hans Ulrich. 2014. *Our Broad Present: Time and Contemporary Culture*. New York: Columbia Univ. Press.

Gupta, Suman, and Tao Papaioannou, eds. 2017. *Media Representations of Anti-Austerity Protests in the EU: Grievances, Identities and Agency*. New York: Routledge.

Gurevich, Aron J. 1985. *Categories of Medieval Culture*. Translated by G. L. Campbell. London: Routledge & Kegan Paul.

Hafferty, Frederic W., and Brian Castellani. 2009. *Sociology and Complexity Science: A New Field of Inquiry*. Berlin: Springer-Verlag.

Hall, Stuart. 2011. "The Neo-Liberal Revolution." *Cultural Studies* 25, no. 6 (November): 705–28.

Hand, Derek. 2011. *History of the Irish Novel*. Cambridge: Cambridge Univ. Press.

Hanna, Adam. 2020. "Habitations: Space, Place, Real Estate." In *Irish Literature in Transition: 1980–2020*, edited by Eric Falci and Paige Reynolds, 121–35. Cambridge: Cambridge Univ. Press.

Harvey, David. 2008. "The Right to the City." *New Left Review* 53 (September–October), https://newleftreview.org/II/53/david-harvey-the-right-to-the-city (accessed 23 May 2022).

———. 2010. *A Companion to Marx's Capital*. New York: Verso.

———. 2015. "The Most Dangerous Book I Have Ever Written: A Commentary on *Seventeen Contradictions and the End of Capitalism*." 19

May 2015. http://davidharvey.org/2015/05/the-most-dangerous-book-i
-have-ever-written-a-commentary-on-seventeen-contradictions-and-the
-end-of-capitalism/.

Hearne, Rory. 2021. "The Government Does Not Want You to Be Able to Afford to Buy a Home." Thejournal.ie, 5 May 2021. https://www.the journal.ie/readme/ireland-investment-housing-5428746-May2021/.

Hebdige, Dick. 1979. *Subculture: The Meaning of Style*. London: Routledge.

Heise, Ursula. 2008. *Sense of Place and Sense of Planet*. Oxford: Oxford Univ. Press.

Herman, David. 2004. *Story Logic: Problems and Possibilities of Narrative*. Lincoln: Univ. of Nebraska Press.

Hershinow, Stephanie Insley. 2018. "*Clarissa*, by the Numbers." Paper presented at the MLA 2018 Convention, 7 January 2018.

Higgins, Rita Ann. [1988] 1993. "Be Someone." In *The Witch in the Bushes*, 40–41. Galway: Salmon.

Hitchings, Henry. 2013. "Those Irritating Verbs-as-Nouns." *New York Times*, 30 March 2013. https://opinionator.blogs.nytimes.com/2013/03 /30/those-irritating-verbs-as-nouns/.

Honig, Bonnie. 1988. "Arendt, Identity, and Difference." *Political Theory* 16, no. 1: 77–98.

———. 2017. *Public Things*. New York: Fordham Univ. Press.

Howard, Jennifer. 2018. "What We Lose by Reading 100,000 Words Every Day." *Washington Post*, 4 October 2018. https://www.washingtonpost .com/outlook/what-we-lose-by-reading-100000-words-every-day/2018 /10/04/72dea000-b212-11e8-a20b-5f4f84429666_story.html.

Huber, Irmtraud. 2016. *Present Tense Narration in Contemporary Fiction: A Narratological Overview*. London: Palgrave Macmillan.

Huehls, Mitchum. 2017. "Juggling the Dialectic: The Abyss of Politics in Charis Abani's Fiction." In *Literatures and the Global Contemporary*, edited by Sarah Brouillette, Mathias Nilges, and Emilio Sauri, 157–75. Cham: Palgrave Macmillan.

Hughes, Declan. 2006. *The Wrong Kind of Blood*. New York: HarperCollins.

———. 2007. *The Color of Blood*. New York: HarperCollins.

Hughes, T. J. 2020. "Situating Marginalised Human Geographies: A Human Security Approach to Direct Provision." In *Haven: The*

Mediterranean Crisis and Human Security, edited by John Morrissey, 93–109. Cheltenham: Edwin Elgar.

Hume, Angela. 2016. "Toward an Antiracist Ecopoetics: Waste and Wasting in the Poetry of Claudia Rankine." *Contemporary Literature* 57, no. 1 (Spring): 79–100.

Huyessen, Andreas. 1986. *After the Great Divide: Modernism, Mass Culture, Postmodernism*. Bloomington: Indiana Univ. Press.

Johnson, Barbara. 1986. "Apostrophe, Animation, and Abortion." *Diacritics* 16, no. 1: 29–47.

Joyce, James. [1934] 1990. *Ulysses*. New York: Random House.

Kane, Edward J. 1987. "Dangers of Capital Forbearance: The Case of the FSLIC and 'Zombie' S&Ls." *Contemporary Economic Policy*, no. 5: 77–83.

Keena, Colm. 2017. "Jobstown Protest: What Happened on the Day." *Irish Times*, 30 June 2017. https://www.irishtimes.com/news/ireland/irish-news/jobstown-protest-what-happened-on-the-day-1.3138378.

Kelleher, Margaret. 1997. *The Feminization of Famine: Expressions of the Inexpressible?* Cork: Cork Univ. Press.

Kelly, Adam. 2017. "The Re-education of Ross O'Carroll-Kelly." *Éire-Ireland* 52, no. 1: 49–77.

———. 2020. "Ireland's Real Economy: Post-Crash Fictions of the Celtic Tiger." *The New Irish Studies: Twenty-First-Century Critical Revisions*, edited by Paige Reynolds, 195–210. Cambridge: Cambridge Univ. Press, 2020.

Kelly, Morgan. 2006. "How the Housing Corner Stones of Our Economy Could Go into Rapid Free Fall." *Irish Times*, 28 December 2006. https://www.irishtimes.com/business/how-the-housing-corner-stones-of-our-economy-could-go-into-rapid-free-fall-1.1042463.

Kelly, Olivia. 2007. "Car Ownership Reaches All-Time High." *Irish Times*, 15 December 2007. https://www.irishtimes.com/news/car-ownership-reaches-all-time-high-1.991699.

———. 2013. "Ireland's Biggest Homeless Hostel to Close." *Irish Times*, 17 May 2013. https://www.irishtimes.com/news/consumer/wetherspoon-to-open-in-former-dublin-homeless-hostel-1.2853777.

———. 2016. "Wetherspoon to Open in Former Dublin Homeless Hostel." *Irish Times*, 4 November 2016. https://www.irishtimes.com/news

/consumer/wetherspoon-to-open-in-former-dublin-homeless-hostel-1
.2853777.

Kennedy, Seán. 2017. "Fifty Shades of Green: Ireland and the Erotics of Austerity." In "Ireland in Psychoanalysis," edited by Joseph Valente, Seán
Kennedy, and Macy Todd, special issue, *Breac*, no. 7. https://breac.nd
.edu/articles/fifty-shades-of-green-ireland-and-the-erotics-of-austerity
/#_ftnref32 (accessed May 23, 2022).

Kenner, Hugh. 1987. *The Mechanic Muse*. London: Oxford Univ. Press.

Keown, Edwina. 2010. "Irish Aviation, Lemass, and Deferred Anglo-Irish
Modernism in Elizabeth Bowen's *A World of Love*." In *Irish Modern-
ism: Origins, Contexts, Publics*, edited by Carol Taaffe, and Edwina
Keown, 217–25. Bern: Peter Lang.

Kerrigan, Gene. 2009. "No Alternative? You've Got to Be Joking." *Independent*, 19 July 2009. http://www.independent.ie/opinion/columnists
/gene-kerrigan/no-alternative-youve-got-to-be-joking-26552067.html.

Kerrigan, Gene, and Pat Brennan. 1999. *This Great Little Nation: The
A–Z of Irish Scandals and Controversies*. Dublin: Gill & Macmillan.

Kilroy, Claire. 2012. *The Devil I Know*. New York: Black Cat.

Kirby, Peadar. 2010. *Celtic Tiger in Collapse*. 2nd ed. Basingstoke: Palgrave Macmillan.

Kloeckner, Christian, and Stefanie Mueller. 2018. "Financial Times: Competing Temporalities in the Age of Finance Capitalism." *Finance and
Society* 4, no. 1: 1–14.

Kondo, Marie. 2014. *The Life-Changing Magic of Tidying*. Translated by
Cathy Hirano. Berkeley, CA: Ten Speed.

Konigs, Martijn. 2015. *Capital and Time: For a New Critique of Neoliberal Reason*. Stanford, CA: Stanford Univ. Press.

Kreilkamp, Vera. 2006. "The Novel of the Big House." In *The Cambridge
Companion to the Irish Novel*, edited by John Wilson Foster, 60–88.
Cambridge: Cambridge Univ. Press.

Krugman, Paul. 2011. "The Austerity Delusion." *New York Times*, 25
March 2011, A27.

———. 2015. "The Case for Cuts Was a Lie. Why Does Britain Still Believe
It? The Austerity Delusion." *Guardian*, 29 April 2015. https://www
.theguardian.com/business/ng-interactive/2015/apr/29/the-austerity
-delusion.

———. 2016. (@paulkrugman). "Leprechaun economics: Ireland reports 26 percent growth! But it doesn't make sense. Why are these in GDP?" Twitter, 12 July 2016. https://twitter.com/paulkrugman/status/752841 032870551552.

Lanham, Richard. 2003. *Analyzing Prose.* 2nd ed. New York: Continuum.

Lash, Scott. 2001. "Forward: Individualization in a Non-Linear Mode." In Ulrich Beck and Elisabeth Beck-Gernsheim, *Individualization: Institutionalized Individualism and its Social and Political Consequences,* vii–xiii. London: Sage.

Lash, Scott, and Brian Wynne. [1986] 1992. "Introduction." In *Risk Society: Towards a New Modernity,* edited by Ulrich Beck, 1–8. London: Sage.

Lauro, Sarah Juliet, and Karen Embry. 2008. "A Zombie Manifesto: The Nonhuman Condition in the Era of Advanced Capitalism." *boundary 2* 35, no. 1: 85–108.

Leary, John Patrick. 2018. *Keywords: The New Language of Capitalism.* Chicago: Haymarket.

Leersen, Jeop. 2002. *Hidden Ireland, Public Sphere.* Galway: Arlen House.

Leonard, Liam. 2007. "The Galway Water Crisis." *Studies: An Irish Quarterly Review* 96, no. 384 (Winter): 379–89.

———. 2013. "The Water Crisis in Ireland: The Sociopolitical Contexts of Risk in Contemporary Society." In *The Social Life of Water,* edited by John Richard Wagner, 199–216. New York: Berghahn.

Lloyd, David. 1993. *Anomalous States: Irish Writing and the Post-Colonial Moment.* Durham, NC: Duke Univ. Press.

Long, Maebh. 2017. "Black Bile in Bohane: Kevin Barry and Melancholia." *Textual Practice* 31, no. 1: 81–98.

Lord, Miriam. 2020. "Time Gets Mangled as Varadkar Unveils Election Slogan." *Irish Times,* 14 January 2020. irishtimes.com/news/politics /miriam-lord-time-gets-mangled-as-varadkar-unveils-election-slogan -1.4139946.

Löwy, Michael. 2008. "The Current of Critical Irrealism: 'A moonlit enchanted night.'" In *Adventures in Realism,* edited by Matthew Beaumont, 193–206. Malden, MA: Wiley.

"Luas—A Bit to Do Yet." n.d. http://www.railusers.ie/campaigns/luas/ (accessed 6 July 2020).

Luhmann, Niklas. 1990. *Essays on Self-Reference*. New York: Columbia Univ. Press.

Lynch, Paul. [2013] 2014. *Red Sky in Morning*. New York: Back Bay.

———. 2014. "The Story of *Red Sky in Morning*." In Paul Lynch, *Red Sky in Morning*, 1–12. New York: Back Bay.

Maher, Eamonn, and Eugene O'Brien, eds. 2015. *From Prosperity to Austerity: A Socio-Cultural Critique of the Celtic Tiger and Its Aftermath*. Manchester: Manchester Univ. Press.

Martin, Randy. 2002. *The Financialization of Everyday Life*. Philadelphia: Temple Univ. Press.

Martín-Ruiz, Sara. 2017. "Melatu Okorie: An Introduction to Her Work and a Conversation with the Author." *Lit: Literature Interpretation Theory* 28, no. 2: 172–84.

Marx, Karl. [1867] 1990. *Capital, Vol. 1*. Translated by Ben Fowkes. New York: Penguin.

McCabe, Conor. 2015. "False Economy: The Financialisation of Ireland and the Roots of Austerity." In *Ireland under Austerity: Neoliberal Crisis, Neoliberal Solutions*, edited by Colin Coulter and Angela Nagle, 47–65. Manchester: Manchester Univ. Press.

———. 2011. *Sins of the Father: Tracing the Decisions That Shaped the Irish Economy*. Dublin: History Press Ireland.

McCann, Colum. 2009. *Let the Great World Spin*. New York: Random House.

———. 2013. *TransAtlantic*. New York: Random House.

McClanahan, Annie. 2018. *Dead Pledges: Debt, Crisis, and Twenty-First-Century Culture*. Stanford, CA: Stanford Univ. Press.

McCormack, Karen, and Iyar Mazar. 2015. "Understanding Foreclosure Risk: The Role of Nativity and Gender." *Critical Sociology* 41, no. 1: 115–32.

McCormack, Mike. 2016. *Solar Bones*. Dublin: Tramp.

McCulloch, Gretchen. 2014. "A Linguist Explains the Grammar of Doge. Wow." The Toast. http://the-toast.net/2014/02/06/linguist-explains -grammar-doge-wow/ (accessed 12 November 2015).

McDonagh, Terrence, and Terry Dundon. 2010. "Thatcherism Delayed? The Irish Crisis and the Paradox of Social Partnership." *Industrial Relations Journal* 41, no. 6: 544–62.

McDonald, Frank. 1999. "Car Ownership in Dublin Soars but Is Still Below EU Average." *Irish Times*, 19 February 1999. https://www.irish times.com/news/car-ownership-in-dublin-soars-but-is-still-below-eu -average-1.154492.

McGlynn, Mary. 2014. "Greengos: Contemporary Irish Constructions of Latin America." In *Where Motley Is Worn: Transnational Irish Literature*, edited by Moira Casey and Amanda Tucker, 43–64. Cork: Cork Univ. Press.

———. 2016. "Collectivism and Thatcher's 'Classless' Society in British Fiction and Film." *Twentieth-Century Literature* 62, no. 3: 309–36.

———. 2017. "'No difference between the different kinds of yesterday': The Neoliberal Present in *The Green Road*, *The Devil I Know*, and *The Lives of Women*." *LIT: Literature Interpretation Theory* 28, no. 1: 34–54.

———. 2018. "Things Unexploded—The Aesthetics of Social Risk in Two Post-Boom Irish Novels." *boundary 2* 45, no. 1: 181–200.

McInerney, Lisa. 2015. *The Glorious Heresies*. London: John Murray.

McIvor, Charlotte. n.d. "The Absences of the Asylum Archive: Making Reflective Space." Asylum Archive. https://www.academia.edu/13127363 /_The_Absences_of_the_Asylum_Archive_Making_Reflective_Space (accessed 6 July 2022).

McLean, Stuart. 1999. "Touching Death: Tellurian Seduction and the Spaces of Memory in Famine Ireland." *Irish Journal of Anthropology*, no. 4: 61–72.

Meade, Rosemary. 2012. "'Our Country's *Calling Card*': Culture as the Brand in Recessionary Ireland." *Variant* 43 (Spring): 33–35.

Meaney, Gerardine. 2013. "Race, Sex, and Nation: Virgin Mother Ireland." In *Theory on the Edge: Irish Studies and the Politics of Sexual Difference*, edited by Noreen Giffney and Margrit Shildrick, 125–44. New York: Palgrave Macmillan.

Melo, Zurita, Maria de Lourdes, Dana C. Thomsen, Timothy F. Smith, Anna Lyth, Benjamin L. Preston, and Scott Baum. 2015. "Reframing Water: Contesting H_2O within the European Union." *Geoforum* 65: 170–78.

Mercille, Julien. 2014a. *The Political Economy and Media Coverage of the European Economic Crisis: The Case of Ireland*. London: Routledge, 2014.

———. 2014b. "The Role of the Media in Sustaining Ireland's Housing Bubble." *New Political Economy* 19, no. 2: 282–301.

Metzer, Greg. 2015. *Rock Band Name Origins: The Stories of 240 Groups and Performers*. Jefferson, NC: McFarland.

Mianowski, Marie. 2014. "The Space In-Between in Colum McCann's Novel *TransAtlantic* (2013)." *Études britanniques contemporaines* 47. http://ebc.revues.org/1810 (accessed 23 May 2022).

———. 2017. *Post–Celtic Tiger Landscapes in Irish Fiction*. London: Routledge.

———. 2019. "Immaterial matters in *Solar Bones* by Mike McCormack." *Études de stylistique anglaise* 14. http://journals.openedition.org/esa /3553 (accessed 23 May 2022).

Michaels, Walter Benn. 2009. "Going Boom." *Bookforum*, February– March, 2009. https://www.bookforum.com/print/1505/-3274 (accessed 22 May 2019).

Mieszkowski, Jan. 2009. "Who's Afraid of Anacoluthon?" *MLN* 124, no. 3 (April): 648–65.

———. 2019. *Crises of the Sentence*. Chicago: Univ. of Chicago Press.

Mirowski, Philip. 2018. "Neoliberalism: The Movement That Dare Not Speak Its Name." *American Affairs* 2, no. 1 (Spring): 118–41.

———. 2019. "Hell Is the Truth Seen Too Late." *boundary 2* 46, no. 1 (February): 1–53.

Mizruchi, Susan. 2009. "Risk Theory and the Contemporary American Novel." *American Literary History* 22, no. 1 (Spring): 109–35.

Molony, Sinead. 2014. "House and Home: Structuring Absences in the Post–Celtic Tiger Documentary." In *Gendering the Recessions: Media and Culture in an Age of Austerity*, edited by Diane Negra and Yvonne Tasker, 181–202. Durham, NC: Duke Univ. Press.

Monahan, David. n.d. "Leaving Dublin." Photo series.

Moretti, Franco. 1996. *Modern Epic: The World-System from Goethe to García Márquez*. Translated by Quintin Hoare. London: Verso.

Moretti, Franco, and Dominique Pestre. 2015. "Bankspeak." *New Left Review* 92 (March–April): 75–99.

Mulhall, Anne. 2016. "Mind Yourself: Well-Being and Resilience as Governmentality in Contemporary Ireland." *Irish Review*, 53 (Autumn): 29–44.

Mullally, Una. 2014. "Workplace Has Become Terrain of Insecurity and Exhaustion." *Irish Times*, 1 September 2014. https://www.irishtimes

.com/news/social-affairs/workplace-has-become-terrain-of-insecurity-and-exhaustion-1.1913401.

Murphy, Antoin. 2014. "The Fall of the Celtic Tiger: Ireland and the Euro Debt Crisis." Paper presented at Queen's Univ. Belfast, 21 March 2014. https://www.qub.ac.uk/home/ResearchandEnterprise/Business Networks/FileStore/Filetoupload,442419,en.pdf.

Murphy, Kevin. 2005. "The Man Tipped to Become No. 1 on the Irish Rich List." *Irish Independent*, 23 September 2005. https://www.independent.ie/opinion/analysis/the-man-tipped-to-become-no-1-on-the-irish-rich-list-25967743.html.

Murphy, Michelle. 2020. "New Government Will Have to Confront the Need to Raise Taxes." *Irish Times*, 20 February 2020. https://www.irishtimes.com/opinion/new-government-will-have-to-confront-the-need-to-raise-taxes-1.4179775.

Murray, Paul. 2015. *The Mark and the Void*. New York: Farrar, Straus & Giroux.

Mythen, Gabe. 2018. "The Critical Theory of World Risk Society: A Retrospective Analysis." *Risk Analysis* 41: 533–43.

"Myths and Realities about NAMA and Developers' Salaries." 2012. NAMA Wine Lake, 17 July 2012. https://namawinelake.wordpress.com/2012/07/17/myths-and-realities-about-nama-and-developers-salaries/.

Nedeljkovic, Vukašin. n.d. "Direct Provision Centres as Manifestations of Resistance." https://www.academia.edu/13127308/Direct_Provision_Centres_as_Manifestations_of_Resistance (accessed 23 May 2022).

———. 2019. Personal communication. February 28, 2019.

Negra, Diane. 2009. *What a Girl Wants? Fantasizing the Reclamation of Self in Postfeminism*. London: Routledge.

———. 2013. "Adjusting Men and Abiding Mammies: Gendering the Recession in Ireland." *Irish Review* 46: 23–34.

Negra, Diane, and Anthony P. McIntyre. 2019. "Ireland Inc.: The Corporatization of Affective Life in Post–Celtic Tiger Ireland." *International Journal of Cultural Studies*, 60–80 (October), https://doi.org/10.1177%2F1367877919882437.

Negra, Diane, Anthony P McIntyre, and Eleanor O'Leary. 2019. "Broadcasting Irish Emigration in an Era of Global Mobility." *European Journal of Cultural Studies* 22, nos. 5–6 (October): 849–66.

Nietzsche, Friedrich Wilhelm. [1886] 2009. *Beyond Good and Evil.* Translated by Ian Johnston. Arlington, VA: Richer Resources.

———. [1887] 1956. *The Birth of Tragedy and The Genealogy of Morals.* Translated by Francis Golffing. New York: Anchor.

Nixon, Rob. 2011. *Slow Violence and the Environmentalism of the Poor.* Cambridge, MA: Harvard Univ. Press.

Norris, Michelle. 2016. *Property, Family, and the Irish Welfare State.* Cham: Palgrave Macmillan.

Nouvet, Claire, Julie Gaillard, and Mark Stoholski. 2016. "Introduction." In *Traversals of Affect: On Jean-François Lyotard*, edited by Claire Nouvet, Julie Gaillard, and Mark Stoholski, 1–18. London: Bloomsbury.

O'Brien, Timothy. 1998. "A Frenzy of Global Anxiety Kicks Up Dust That Had Been Settling." *New York Times*, 28 May 1998, D1.

O'Byrnes, Stephen 2014. "Time to Expose the Charade of 'Peaceful Protest' over Irish Water." *Irish Times*, 19 November 2014. https://www.irishtimes.com/opinion/time-to-expose-the-charade-of-peaceful-protest-over-irish-water-1.2006020.

O'Callaghan, Cian, Mark Boyle, and Rob Kitchin. 2014. "Post-Politics, Crisis, and Ireland's 'Ghost Estates.'" *Political Geography* 42: 121–33.

O'Callaghan, Cian, Sinead Kelly, Mark Boyle, and Rob Kitchin. 2015. "Topologies and Topographies of Ireland's Neoliberal Crisis." *Space and Polity* 19, no. 1: 31–46.

O'Connor, Joseph. 2007. *Redemption Falls.* New York: Free Press.

O'Donnell, Rory. 2019. "Why No One Shouted Stop: Review of Ciarán Michael Casey, *Policy Failures and the Irish Economic Crisis*." *Dublin Review of Books* 115 (October). https://www.drb.ie/essays/why-no-one-shouted-stop (accessed 23 May 2022).

O'Flynn, Micheal, and Lee F. Monaghan. 2014b. "Scapegoating during a Time of Crisis: A Critique of Post 'Celtic Tiger' Ireland." Slide presentation, Social Policy Conference in University College Cork, The Irish Welfare State in and after Crisis: Resilience, Resistance, Retrenchment, Reform, 28 March 2014. http://irc-equality.ie/?page_id=247.

O'Flynn, Micheal, Lee F. Monaghan, and Martin J. Power. 2014. "Scapegoating during a Time of Crisis: A Critique of Post-Celtic Tiger Ireland." *Sociology* 48, no. 5 (October): 921–37.

Okorie, Melatu Uche. 2018. *This Hostel Life.* Dublin: Skein.

Ó Riain, Seán. 2014. *The Rise and Fall of Ireland's Celtic Tiger: Liberalism, Boom and Bust*. Cambridge: Cambridge Univ. Press.

———. 2017. "The Road to Austerity." In *Austerity and Recovery in Ireland: Europe's Poster Child and the Great Recession*, edited by William K. Roche, Philip J. O'Connell, and Andrea Prothero, 23–39. Oxford: Oxford Univ. Press.

O'Rourke, Liam. "Foreign Investors." 2003. *Vaccuum 5*. http://www.the vacuum.org.uk/issues/issues0120/issue05/is05artforinv.html (accessed 8 August 2020).

O'Toole, Fintan. 1985. "Going West: The Country versus the City in Irish Writing." *Crane Bag* 9, no. 2: 111–16.

———. 1994. *Black Hole, Green Card: The Disappearance of Ireland*. Dublin: New Island.

———. 2002. "The Clod and the Continent: Irish Identity in the European Union." EURUnion publication, Irish Congress of Trade Unions, Dublin, Spring 2022. www.ictu.ie/publications (accessed 15 January 2019).

———. 2010. *Ship of Fools*. New York: Public Affairs.

Papaioannou, Tao and Suman Gupta, eds. 2018. *Media Representations of Anti-Austerity Protests in the EU*. New York: Routledge.

People before Profit. 2019. "Why Does the State Pamper Sean Mulryan?" 29 January 2019. https://www.pbp.ie/why-does-the-state-pamper-sean -mulryan/.

Piketty, Thomas. 2014. *Capital in the Twenty-First Century*. Translated by Arthus Goldhammer. Cambridge, MA: Harvard Univ. Press.

Power, Martin, Eoin Devereux, and Amanda Haynes. 2018. "Discursive Constructions of the Anti-Water Charges Protest Movement in Ireland." In *Media Representations of Anti-Austerity Protests in the EU*, edited by Tao Papaioannou and Suman Gupta, 27–46. New York: Routledge.

Prasad, Monica. 2006 *The Politics of Free Markets: The Rise of Neoliberal Economic Policies in Britain, France, Germany, and the United States*. Chicago: Univ. of Chicago Press.

Quinlan, Ronald. 2008. "High-Flying Builder Puts Chopper on Market, but Sky Still the Limit." *Independent*, 30 November 2008. https:// www.independent.ie/irish-news/high-flying-builder-puts-chopper-on -market-but-sky-still-the-limit-26495920.html.

Rajan, Tilottarna. 2002. *Deconstruction and the Remainders of Phenomenology: Sartre, Derrida, Foucault, Baudrillard.* Stanford, CA: Stanford Univ. Press.

Rasborg, Klaus. 2017. "From Class Society to the Individualized Society? A Critical Reassessment of Individualization and Class." *Irish Journal of Sociology* 25, no. 3 (December): 229–49.

Rasch, William. 2000. *Niklas Luhmann's Modernity: The Paradoxes of Differentiation.* Stanford, CA: Stanford Univ. Press.

Reilly, Gavin, 2010. "Developers Score €200,000 Salaries from NAMA." Thejournal.ie, 21 October 2010. https://www.thejournal.ie/developers-score-e200000-salaries-from-nama-38470-Oct2010/.

Ricks, Christopher. 1989. *Tennyson.* 2nd ed. Houndmills: Macmillan.

Riffaterre, Michael. 1978. *Semiotics of Poetry.* Bloomington: Indiana Univ. Press.

Roche, William K., Philip J. O'Connell, and Andrea Prothero. 2017. "Introduction 'Poster Child' or 'Beautiful Freak?' Austerity and Recovery in Ireland." In *Austerity and Recovery in Ireland: Europe's Poster Child and the Great Recession,* edited by William K. Roche, Philip J. O'Connell, and Andrea Prothero, 1–22. Oxford: Oxford Univ. Press.

Royle, Nicholas. 2003. *The Uncanny: An Introduction.* Manchester: Manchester Univ. Press.

Rubenstein, Michael. 2010 *Public Works: Infrastructure, Irish Modernism, and the Postcolonial.* South Bend, IN: Notre Dame Univ. Press.

———. 2018. "Aquacity versus Austerity: The Politics and Poetics of Irish Water." In *Planned Violence: Post/Colonial Urban Infrastructure, Literature and Culture,* edited by Dominic Davies and Elleke Boehmer, 305–22. New York: Palgrave Macmillan.

Ryan, Donal. [2012] 2014. *The Spinning Heart.* Hanover, NH: Steerforth.

———. [2013] 2014. *The Thing about December.* Hanover, NH: Steerforth.

Schussler, Jennifer. 2017. "Number-Crunching the Novel." *New York Times,* 30 October 2017, C6.

Sen, Malcolm. 2019. "Risk and Refuge: Contemplating Precarity in Irish Fiction." *Irish University Review* 49, no. 1 (May): 13–31.

Shakespeare, William. [1623] 2020. *Timon of Athens.* New York: Simon & Schuster.

Shapiro, Stephen. 2008. "Transvaal, Transylvania: *Dracula*'s World-System and Gothic Periodicity." *Gothic Studies* 10, no. 1 (May): 29–47.

Share, Perry. 2011. "The Rise and Fall of the Jumbo Breakfast Roll: How a Sandwich Survived the Decline of the Irish Economy." *Sociological Research Online* 16, no. 2: 143–49.

Shear, Michael D., Maggie Haberman, and Astead W. Herndon. 2020. "Trump Rally Fizzles as Attendance Falls Short of Campaign's Expectations." *New York Times*, 20 June 2020. https://www.nytimes.com/2020/06/20/us/politics/tulsa-trump-rally.html.

Sheridan, Kathy. 2007. "Money Talks Louder than the 'Quiet Man.'" *Irish Times*, 22 October 2007. https://www.irishtimes.com/culture/money-talks-louder-than-the-quiet-man-1.974893.

Slovic, Paul. 2000. "Trust, Emotion, Sex, Politics, and Science: Surveying the Risk-Assessment Battlefield." In *The Perception of Risk*, edited by Paul Slovic, 390–412. London: Earthscan.

Soni, Vivasvan. 2017. "Energy." In *Fueling Culture: 101 Words for Energy and Environment*, edited by Imre Szeman, Jennifer Wenzel, and Patricia Yaeger, 132–35. New York: Fordham Univ. Press.

Spencer, Douglas. 2016. *The Architecture of Neoliberalism: How Contemporary Architecture Became an Instrument of Control and Compliance*. London: Bloomsbury.

Spivak, Gayatri C. 2012. *Outside in the Teaching Machine*. New York: Routledge.

Staten, Joseph Henry. 2017. "What Exists Is Good: On *The Architecture of Neoliberalism* by Douglas Spencer." *Los Angeles Review of Books*, 25 March 2017. https://lareviewofbooks.org/article/what-exists-is-good-on-the-architecture-of-neoliberalism/.

Thatcher, Margaret. 1987. 'Interview for "Woman's Own" ("No Such Thing as Society").' In *Speeches, Interviews and Other Statements*. https://www.margaretthatcher.org/document/106689 (accessed 5 June 2012).

Townsend, Sarah. 2020. "Writing the Tiger: Economics and Culture." *Irish Literature in Transition: 1980—2020*, vol. 6, edited by Eric Falci and Paige Reynolds, 246–62. Cambridge: Cambridge Univ. Press.

Urry, John. 2007. *Mobilities*. Cambridge: Polity.

———. 2000. *Sociology beyond Societies*. London: Routledge.

Wacquant, Loïc. 2009. *Punishing the Poor: The Neoliberal Government of Social Insecurity*. Durham, NC: Duke Univ. Press.

Warwick Research Collective (WReC). 2015. *Combined and Uneven Development: Towards a New Theory of World-Literature*. Liverpool: Liverpool Univ. Press.

Webb, Nick. 2017. "Mulryan Noses ahead with Sweet Revenge." *Sunday Times* [London], 20 August 2017, 12.

Wekker, Gloria. 2016. *White Innocence: Paradoxes of Colonialism and Race*. Durham, NC: Duke Univ. Press.

Wenzel, Jennifer. 2019. *The Disposition of Nature: Environmental Crisis and World Literature*. New York: Fordham Univ. Press.

Whitney, Karl. 2014. "Nice Gaff: Abbeville." Totally Dublin. https://www.totallydublin.ie/more/nice-gaff-abbeville/ (accessed 28 September 2020).

Williams, Jeffrey. 2013. "The Plutocratic Imagination (On Contemporary American Fiction)." *Dissent* (Winter 2013): 93–97.

Williams, Raymond. 1977. *Marxism and Literature*. Oxford: Oxford Univ. Press.

Yeats, William Butler. 2008. *Collected Poems of W. B. Yeats*. Edited by Richard J. Finneran. New York: Scribner.

Zimmer, Ben. 2020. "'The "Before" Time': A Sci-Fi Idea That Has Made Its Way to Real Life; the Shorthand Phrase for an Era before a Catastrophe Has Now Become Part of Our Pandemic Vocabulary." *Wall Street Journal*, 19 June 2020. https://www.wsj.com/articles/the-before-time-a-sci-fi-idea-that-has-made-its-way-to-real-life-11592580133.

Index

Mary M. McGlynn is Professor of English at Baruch College, CUNY, and the CUNY Graduate Center, as well as cochair of the Columbia University Seminar for Irish Studies. She writes about contemporary English, Scottish, and Irish fiction, and also about film, detective fiction, and country music. She is the author of *Narratives of Class in New Irish and Scottish Literature.*